Becoming the Tupamaros

BECOMING THE TUPAMAROS

*Solidarity and
Transnational Revolutionaries
in Uruguay and the United States*

Lindsey Churchill

Vanderbilt University Press | Nashville

This book is printed on acid-free paper.
Manufactured in the United States of America

Library of Congress Cataloging-in-Publication Data on file
LC control number 2013007211
LC classification F2728.C535 2014
Dewey class number 989.506—dc23

ISBN 978-0-8265-1944-3 (cloth)
ISBN 978-0-8265-1946-7 (ebook)

Contents

Acknowledgments

RESEARCHING AND WRITING *BECOMING the Tupamaros* was an exciting and at times challenging process. I received the help of many wonderful people while writing this book.

Furthermore, the overseas and in country research I conducted for this project would not have been possible without outside support. Special thanks to the Graduate School at Florida State University for awarding me a research fellowship for the Spring and Summer semesters of 2009. This fellowship allowed me to conduct research in Uruguay and Argentina. I also was able to explore the US side of solidarity in both 2007 and 2008 because of the Mary Lily Research Grant from Duke University. Thanks especially to Kelly Wooten at the Sallie Bingham Center for Women's History and Culture, at the David M. Rubenstein Rare Book and Manuscript Library at Duke University, for supporting my work.

My time as a Research Associate at the Five College Women's Studies Research Center at Mount Holyoke College in 2010–2011 allowed me to deepen this project by accessing the archives at Amherst College. At the Center I met many people who passionately supported this project. Thanks especially to Elizabeth (EB) Lehman and Laura Lovett for believing in my project enough to invite me to the FCWSRC. Megan Elias, Glenda Nieto-Cuebas, Japonica Saracino-Brown, you went out of the way to help me and showed an incredible amount of enthusiasm for my work. During this time I also got to know a wonderful community of scholars that included Karin Ekström, Amy Mittleman, Jennifer Hamilton, Johanna Hiitola, Minna Nikunen, and Ceyda Kuloğlu-Karsli. I will never forget these amazing, helpful, and fun cohorts!

I would also like to thank Robinson Herrera for his input and help concerning this project and its development.

A special thanks to Eli Bortz, my editor at Vanderbilt, for his unfaltering support of this manuscript.

Thanks to all of my new and wonderful colleagues at the University of Central Oklahoma for giving me the best job ever. I appreciate Jeff Plaks, Katrina Lacher, Patricia Loughlin, Tim Tillman, and Lindsey Osterman for going out of their way to make me feel included in this new community. Also, thank you to my students, many of whom have shown a great deal of enthusiasm for this project.

My family and friends have helped me immensely throughout this process. Thank you, Mom, Dad, and Nana for being the most loving and encouraging family imaginable. I honestly could not have done this without you. I appreciate the emotional support and encouragement offered to me throughout the years by Jessica Marion. Thanks also to Eileen O'Hara. Last but definitely not least, thank you Jeremy Holcombe for being there every step of the way.

Becoming the Tupamaros

Introduction

"Como el Uruguay no hay! There is nothing like Uruguay!"

ON MAY 29, 1970, around two o'clock in the morning, an assistant guard at a Uruguayan military training center in the capital city of Montevideo, Fernando Garin, inconspicuously removed his helmet and then quickly placed it back on his head. Though this small gesture seemed insignificant to Garin's fellow guards, three men in a nearby car took notice and began to drive slowly down Washington Street. The car stopped in front of the gate of the military training center.

Two men wearing police uniforms emerged from the vehicle. Though the guards believed the men worked in law enforcement, in actuality, the "policemen" were soldiers in Uruguay's national liberation army, el Movimiento de Liberación Nacional-Tupamaros (MLN-T), also known as the Tupamaros.

"We're from police headquarters and need to see the officer on duty," one of the Tupamaros commanded in a booming, authoritarian voice. The guard called for Garin, who pretended he didn't know anyone in the group.

Garin walked to one side of the car and inspected the papers of the alleged police officers. He told the Tupamaros they had permission to enter the center, which housed around sixty people, mostly officers and sailors. Other Tupamaros, hiding in the darkness across the street, covertly witnessed this scene and waited for their chance to strike.

Indeed, the Tupamaros were known for their clandestine actions against the Uruguayan government and by 1970, committed new, violent actions nearly every day.

The hiding Tupamaros observed a soldier on the rooftop put down his rifle and adopt a more relaxed position. At the same time, a couple who appeared to be passionately in love walked down Washington Street. As they passed by the center's high gray wall, one of the recently arrived Tupamaro "police officers" stopped the happy couple.

"Identification," the Tupamaro "police officer" demanded. With nervous hands, the young man searched his pockets and the girl sifted through her purse.

"We don't have any identification," the young man stuttered. "We're students, and we can prove it."

"We'll see about that," the Tupamaro policemen said, and he ordered the two undercover Tupamaro students to go inside the building.

Meanwhile, Garin approached the rooftop guard and told him he had permission to leave for the remainder of the evening. The guard expressed suspicion about all of the late night activity. In response, Garin struck the guard in the stomach with his Colt .45 and confiscated his rifle. The Tupamaro policemen and the two students surrounded another guard who stood in front of the entrance gate to the center. From above, Garin pointed his newly acquired rifle at the guard.

After restraining the remaining outside guards, Garin changed into a police uniform and, along with the two fake police officer Tupamaros, entered the military base. The corporal inside the base called another officer on duty but failed to question the "police officers." The corporal saw no need to set off the alarm that alerted the military men who slept in the center's dormitories. The Tupamaros quickly overtook the officer and corporal on duty and tied them up. The Tupamaros then performed another costume change—they slipped into the ponchos worn by Uruguayan sailors. These types of disguises and costumes only fueled the mythology of the Tupamaros as hip and creative revolutionaries.

The group quietly allowed seventeen more awaiting Tupamaros into the building courtyard. The Tupamaros easily garnered control of an area where thirty sailors slept, the infirmary, the dining room, and the recruiting office. The surprised sailors were lined up in the central patio, most still in their sleepwear. Tensions ran high as it took nearly twenty minutes for a commando to arrive with keys to the cells inside the center. In spite of the delay, the Tupamaros successfully locked up the sailors without any overt violence from either side.

A truck entered through the center's front gate and pulled up close to the building. The commandos emptied the navy's arsenal and gathered up all available arms stored in the dormitories. The Tupamaros acquired three hundred rifles, two .30 caliber machine guns, 150 Colt .45 pistols, sixty thousand bullets, a cache of submachine guns, and six R-15 rifles, ostensibly used by the United States in Vietnam. While the Tupamaros loaded the arsenal into their truck, two sailors arrived at the entrance.

They greeted the disguised Tupamaros and walked into the center. A Tupamaro awaited the sailors and trapped them as they entered the building. In this and other actions, the Tupamaros claimed to try to avoid gratuitous violence. In fact, the group prided itself on using violence only against specific targets or in self defense.

Around 3:30 a.m., the truck carried the arsenal and all but six Tupamaros from the center. One of the remaining Tupamaros removed the Uruguayan flag and in its place raised the flag of the Tupamaros. He took pictures of the jailed officers and sailors and the many revolutionary slogans that were sprayed across the center's walls. Garin, the son of a textile union organizer, left a letter explaining that he had betrayed the Uruguayan military because he could no longer endure the oppression that the military inflicted upon labor unionists.

At 4:15 am, the remaining few Tupamaros vacated the building and drove away in a number of cars parked nearby for their convenience. Several hours passed before a group of navy officers finally managed to open the cell locks and alert the government about the Tupamaros' latest mission.[1] In this action and others, the Tupamaros believed they were fulfilling their promise that "no one would be immune" to what they deemed "popular justice."[2]

This occupation of the Uruguayan Navy training center, described in the US leftist newsletter *Liberation News Service* (*LNS*), was just one of hundreds of missions that the Tupamaros performed throughout the 1960s and the early 1970s.[3] During these highly publicized missions, the Tupamaros wore many different disguises, including police uniforms, army fatigues, and wigs. They attacked their government enemies with a creative arsenal of weapons and used everything from vans to hearses to motorcycles in their missions. They placed tacks on the ground to slow down their police pursuers. They once took over an upscale nightclub in Montevideo and reportedly spray-painted slogans such as "All will dance or none will dance" (a creative revision of their motto "There will be a country for all or a country for none").

In 1970, MLN-T members committed the most profitable bank robbery on record. The successful prison breaks of the Tupamaros seemed always to have a cinematic flair to them. For example, one female Tupamaro, more properly Tupamara, prison break occurred while the Tupamaras attended mass at a church next door to their prison. Someone in the center of the church began rehearsed clapping, which inspired all prisoners to join in making noise. The loud noise confused the guard, and the women easily overtook their only security. Outside the church, an ambulance, fake police car, two taxis, and three other cars waited to pick up the thirteen escaped Tupamaras. For outrageous and usually successful rebellions such as these, the Tupamaros have frequently been romanticized by their admirers. Many radical and moderate leftists throughout the world envisioned the Tupamaros as passionate, committed, and most of all, hip revolutionaries capable of outsmarting the police and the increasingly authoritarian Uruguayan government.

Beyond these romantic portrayals, little work has been done concerning the quotidian realities of the organization or its international connections and solidarity with other leftist groups. This manuscript constitutes the first in-depth analysis of the often contradictory ideologies of the Tupamaros, the transnational connections between Tupamaro revolutionaries and leftist groups in the US, and issues of gender and sexuality within the MLN-T.[4] I investigate how the Tupamaras combated patriarchy and how gender structures in the organization compared with the role of women in Uruguayan society at large.[5] I demonstrate how issues of gender and sexuality permeated almost all representations of women in the MLN-T. The Tupamaros, the Uruguayan and the US left in general, human rights groups in the United States, and the Uruguayan government have all had specific conceptions of what it means to be a female militant.[6]

In addition, I further examine the experiences and ideologies of the Tupamaro guerrillas by exploring the transnational connections between the Tupamaro revolutionaries and leftist groups in the US. I reveal how both the Tupamaros and the greater Uruguayan left formed connections with their counterparts in the US and the transnational nature of these alliances. My research demonstrates that international conceptions of revolution and solidarity influenced the Uruguayan left and the Tupamaros in particular to forge ties with radical groups, including in the US, the very country whose ruling government they hoped to help destroy. The Uruguayan left's political and cultural solidarity with radicals in the United States showed a variant and complicated kind of exchange that did not replicate traditional models of dominance and acquiescence.

My work primarily examines the Tupamaros but also looks at the Uruguayan left in general. While the Uruguayan left and the Tupamaros are not interchangeable and were incredibly diverse, many Uruguayan leftists admired the actions of the Tupamaros. The Tupamaros derived from dozens of disparate leftist groups and read newspapers such as

Marcha, a periodical also purchased by the moderate left. However, some members of the Uruguayan left, particularly those in the Communist Party and the pacifist left, did not approve of the tactics of the Tupamaros. This book examines some of the schisms within the Uruguayan left, particularly between communists and proviolence groups such as the Tupamaros.

Furthermore, when referencing the US left, periodicals from the Uruguayan left often conflated various groups. The Uruguayan left commonly listed the US civil rights movement, workers, and students in the same sentence when expressing political solidarity. Though these groups were sometimes at odds with one another, the Uruguayan left focused on the unity of the US left in its battle against the US government. Groups such as the Tupamaros also participated in the invocation of many different national and international heroes for inspiration. In a letter written to the Uruguayan leftist publication *Marcha*, one activist called upon the memory of South American independence hero José Artigas as well as Che, Castro, Brazilian revolutionary Carlos Lamarca, Vietnamese guerrillas, and the US-based Black Panthers.[7] This letter exemplifies how members of the Uruguayan left passionately spoke about international radical groups and individuals and hoped to express solidarity with others working for revolutionary social change.[8]

This work occasionally includes sources from European activist groups. The French in particular took an interest in Uruguayan politics and human rights abuses in the country between the years 1973 and 1984.[9] However, in general, the Uruguayan left seemed more interested in US radicals' politics and culture in the 1960s and 1970s than that of their European counterparts. Though this work focuses primarily on the influences and connections between the US and the Uruguayan left and on their imagining of each other, it is impossible to tell the complex story of the Tupamaros in a constricted and insular narrative. Indeed, the transnational, global left was interconnected and extensive.

Therefore, in addition to previously unexplored transnational contacts and networks, this work reveals the specific imagined conceptions that the Uruguayan and US left developed about each other.[10] In his work *Imagined Communities: Reflections on the Origin and Spread of Nationalism*, Benedict Anderson defines the nation as an imagined political community. He argues that the nation is imagined because citizens will never personally know most of the other people within their nation, yet they maintain an idea or image of their shared identity.[11]

While Anderson's work specifically focuses on the "nation," my work addresses how groups and individuals imagined one another across nations. My analysis explores more than the concrete connections between activists. It is an intellectual history that investigates how leftists in the US and Uruguay conceptualized one another and saw themselves as part of an international, and largely imagined, community. Anderson writes about this type of community, "It is imagined as a community because, regardless of the actual inequality and exploitation that may prevail in each, the nation is always conceived as a deep horizontal comradeship."[12] Indeed, despite racial, gender, and class differences, many in the Uruguayan left claimed communal bonds with members of the US left.

Language and print helped to create this imagined community. Many Uruguayan leftists spoke English, and radical presses helped to translate Spanish documents for revolutionaries in the US. However, it was not a particular language that enabled the creation of community—it was how they conceptualized the revolution that bonded activists. Uruguayan and US radical leftists employed a language of social justice, called for extreme political change, and characterized the US as oppressive. This common language allowed activists to connect and share information. As Anderson asserts, "Print language is what invents nationalism, not *a* particular language per se."[13]

Anderson claims that two forms of imagining the nation blossomed in Europe in the eighteenth century—the novel and the newspaper.[14] In the 1960s and 1970s, for US and Uruguayan activists, newspapers and pamphlets became the most powerful way to share ideas and create community bonds with individuals they had never met. Uruguay presents a fascinating case because of its citizens' frequent interactions with the shared world of print. In 1970, the Uruguayans had a ratio of 310 periodicals for every one thousand citizens.[15] Such a wide circulation of written materials enabled middle-class members of the Uruguayan left and the Tupamaros to imagine themselves as part of a larger community of international leftist radicals.[16]

Many leftist publications in Uruguay and the US shared information and often reprinted the same articles. The aforementioned US-based radical newsletter *Liberation News Service* (*LNS*) distributed information to over two hundred small newspapers in North America, Europe, and Latin America.[17] The Chicago Area Group on Latin America (CAGLA) sought solidarity with the "struggle for liberation" throughout Latin America. The organization included members from both the US and Latin America. The group promoted solidarity primarily through the translation of leftist documents from Latin America for US activists. CAGLA translated and reprinted articles from the popular Uruguayan publication *Marcha*. They housed copies of *Marcha* in their library along with other documents from Uruguay. In turn, *Marcha* featured articles written by leftists in the US, particularly from the Black Power movement.[18]

Inspiration from international, proviolence radicals and movements derived in large part from improvements in print technology and lower cost printing options, which allowed for the worldwide distribution of pamphlets and books.[19] State funding in communist countries also helped support the international circulation of leftist materials in numerous countries. Both Cuba and China participated in aggressive publishing and distribution campaigns and focused a great deal of their attention on the Western Hemisphere. By the mid-1960s, inexpensive copies of Mao Tse-tung's *Little Red Book* and the writings of Fidel Castro, Friedrich Engels, Vladimir Lenin, Karl Marx, Joseph Stalin, and Ernesto "Che" Guevara could be found in every big city and college town in the US and Uruguay and throughout the world.[20] In *Soul Power: Culture, Radicalism, and the Making of a Third World Left*, Cynthia Young discusses the phenomenon of transnational literature and heroes inspiring leftist activism. She writes, "The greater circulation of radical literature from around the globe depended on print and media technologies, national infrastructures, and transnational networks that, in a very real sense, shrank the distance between national contexts and the people in them."[21]

Networks of radicals emerged in large part because of leftist activism within the burgeoning university population. In Uruguay specifically, between 1955 and 1975 the number of students receiving university educations increased by 117 percent.[22] The university offered a forum for Uruguayan and US leftists to organize and debate various strategies and ideologies for political success. It allowed students an opportunity to discuss the Cuban Revolution and its significance to global politics. Furthermore, middle-class students in Uruguay and the US turned to leftist politics in part because they viewed their countries' once democratic ideals as disintegrating into a quagmire of repression and violence because of Cold War politics and free market economic policies.[23]

Both the US and Uruguay have traditionally been portrayed as beacons of democracy in an unstable hemisphere.[24] Throughout the twentieth century, Uruguay boasted a high standard of living in comparison with other countries in Latin America. By the 1950s, it contained the highest rate of urbanization (75 percent of the population), the highest life expectancy (sixty-nine years) and one of the lowest infant mortality rates (forty-seven deaths per one thousand live births).[25] One article from the US about Uruguay referred to the country as a "bastion of good living." Adding to the myth, author R. C. Longworth claimed that life was good for Uruguayans, who supposedly worked six-hour days and retired at forty-five with full salary and benefits. Longworth bragged about Uruguay, "It has few Indians and suffered none of the problems that plague other Latin American countries."[26] Despite these portrayals, according to reports from the leftist media, by the late 1960s Uruguay had transformed into a site of intense government repression of students, labor union members, and other suspected subversives.[27]

The Setting

Though the Uruguayan people endured unrest and war throughout the nineteenth century, for the first five decades of the twentieth century, overall political stability and democratic procedures bolstered secular ideas of consensus, fairness, and citizenship within the country. This, along with a sizeable urban middle class, shaped Uruguayans' image of themselves as an exceptional nation with a unique history. Indeed, beginning in the 1880s, Montevideo and the rest of Uruguay dramatically transformed. An influx of European immigrants, largely from Italy and Spain, helped to increase urban growth and responded to the growing need for industrial labor.

As they had in the nineteenth century, two political parties, the Colorados and the Blancos dominated the political scene and sometimes resorted to violence against one another.[28] The predominately urban Colorados consistently garnered more support than the rural Blancos. Colorado Party members have typically been more urban, liberal, and anticlerical than the predominately rural Blancos and consequently much more successful in Uruguayan politics. However, both parties contributed to the development of democracy in Uruguay. At the beginning of the twentieth century, the Blancos called for free elections, the secret ballot, and proportional representation. The Colorados wanted provisions for the so-called weaker elements of society, protections against foreign exploitation of the Uruguayan economy, and a powerful bureaucratic state.

A civil war broke out in 1904, with the Blancos rebelling against the ruling Colorados. José Batlle y Ordóñez, president at that time, sent Colorado troops to squelch the rebellion, which incited nine months of intense fighting. Afterward, both parties attempted to work toward a democratic solution to their problems. Starting in 1905, largely because of increased exportation of wool and frozen beef, Uruguay's economy steadily grew for fifteen years.[29]

The Batllista epoch, influenced by modernization, started at the beginning of the twentieth century and lasted into the 1930s. During this time, the government implemented many progressive reforms that demonstrated forward thinking for their time. Between 1910 and 1915, the regime granted pensions for older workers, an eight-hour workday, and free secondary education and created national public assistance in order to give care to the indigent and sick. The state also became involved in the economy by creating a national railroad and restricting the extent to which foreigners could hold land. Other laws extended domestic, political, and workplace rights to women.[30]

By the 1930s, however, global trade stagnated. Uruguay's economy depended primarily on international markets, with the majority of its exports going to the US and Europe. Furthermore, British and US capital made up 90 percent of all foreign investments. The government attempted to protect the "weaker" sectors of society from the economic crisis by safeguarding employment, discouraging imports, and raising taxes. The actions of the government ignited the opposition and resulted in a coup in 1933 by newly elected president Gabriel Terra. Terra dissolved the legislature and suppressed the opposition but did not completely undermine civil rights. The Terra administration also continued some Batlle-style protection of the weaker elements of society.

The government allowed the 1938 elections as scheduled, and a pro-Terra candidate won. Many on the left criticized the transition to democracy, including Carlos Quijano, founder of the weekly periodical *Marcha*. By the 1940s, the Colorados had reclaimed their influence, winning 47 percent of the vote in the national elections in 1946 and maintaining their power until 1958.[31] During this time, the Socialist and Communist Parties lost the small amount of support they had because of Cold War politics and the prolabor government.

In the early 1950s, Uruguay's yearly export earnings totaled over

US$240 million, but by the end of the decade, earnings had decreased to US$132 million. This economic downturn occurred in large part because of the cessation of the Korean War and the stagnation of industrial growth. During this time, wages also decreased while inflation grew. In order to fix the country's dire economic problems, in 1958, the newly elected Blanco Party, which had finally triumphed over the Colorados, implemented laws inspired by economic liberalism ostensibly in order to manage the failing economy.

However, these policies seemed only to contribute to more unemployment in Uruguay. The second Blanco administration, after seeing the failed policies of their predecessors, attempted other measures such as increasing state expenditures, which also did little to improve the economy.[32] In 1959, six Uruguayan pesos equaled one US dollar. By November 1967, the rate rose to two hundred pesos per dollar, and by October 1970, Uruguayan pesos sold for as much as four hundred per one US dollar.[33] The Tupamaros believed that Uruguay's economic crisis offered the group a chance to ally with the Uruguayan people. Therefore, according to the Tupamaros and many other Uruguayans, government solutions proved ineffectual at ending the economic crisis. The ineptitude of the government inspired the Tupamaros to take radical measures in order to change the increasingly dire economic and political situation in Uruguay.

An important aspect of the transformation of the Uruguayan left during the 1960s concerned moving toward more violent means of political expression in order to challenge the increasingly repressive Uruguayan government. Like many throughout the world who came to support violent means of political action during the 1960s, the MLN-T criticized the left for its insularity and over-reliance on theoretical debates. According to the Tupamaros, who first emerged in 1963, the "old" Uruguayan left had failed to change society through manifestos and electoral solutions. Indeed, the Tupamaros knew that the left in Uruguay never received more than 10 percent of the vote in national elections.[34] For example, in the 1962 national elections, the Uruguayan Communist Party received 3.6 percent of the vote, and the socialist-led Unión Popular only 2.3 percent.[35] Partially because of the left's lack of electoral success, the MLN-T argued that direct and violent political action represented the best way to challenge the Uruguayan government.

Besides the economic crisis and political stagnation, the Cuban Revolution also had an important impact on the radicalization of the Uruguayan left, particularly young people. The Cuban news agency Prensa Latina established itself in Montevideo soon after the revolution on June 16, 1959. Prensa Latina forged close ties with journalists in Montevideo, and many of the agency's reporters maintained an office in the city for over a decade. In 1971, however, the Uruguayan government shut down Prensa Latina on charges that it "conspired against the security of the state." After the closing down of the Prensa Latina office in Montevideo, the Cuban government expressed a specific antipathy for the regime in Uruguay and promised to one day return to the "land of Artigas."[36]

In addition to the influence of Prensa Latina, in 1961, Uruguayan students protested the expulsion of Cuban ambassador Mario García Incháustegui from the country and their government's support of Cuba's ejection from the Organization of American States (OAS). The Uruguayan military further continued to show their disdain for Cuban politics by stopping a crowd of sympathizers who went to bid farewell to Cuban diplomats at the airport. In protest, students, along with all sectors of Uruguayan society, held meetings and marched in solidarity with the Cuban Revolution. In these early meetings, Uruguayan students became radicalized and began to question the effectiveness of traditional electoral solutions.[37]

The reactions of the Uruguayan government to the people's solidarity with Cuba as well as its increasing repression of organized labor represented to the leftists the beginnings of a future authoritarian police state. This inspired many in the Uruguayan left to rethink their political tactics. The support or rejection of tactics used to implement the Cuban Revolution also inspired schisms in the Uruguayan left.[38] Most in the Uruguayan Communist Party disdained violence as a means of political change. In support of this, some cited Che Guevara's aforementioned speech at the Universidad de la República on August 17, 1961. Guevara told the crowd that no place in Latin America except Uruguay allowed so many democratic freedoms. Guevara advised that the Uruguayan left should try to use all available democratic tactics to incite change before resorting to violence.[39] Ironically, before Che's speech, counterrevolutionaries sprayed the auditorium with stink bombs. Afterwards, as he walked out of the auditorium, an assassin tried to kill Guevara but ended up fatally shooting educator Arbelio Ramírez. Journalist Niko Schvarz wrote that Che was "inconsolable" the night of Ramírez's death. Some Uruguayans referred to Ramírez's killing as Uruguay's first modern political assassination.[40] Senator Alba Roballo even published a poem in tribute to Ramírez entitled "El Primer Disparo," which claimed, "It all started with the first shot / the first death / killed the first innocent / Who remembers his name / Arbelio, Arbelio, Arbelio Ramírez."[41]

Factions of the Uruguayan left, such as the Communist and Socialist Parties, applauded the Cuban Revolution but also expressed opposition to armed struggle in their country. According to many Uruguayan communists and socialists, the left needed to create a popular front and search for electoral solutions to the problems within Uruguay. Secretary of the Communist Party in Uruguay, Rodney Arismendi, spoke on this issue in Cuba as early as 1967 when he participated in a Latin American solidarity conference. As chief of his delegation from Uruguay, Arismendi gave a speech about the people of Uruguay and their support for Cuba. He also argued for the importance of the masses in the struggle for revolution. Arismendi asserted that to support acts of solidarity in only their most "extreme terms" ignored the importance of comparatively moderate strikes and demonstrations taking place in Uruguay. By discounting those who took solidarity to the "extreme," Arismendi took an obvious jab at the tactics of the Tupamaros. Arismendi criticized violent action, claiming he only wanted the Uruguayan people to take the path of least suffering. While Arismendi purported to understand the need for armed struggle against the bloody realities of repression in Latin America, he did not believe countries such as Uruguay were ready for such battles. Arismendi told his Cuban audience, "It is a mistake to say that we must be prepared for every method of struggle, for we thereby avoid defining the basic aspects of the revolutionary process."[42]

Opposition to traditional communist and socialist organizations and beliefs such as Arismendi's came from activists in groups such as the Movimiento Revolucionario Oriental (MRO), disillusioned young people in the Socialist Party, and communists who formed the Movimiento de Izquierda Revolucionaria (MIR). The MRO, founded in 1962, consisted of young Uruguayans who studied guerrilla warfare and rejected the tactics of the traditional Uruguayan left. Inspired by both the Cuban Revolution and their country's dire economic situation, the group offered solidarity in the form of people and arms to radicalized labor movements.[43]

Similarly, disenchanted members of the Socialist Party also rejected the electoral left, citing its powerlessness to fight against the repressive Uruguayan state. They grew tired of their party focusing solely on electoral work and critiqued its supposed alienation from the masses. These splinter groups expressed disillusionment with the poor electoral show-ing of the Uruguayan left and argued that conventional political solu-tions failed to truly confront the Uruguayan government. Disenchanted members of the Socialist Party finally completely abandoned electoral solutions after the left received only 6 percent of the vote in the 1962 election. Legal work also seemed futile in the fight against increasing repression from the state and radicalized right wing organizations.[44]

Members of the MIR, founded in 1963, also expressed solidarity with the Cuban Revolution and supported the use of guerrilla tactics in Uruguay. These young former communists disavowed the Uruguayan Communist Party's theories of nonviolence and their alliance with the Soviet Union. Denouncing the Soviet Union as fraudulent and bureau-cratic, disillusioned militants searched for alternative political and tacti-cal inspiration. During their inquiry, they found other young activists who broke with the Communist Party during debate of the early 1960s concerning the authenticity of the USSR's and China's revolutions. These comrades perceived the Chinese Revolution as more authentic and truly revolutionary. Inspired by the Cuban and Chinese Revolutions and re-belling against the nonviolent ideology of the staid Uruguayan Commu-nist Party, the splinter group, including future Uruguayan president José Mujica, formed the MIR.[45]

Various types of exchange between members of the proviolence and nonviolent Uruguayan left and Cuba occurred during the 1960s and 1970s. For example, Ruben Abrines, a Uruguayan member of the 1970 Latin American Brigade Victoria de Girón noted that his time in Cuba brought him a higher level of political awareness. Abrines was a car-penter and student who visited Cuba along with four other Uruguayan delegates. After taking part in the sugarcane harvest, Abrines felt that helping with the harvest could never repay what the Cubans had done for him and Uruguayan liberation movements in general. The volunteer promised to tell others in Uruguay what he had experienced in Revolu-tionary Cuba. According to Abrines, spreading the ideas of the revolu-tion at home would be the real contribution of the Uruguayan delegates to Cuba.[46]

The Cuban Revolution also specifically influenced the Tupama-ros, and some exchange occurred between the Cuban government and the group.[47] Many Tupamaros eventually escaped to Cuba, and others trained in the country before coming back to Uruguay to join the Tupa-maros.[48] While the group's secrecy makes it difficult to uncover all of its connections with Cuba, the Tupamaros reached out to the Cuban press with messages for the "heroic Cuban youth." In one communiqué they sent to the Second Congress of the Young Communist League of Cuba, the Tupamaros assured, "We know of your past and present successes, these being the motivating force of our own struggle and it is our fervent desire that the present Congress be the dawn of new revolutionary conquests. Our people, following the same path that began in your homeland . . . are nearing day by day—and today with an uncontainable impulse—its complete liberation."[49]

However, the Tupamaros also accentuated their ideological independence and strategic differences from Cuba, particularly in the form of urban guerrilla warfare. Some Tupamaros engaged in a debate with Cubans about the true possibilities of the successes of urban guerrilla warfare.[50] Richard Gillespie writes about the Tupamaros, "Originally Cuban influenced, their subsequent expertise in urban guerrilla warfare owed more to collaboration with Argentine Peronist guerrillas, the strategic thinking of Spanish Civil War veteran Abraham Guillén and the study of the Algerian guerrilla."[51] Therefore, while the Cuban Revolution had an important influence on the Tupamaros, they also developed their own unique revolutionary tactics.

Indeed, during the 1960s, leftists in Uruguay took many paths. As the Tupamaros formed their organization, Uruguayan unions organized strikes and marches in increasingly large numbers. In response to organized labor, the Uruguayan government declared an internal "state of siege" several times, first in 1963 during an electric company workers strike. Conveniently, within the next few years, government declared "states of siege" coincided with the marches of the sugarcane worker's Unión de Trabajadores Azucareros de Artigas (UTAA) and strikes of other state and bank employees.[52] Thus, for leftist activists, the reactions of the Uruguayan government to the people's solidarity with Cuba as well as their repression of organized labor demonstrated that the police state they had been trying to fend off was actually taking hold.[53]

Members of the UTAA further challenged traditional leftist politics in Uruguay. In the early 1960s, socialist attorney and future founder of the Tupamaros Raúl Sendic joined with the UTAA to act as their legal representative. Under his direction, the UTAA launched two strikes, the second of which received a response from the management of one company, who signed an agreement with the UTAA and implemented the workers' demands. However, the union remained dissatisfied with workers' conditions, and under Sendic's leadership they marched to Montevideo to confront the Uruguayan parliament. UTAA workers, along with their wives and children, marched nearly four hundred miles from Artigas to Montevideo in protest.[54] The march proved futile as the government failed to respond to protestors' pressure. In turn, Sendic suggested that union members and other social activists occupy an unused piece of land as a more radical action. While Sendic prepared for the occupation with the UTAA, the Uruguayan government arrested and imprisoned him in order to squelch the union's plans.[55]

After his release, Sendic began to see what he called the "futility" of the legal and political process. Sendic later wrote about legal institutions, "A gun well loaded gives more guarantees than the whole Uruguayan institution and laws."[56] Inspired to take a different course of action, Sendic led what most consider the Tupamaros' first revolutionary action on July 31, 1963. Sendic, along with a few other sympathizers, "expropriated" arms from an upper-class shooting club at Colonia Suiza. Although the getaway van overturned during the mission and the police arrested some of the people involved in the action, many on the left viewed the robbery as a success because they had changed their tactics from debate to violent action. The MLN-T followed this act with hundreds of other more successful actions, several of which other activists admired and hoped to emulate.

Some who took part in the action came from the Movimiento de Ayuda al Campesino (MAC), which formed after members left the aforementioned MRO in protest. Activists specifically broke with the MRO and joined the Tupamaros after the MRO promised to use its funds to help with the UTAA's land occupation but instead funneled resources to electoral campaigns. Angry MAC members contended that by supporting electoral politics the MRO had not fulfilled its revolutionary promises. The MAC instead focused on assisting the struggle of rural workers by emulating the tactics of the Cuban Revolution. One member even traveled to Cuba to study guerrilla warfare.[57] While critiquing the Uruguayan left's over-reliance on theory, the group also encouraged discussions of international events including national liberation in Algeria, the Vietnam War, and Marxism.

Besides members of Sendic's group, the Tupamaros eventually subsumed other revolutionary groups disaffected by the politics of the Uruguayan left. This included the aforementioned MAC, MIR, and members of the Socialist Party. Tupamaro and former MRO member Eleuterio

Fernández Huidobro commented about the break of the new revolutionary left with the old, "We broke with certain deep rooted vice in the Left. And it is true that the traditional Left broke with us."[58] Young leftists began to see what they believed represented the corruption of the "old" electoral left. By the mid-1960s, disaffected members from the Uruguayan left, Trotskyites, Christians, and Independents also joined the Tupamaros. These varied members sought a different path of resistance than traditional leftist politics offered. In one Tupamaros manifesto, the group acknowledged, "We must recognize there are authentic revolutionaries in all leftist parties and many more that are not even organized."[59] Joining former members of the UTAA, MRO, and MIR, these activists allied and began to discuss various tactics and train in self-defense.

In 1964, the variant groups met formally at a symposium at the beach resort of Parque de la Plata. In one of the MLN-T's first known documents, the group condemned the alleged inaction of the left by titling their paper "No Lamb Ever Saved Itself by Bleating." In this document, the Tupamaros asserted the importance of armed struggle in Uruguay, particularly because of political and economic crisis. They characterized their armed struggle as predominately urban and part of a continental strategy of revolution. The MLN-T also claimed that their armed struggle operated only within the unique context of Uruguay. In this way, the newly formed group accentuated their independence from other movements. The group somewhat articulated their goal of achieving both national liberation and socialism. The document chided the "old" left as misguided and alienated from the people. However, it would take several years before the MLN-T provided a detailed plan concerning what they wanted from a revolutionary government.

Not everyone expressed approval toward the vague proposals of 1964. A group of anarchists demanded a formal ideological position for the group but were told that strict definitions produced only divisions and not revolutionary results. After the anarchists abandoned the group, the remaining militants agreed to form a new organization and unify all of their financial resources and members under one single executive committee. Although the name had been used occasionally by MAC in leaflets, the newly formed group called themselves the Tupamaros.[60] After the symposium, the organization broke up into various cells. These cells, set up in a tightly controlled hierarchy, contained coordinators who debated tactical and ideological issues. More significantly, the Tupamaros began to create and maintain hideouts and other infrastructure for their organization. They trained in the preparation and handling of explosives and weapons and performed a major inspection of the sewer system in Montevideo.[61]

The group also began performing some violent actions, such as the bombing of the offices of Bayer Pharmaceutical Company on August 9, 1965. After the explosion, officials found a leaflet with a message, "Death to Vietnam's Yankee assassins. The assassin's intervention in Vietnam must be answered by a union of all oppressed people. The common enemy must be crushed. Bayer, a Nazi enterprise, supports the gringo's intervention. Viva Vietnam. Viva la revolución. TUPAMAROS."[62]

At their so-called formal founding at El Pinar beach resort in 1966, the Tupamaros again reiterated their distance from the conventional Uruguayan left and their support of violent tactics, such as the Bayer Company bombing. They argued that the Uruguayan left would never grow by engaging in armchair debates and supporting electoral solutions. Even if the left won the elections (which seemed improbable in the 1960s), the Tupamaros anticipated repressive forces squelching the left's rise to political power. The Tupamaros claimed that the majority of Uruguayan leftist groups "appear to have more confidence in manifestos, in issuing theoretical statements referring to the Revolution . . . without understanding that it is basically revolutionary action that precipitates revolutionary situations."[63] According to the MLN-T, inciting true change in Uruguay required violent and direct action. After another series of intense debates during the convention, some socialists and members of the MIR abandoned the cause of the Tupamaros. The issue of double militancy, or being part of a political movement, feminist group, or both, caused schisms in the group.[64] Members of the MIR also left the group when the Tupamaros rejected their proposal to form a Maoist party.

After the volatile meeting in 1966, which alienated some militants, factions of the MIR and Socialist Party decided to stay, joining with Sendic's group and the MAC. The group decided to focus its attention primarily on not theories but violent actions, which they felt offered the best possibility for radically changing Uruguayan society. In reflection, one Tupamara asserted that many who joined the organization were in a post-adolescent period or a late-adolescent phase of life. Such youthful idealism, which supported the construction Che's "New Man" in Uruguayan society, inspired Tupamaro members to give themselves completely to the cause. In part, some Tupamaros believed that their members' youthful idealism and passion substituted for the lack of cohesive revolutionary theory. Thus, the notion of the mythical and romantic revolutionary in action often replaced the theoretical education of militants.[65]

The majority of the founding members of the Tupamaros were between nineteen and thirty-four years old and male. Most came from the middle and lower classes. Students made up nearly half of the organization from 1966 to 1969, but their numbers dwindled to 20 percent by 1972. The proportion of Tupamaro members who were female increased from only 10 percent in the mid-1960s to nearly 30 percent by 1970.[66] The ability of radical youth to make change in the world was reflected in Uruguayan Carlos Molina's song "Coplas y revolucion" or "Poems and revolution." In the song, Molina claimed, "Youth is life and is beauty. It is spirit, light, blood, hope. Youths are those that always keep going, with the light of triumph in their gaze. Those are not youths, no, those who waver. They are not youth who drag behind. Youth is in rebellion against everything."[67]

Over the next two years, group members engaged in a few clashes with police, resulting in the death of two Tupamaros. According to one supporter of the Tupamaros, the group achieved "political maturity" between 1966 and 1968, which coincided with the public's increasing awareness of the decline of Uruguay's civil rights.[68] Beginning in 1968, the varied actions of the Tupamaros included bombing buildings and vehicles connected to the US, abducting officials from several different nations, broadcasting manifestos on radio stations, besieging the city of Pando, harassing police officers, robbing various banks and casinos, and stealing documents from a financial firm and exposing them to the public and judiciary. By the late 1960s, these varied and frequent actions garnered support for the MLN-T and reinforced their popular nickname: Robin Hood.[69] One Tupamaro explained about the group's robberies, "Tactically, we always characterize the bank robberies as 'taking the money back.'"[70]

By 1970, the Tupamaros had several thousand members (this includes the hundreds of individuals who aided the group without officially joining). These "peripheral" cells helped with propaganda, monetary issues, and recruitment. Other sympathizers supplied resources, information, and medical help and sometimes offered their homes and property for the Tupamaros to hide in. The group understood the significance of these peripheral cells, claiming that "all tasks that support a strategic plan are equally important for the revolution. He who purchases the material necessary for a base of operations, he who collects funds, he who lends his automobile for a mobilization, he who lends his house, is running as great a risk and sometimes a greater one, than the commando group in action."[71] The Tupamaros "request" of civilian cars to help with their actions also became legendary during the 1960s. The popular myth claimed that the civilians who allowed the Tupamaros to borrow their cars rarely put up a fight. Some even supposedly told the revolutionaries peculiarities or issues about their cars in order to help them. While his or her car was in use, many times the civilian wandered throughout Montevideo, eating a meal or going to the movies. However, Tupamaro members did often watch the civilians discreetly to make sure they did not inform the police of the theft of their car. Usually, civilians waited patiently for their car to be returned.[72]

The actions of the government further strengthened the public's support of the Tupamaros. When Uruguayan president Oscar Gestido died in December 1967, his replacement Jorge Pacheco Areco began a campaign against the noncommunist left. Pacheco banned several leftist groups and even shut down newspapers such as the socialist weekly *El Sol*. Pacheco's actions earned him the nickname "Paco" Areco because according to the people, the Uruguayan president did not deserve the inclusion of the word "Che" in his name.[73] In 1968, after the police responded with excessive violence during a May Day demonstration, teachers, students, and workers protested in solidarity. By June, almost all university and high school students and teachers in Montevideo were on strike. Hundreds of leftists also responded violently, creating barricades and confronting the police with slingshots.

In this tense political climate, on August 7, the Tupamaros kidnapped Ulysses Pereira Reverbel, a government official and friend of Pacheco. Reverbel was the director of the state-owned Power and Telephone Enterprise (UTE) and supported a strong anti-union policy. Tupamaro commandos abducted Reverbel outside of his home and wounded the companions who attempted to help him. The Tupamaros left a note behind that explained, "Today Mr. Reverbel has been detained by decision of the MLN." The note also told why the group kidnapped Reverbel and that his physical well-being depended on "the conduct of the repressive forces and the fascist groups at their service."

Before Reverbel was found five days later, unharmed, in a Land

Rover parked near Montevideo's soccer stadium, the government deployed more than three thousand police officers to search for him, nearly half of the entire police force in Montevideo. Pacheco ostensibly believed that his friend was being held in one of the "subversive grottos" of the university. Convinced that students and professors supported the Tupamaros, the police occupied the Universidad del la República and confronted student protestors in a street battle that lasted over twelve hours. After the police killed several students, including a young man named Liber Arce (who would become a symbol of the subversion against government repression), student resistance intensified until the military occupied all universities and high schools in Montevideo. Critics claimed that the government used the situation with the Tupamaros as an excuse to occupy the university, a stalwart of resistance to Pacheco's regime.[74] The occupation of public schools in Montevideo only served to further radicalize students and intensify their support of the actions of the Tupamaros.

While human rights in Uruguay steadily declined in the late 1960s, an official coup and complete cessation of democracy occurred when President Juan María Bordaberry, assisted by the armed forces, indefinitely suspended constitutional rights on June 1, 1973. Part of this suspension allowed for the continuous detention of those perceived as a national security threat, which was broadly interpreted as anyone who disagreed with the government's actions. Weeks later, on June 27, Bordaberry dissolved the elected General Assembly and soon after declared all political parties and student organizations of the left illegal.[75] The MLN-T undertook numerous operations to combat the increasingly bloody repression. However, by the end of 1973, the Uruguayan state, with the assistance of the US government, had imprisoned the majority of the Tupamaros and any others who dared to speak out against the government.[76]

More than 14 percent of the population fled Uruguay between 1964 and 1981.[77] Fifty percent left between 1973 and 1977, directly after Bordaberry's coup. By the end of 1972, an estimated one thousand Tupamaros had already gone to Cuba, Argentina, or Chile. In Cuba and Chile, Fidel Castro and Salvador Allende offered the Tupamaros economic and political support.[78] The Tupamaros went to Chile en route to Cuba, where the Allende government allowed them to rest and reorganize. Many MLN-T members also fled to nearby Argentina. The short-lived Cámpora government in Argentina in 1973 became a refuge for a number of Uruguayan leftists who needed time to regroup and ponder new strategies about how to combat the authoritarian regime.

During their exile in Argentina, some Tupamaros superficially strengthened their bonds with guerrilla groups such as the Montoneros. They also participated in debates about ideological and tactical failures and successes. Other Tupamaros tried to align themselves with Marxism-Leninism and become more doctrinaire. They formed small splinter groups, such as Nuevo Tiempo, founded in 1975 in Buenos Aires. Nuevo Tiempo hoped to develop a stronger Marxist ideological base, broader international alliances, and a political solution to the problems in Uruguay.[79]

By late 1975, the Uruguayan government intensified its persecution of the Communist Party, forcing hundreds of activists to leave the country. By this point Argentina was not a safe refuge for Uruguayan exiles, so communists fled to Mexico, East Germany, Cuba, Czechoslovakia, and the Soviet Union. By 1976, the Cuban government urged the Tupamaros to leave the country as they hoped to distance themselves from Latin American guerrillas in order to reinforce their new "pro-Soviet" turn. Some Tupamaros who still believed in the validity of armed struggle went to Colombia, El Salvador, and Nicaragua, where they allied with guerrilla groups. Other MLN-T members moved to Europe and attempted to redefine their once proviolence politics.[80]

Sources and Methodology

Since the Tupamaros were a clandestine organization, there is a paucity of sources directly written by group members. Therefore, this work relies heavily upon interviews of Tupamaros in leftist publications in Latin America and the US, testimonials from kidnapping victims, songs, poems, communiqués, government reports, various mainstream and countercultural newspapers in the US and Uruguay, and information written by other leftist organizations about the MLN-T. When checked against one another and analyzed in aggregate, these sources offer information about the cultural interests, tactics, day-to-day life, political inspiration, and gender organization of the Tupamaros. Furthermore, as this work is largely an intellectual history, these sources reveal how the Uruguayan and US left imagined one another. Although I explore concrete connections between groups, this work prioritizes the ideas and perceptions of the Tupamaros and the greater Uruguayan left.

Using previously ignored sources located in Latin American and US archives and special collections, this manuscript uncovers connections between the MLN-T and radical groups in the US through a web of seemingly disconnected archival materials. The Biblioteca Nacional del Uruguay (BNU) in Montevideo, Uruguay, and the Centro de Documentación e Investigación de la Cultura de Izquierdas en la Argentina (CEDINCI) in Buenos Aires, Argentina, provided sources related to the Tupamaros and the greater Uruguayan left. The BNU housed the Uruguay publication *Marcha*, a newspaper edited by Carlos Quijano that was integral to leftist politics in Uruguay through 1974, as well as documents authored by the Tupamaros. The CEDINCI provided rare pamphlets, bulletins, journals, and posters from the Uruguayan left. Materials from the Sallie Bingham Center for Women's History and Culture at the David M. Rubenstein Rare Book and Manuscript Library at Duke University and from the expansive Marshall Bloom Alternative Press Collection at the Amherst College Library revealed the depth and significance of the US side of solidarity with Uruguayans. These sources contradict established thinking about the supposed lack of transnational alliances forged between US and Uruguayan revolutionaries during the 1960s through the 1980s. The sources at the BNU, the CEDINCI, Duke University, and Amherst College demonstrate that leftists in the US not only acknowledged but in some instances initiated contact, asked for help, and forged ties with the Uruguayan left. Conversely, these sources reveal the previously unexplored history of how the Uruguayan left and the Tupamaros looked specifically to the Black Power movement and the US left for revolutionary inspiration.

Feminist scholar Judith Butler's assertions of gender as a performance also influenced my approach to the construction of femininity and masculinity among the Tupamaros. According to Butler, there exists no "original" gender or sexuality—all function as an impersonation of some sort, an act that has been reinstituted and imitated throughout time.[81] Butler argues that drag demonstrates how genders are "appropriated, theatricalized, worn and done," which implies that all gender is a sort of impersonation. She asserts, "Gender is a kind of imitation for which there is no original."[82] Therefore, while the dominant discourse in Uruguay supported notions of gender as an intrinsic phenomenon, constructions of masculinity and femininity in the Tupamaros exemplified how gender represents a type of performance. In order to be accepted as viable militants, the Tupamaras needed to lose their femininity and "perform" masculine gender roles. Most Tupamaras had to reaffirm the so-called masculine attributes of aggression, physical control, and mastery of weaponry on a daily basis to be included in the group and considered true revolutionaries.

Furthermore, my analysis of gender employs María Josefina Saldaña-Portillo's work *The Revolutionary Imagination in the Americas and the Age of Development*, which suggests that revolutionary icons of the 1960s and 1970s shared notions of masculinist transformation while attempting to transcend ethnic identity. Saldaña-Portillo posits, "The whole guerrilla experience served as a trope for fantasmatic recuperation of full masculinity."[83] Building on this characterization of revolution and gender, I argue that the Tupamaros idealized transformative masculine identity and also ignored racial and ethnic differences in the name of the MLN-T's political struggle.

Revolution in Twentieth-Century Latin America

Many significant revolutions and proviolence revolutionary movements emerged in Latin America during the twentieth century. Scholars have explored the unique national character of revolutions in Latin America, particularly the Mexican Revolution of 1910, Cuba's revolution in 1959, and Nicaragua's in 1979.[84] These revolutions followed exceptional patterns and definitions of liberation that did not emulate strict Marxist definitions for when, how, and where radical change would occur. During the 1960s, twenty-five proviolence revolutionary groups emerged in Latin America; one of these groups was the Tupamaros. By the 1980s, armed groups existed in seventeen of the nineteen countries in Latin America. A majority of these guerrilla movements found inspiration in the writings and life of Ernesto "Che" Guevara.

One of the most important works on Latin American revolution in the twentieth century is Guevara's *Guerrilla Warfare* (first published in 1960), which inspired revolutionary groups not only in Latin America but throughout the world. In *Guerrilla Warfare*, Guevara moved away from traditional ideas of how to create a communist revolution by arguing that a small group of about thirty to fifty armed guerrillas could instigate revolution. This small group of revolutionary fighters in the countryside or "foco" would create the conditions for revolution by sparking a rural-based revolt. The guerrilla foco was an important part of the struggle to defeat imperialism (believed by Marxists to be the last stage of world capitalism). Though inspired by Marxism, Che's methods were criticized by traditional communists who felt that the masses should lead the revolution.

Other writers of revolution, however, objected to Guevara's argument that rural peoples constituted the most important social force for radical change. In *The Philosophy of the Urban Guerrilla*, Spanish-born Abraham Guillén argued for the strategy and tactics of the urban guerrilla. Though Che's ideas for revolution worked for Latin American countries with large rural populations, many Southern Cone countries (particularly Brazil, Argentina, and Uruguay) contained an urban majority. Most famously implemented by the Tupamaros, Guillén's strategy offered the principal challenge to Guevarist revolutionary techniques. He advocated bank robberies, kidnappings, and bombings as the primary tactics for the urban guerrilla.

Other writers of revolution in twentieth-century Latin America have focused on the level of "success" of revolutions in Latin America. They attempt to uncover why certain revolutions succeeded and why others failed. Timothy Wickham-Crowley's book *Guerrillas and Revolutions in Latin America* contends that the Sandinista Revolution in Nicaragua and the Cuban Revolution succeeded because they both engendered national, cross-class alliances. Thus, alliances of "convenience" formed between radical and more moderate opponents of the authoritarian Batista and Somoza regimes. Wickham-Crowley also contends that although the revolutionaries "made" the revolution, they did so largely because of structural weakness. In *Modern Latin American Revolutions*, Eric Selbin argues that revolutions can be successful only when consolidation and institutionalization occur. He defines consolidation as convincing the people to embrace the revolutionary project while institutionalization consists of dismantling old-regime institutions and reconfiguring new ones. Selbin conceptualizes the Sandinista Revolution as an excellent example of both institutionalization and consolidation.

In Nicaragua, after the Sandinista Revolution, the enactment of new laws and institutions occurred relatively smoothly. The revolutionaries understood the limits of their authority and peacefully transferred power to another political party after the 1990 elections. According to

Selbin, Cuba experienced consolidation without institutionalization. By holding so much political influence, leader Fidel Castro seemed unwilling to share power. Therefore, Selbin argues that the Cuban Revolution was overall "unsuccessful." Conversely, in his 1993 work *Utopia Unarmed: The Latin American Left after the Cold War*, Jorge Castañeda contended that "with the exception of Cuba [the left] has failed miserably in its efforts to take power, make revolution and change the world." If these definitions represent the criteria for a successful revolution, then the Tupamaros completely failed in their ability to incite revolution in Uruguay during the 1960s and 1970s. In fact, some critics explicitly blame the Tupamaros for the rise of Bordaberry's authoritarian regime in 1973, which incarcerated or killed most of Uruguay's revolutionaries. However, after examining the 2009 democratic election of former Tupamaro leader José Mujica, only the narrowest definition of "success" eliminates the Tupamaros as a group that incited substantial change in their country's political system. The road to power took a significant period of time—nearly fifty years. By the turn of the century, however, the revolutionary vision of the Tupamaros manifested in profoundly different ways than it did in the 1960s.

Chapter Overview

This work consists of four chapters. I begin with an exploration of how and why the Tupamaros came to occupy such an influential position in the imagination and activism of the US left. From there I examine how during the late 1960s and early 1970s the Uruguayan left and the Tupamaros offered solidarity to the US left, particularly the Black Power movement. Next, I analyze the political strategies that US activists employed on behalf of Uruguayans under authoritarian rule. Following an analysis of the gendered forms of representations of Tupamara political prisoners by US activists, in the final chapter I look specifically at the construction of gender roles and sexual mores in the group.

Chapter 1 reveals the romanticism and representations of the Tupamaros, specifically from the perspective of the US left, during the 1960s and 1970s. I explore why the Tupamaros maintained a special position of influence in the imagination and activism of the US left. To their admirers, the Tupamaros ostensibly represented a case of more "successful" revolutionaries. I posit that this occurred in large part because of the popular notion that the group had perfected the art of urban guerrilla warfare, particularly in the form of technical superiority. The film *State of Siege* also influenced the US left's perception of the Tupamaros. Though *State of Siege* was a foreign film, it influenced the politics and discourse of various types of leftists in the US. The controversial film, which portrayed the Tupamaros in a positive manner, garnered the attention of leftists and taught a whole new audience about the politics of the MLN-T. Along with romanticism from the left, I analyze the multifaceted critiques of the Tupamaros, which demonstrate how the group pervaded both the activism and imagination of the US left. Some in the left who supported political violence also viewed the Tupamaros as lacking a sufficiently strong Marxist ideological base. Pacifist leftists objected to the Tupamaros, whom they saw as fueling the fire of oppression through their violent acts. An analysis of these critiques also reveals the tensions that existed within the group and the left in Uruguay.

Chapter 2 shows the various ways the Uruguayan left conceptualized their US counterparts. Looking specifically at the Uruguayan leftist publication *Marcha*, I argue that both the Tupamaros and the greater Uruguayan left showed particular admiration for the Black Panther Party and other civil rights organizations in the US. The Uruguayan left saw the US as divided into two separate and warring nations—one imperialist (the US government) and the other both oppressed and radicalized (students, the Black Power movement, and so on). The Uruguayan left consistently allied itself with the oppressed "nation" in the US in hopes of overthrowing the current US government. This chapter also examines how the Tupamaros specifically consumed US leftist and Black Power cultural products such as songs and movies. However, while the primarily white, middle-class Uruguayan left demonstrated solidarity for the US Black Power movement, they often ignored the very existence of those of African descent in their own country.

Chapter 3 examines the multifaceted forms of US activism on behalf of Uruguay and the instances of international reciprocal connections between activists. I demonstrate that numerous types of activism emerged during the 1970s and 1980s concerning Uruguay and its declining democracy. While some US groups focused primarily on human rights issues, others criticized human rights violations and also offered leftist solidarity to Uruguayans. I demonstrate that in order to criticize the authoritarian regime in Uruguay, some from the left also denounced US capitalism as well as apartheid in South Africa. These groups, however, failed to offer any form of gendered analysis of the treatment of male and female political prisoners in Uruguay and sometimes ignored the existence of women prisoners all together. Despite the overall ignorance of the existence of female political prisoners, a few activists in Uruguay reached out to groups in the US on behalf of Tupamaras.

Chapter 4 investigates the construction of gender roles and sexuality within the Tupamaros and the greater Uruguayan left. I argue that while the Tupamaros undeniably opened a political space for Uruguayan women and deviated from traditional understandings of women as passive, maternal, and nonviolent they nevertheless marginalized female militants in other ways. My research reveals that despite the Tupamaros offering a unique mechanism for women's public participation, the group overall denied female militants the opportunity to speak about their own liberation and required women to assume socially constructed traits of masculinity in order to participate as revolutionaries. Furthermore, while the Tupamaros and the greater Uruguayan left may have harbored somewhat more open ideas about sexuality than the rest of Uruguay, they remained nowhere near radical.

This manuscript challenges long-held notions about the Tupamaros. It shows that rather than disconnected from leftists in the US, the Tupamaros and others in the Uruguayan left engaged in an active discussion with US-based revolutionaries. The Tupamaros influenced groups in the US, and in turn, revolutionaries from the US influenced the MLN-T. Beyond issues of transnationalism, my research also illuminates the complexity of gender relations within the Tupamaros, which included both instances of liberation and subjugation for female militants.

1

"Digging the Tupes"
The Unique Revolutionary Contributions of the Tupamaros

[There will be] a country for all, or a country for none.
  —Tupamaros popular slogan

IN A 1969 BOOK describing the strategy and actions of the Tupamaros, Antonio Mercader and Jorge de Vera depicted MLN-T members as "total samurais, with muscles of steel, mentally alert, instant reflexes, an exact knowledge of weapons and resistance to pain."[1] This romanticized description is one of numerous examples of the admiration that the left had for the Tupamaros. The Tupamaros garnered international attention in the late 1960s, a time when leftists throughout the world turned to more violent means of activism in order to inspire political change. Because of their violent actions against an increasingly repressive state, for their admirers, the Tupamaros were successful revolutionaries who challenged their country's dictatorship and won the support of a large portion of the Uruguayan people. With their seemingly creative and usually dangerous actions, the group specifically garnered the attention of the left in the United States. Scholars of the left occasionally and briefly acknowledge the international impact of the Tupamaros, but their influence and importance has not been explored in depth in historical literature. Despite frequent references and stories about the Tupamaros within leftist activism, scholars have tended to focus on Cuba as the romanticized country for leftist organizations in the US in the 1960s and 1970s.

While the Tupamaros performed actions not drastically different from other guerrilla groups such as the Brazilian Ação Libertadora Nacional and Cuba's urban guerrillas, the left perceived the Tupamaros as more successful, egalitarian, and creative.[2] The Tupamaros' victories occurred in part because of the Uruguayan state's initially weak response to the group. During the 1960s, the Uruguayan government lacked the ability to repress its citizens as violently as other nations in Latin America, allowing the Tupamaros to have more staying power and perceived successes. Because of the democratic and essentially nonviolent tradition within Uruguay during the twentieth century, initially the ruling government had neither the resources to neutralize the group nor the historical framework to conceptualize their violent attacks.

In order to demonstrate the supposed superiority of the Tupamaros, their leftist admirers pointed to the Tupamaros' use of urban guerrilla warfare, which included actions such as the kidnapping of several government officials (including US foreign agent Dan Mitrione) and the making and distribution of the controversial movie about the group, *State of Siege*. These romantic representations enabled the Tupamaros to invade the consciousness of the action-oriented left more than other urban based Latin American revolutionary groups. Thus, the left often *imagined* the MLN-T as more successful and egalitarian than other revolutionaries.[3] This romantic perception inspired leftists to study the tactics and practices of the group in order to start similar revolutions in their own countries. However, while idealized portrayals proved common, the left also had a wide range of reactions to the accomplishments of the Tupamaros, some of which included criticism of the group's lack of a coherent ideology. Others rejected the MLN-T's advocacy of violence as a proper means of societal and political change. However, even strong critics of the Tupamaros recognized the group's achievements in their practice of urban guerrilla warfare.[4]

Urban Guerrilla Warfare

A primary reason many North American groups and movements throughout the world admired the Tupamaros was the perception that the group more successfully implemented urban guerrilla warfare tactics than did their colleagues in other countries. Tupamaro supporters argued that Uruguay represented an ideal place to practice urban guerrilla warfare. By the 1960s, half of Uruguayans lived in the capital city of Montevideo, and 30 percent more resided in other urban areas.[5] The Tupamaros' inspiration for urban guerrilla warfare derived in part from the so-called theoretical brain of the group, Abraham Guillén. Along with Guillén, Brazilian militant Carlos Marighella also inspired the urban guerrilla strategies of the Tupamaros and other leftists throughout the world. However, Guillén had a specific impact on and association with the Tupamaros.[6] Though the relationship between Guillén and the Tupamaros is not completely clear, the left considered Guillén the Tupamaros' theoretical mastermind as he wrote extensively about the group's revolutionary development. While not an official member of the Tupamaros, in 1966 Guillén participated in series of discussions with Tupamaros and a cell of Argentine guerrillas in Montevideo.[7] He later published his contributions to these meetings and also expressed the Tupamaros' ideas concerning urban guerrilla warfare in a book entitled *Estrategia de la guerrilla urbana*.[8] Publishing information from these meetings proved to be an important task as the group rarely articulated their theories to a larger audience.

Guillén, originally from Spain, immigrated to Argentina when he was thirty-five. He earned fame as a commentator on international politics but never joined a Marxist party. He was associated with the Uturunos leftist guerrilla movement in Northwest Argentina until the Argentine government arrested him for his involvement with the group.[9] When he was released from jail three months later in 1962, Guillén escaped to Montevideo. There he established himself with Fidelista strategy groups but soon realized that the topography and urban demography of Uruguay was not conducive to rural strategies.[10] This realization supported Guillén's argument that topography should never be the foremost element of consideration for revolutionary movements. Instead, Guillén asserted that ultimately people make the revolution.[11]

Guillén's critical work, *Estrategia de la guerrilla urbana*, helped provide a theoretical model for the Tupamaros. Guillén's notion of urban guerrilla warfare posited an alternative to Che Guevara's ideas of guerrilla warfare in the countryside. Inspired by the actions of the Tupamaros, Guillén later contended that the group demonstrated the struggle between "capitalism and socialism with its epicenter in the great cities."[12] Guillén even went so far as to criticize the ostensibly poor strategy of carrying out a revolution in the middle of the countryside as "peasants did in the middle ages."[13] Guillén suggested instead that guerrillas in countries such as Uruguay and Argentina should engage in prolonged urban warfare and focus on small victories that would eventually destroy existing governments.

Large cities would ideally contain hundreds of revolutionary cells living separately but fighting together (which the Tupamaros accomplished at the height of their success). Guillén advocated that urban guerrillas rob banks and kidnap important figures for ransom. Such strategies appealed to those that lived in large cities and had trouble relating to notions of guerrilla warfare focused on the countryside. Therefore, within this symbiotic relationship, the Tupamaros came to represent Guillén's idea of urban warfare.[14] Guillén also called for the union of as much as 80 percent of the population in a broad front to create revolution. Thus, revolution in Latin American urban settings also needed to include the middle class along with exploited workers and peasants. The call for a cross-class alliance also fit well with the Tupamaros as the majority of the group derived from the middle class.[15]

Therefore, Guillén's methods enticed revolutionaries dealing with variant terrain, such as cities. For Guillén, it was the Tupamaros who exemplified the best model of urban guerrilla warfare.[16] In an English-language translation of Guillén's work, US professor Donald Hodges notes that the Tupamaros' organizational model influenced the Quebec Liberation Front, the Black Panthers, and Weather Underground. Hodges posits that these groups maintained revolutionary tactics similar to the Tupamaros in part because they too operated in more "advanced" countries with similar terrain.[17] Indeed, revolutionaries throughout the world, particularly in urban settings, continuously imagined the Tupamaros as more successful practitioners of urban guerrilla warfare and hoped to emulate their tactics.

Tupamaros as Inspiration

The Tupamaros' inspiration of radical action spanned the globe during the late 1960s and early 1970s. The proviolence West German Baader-Meinhof group or Red Army faction called themselves the "Tupamaros of West Germany" and released statements asserting that they must learn from revolutionary movements such as the Tupamaros.[18] One article in the mainstream press even went so far as to claim that a handbook explaining the armed resistance strategy of the Tupamaros had been the Baader-Meinhof's "only ideological basis."[19] The US leftist press sometimes described the Baader-Meinhof as "West Germany's version of the Tupamaros."[20] Furthermore, in the late 1960s, two small, proviolence organizations named after the Uruguayan Tupamaros emerged in Germany—the Tupamaros West Berlin and the Tupamaros Munich.[21]

A group of leftist guerrillas in Greece also found inspiration from the small Uruguayan organization as they planned to overthrow the military backed government by using the tactics of the "South American Tupamaros."[22] The influence of the Tupamaros extended to the Voice of Palestine, a group of Palestinian volunteers who broadcasted a two-hour show about politics and ostensibly transmitted coded messages to guerrilla members in Israel. The radio show sometimes gave details about the successful tactics of the Tupamaros as a teaching tool.[23] Therefore, to those who admired the Tupamaros, the group offered an excellent example of the growing strength of leftist revolutionary movements.[24]

Because of their status as international symbols of revolutionary triumph, French-born Régis Debray, who theorized about revolution and fought with Che Guevara in Bolivia, found inspiration from the Tupamaros. Debray wrote about what he perceived as the group's success in comparison to other revolutionary groups in Latin America. Debray had first visited Cuba in 1959 after Castro and the 26 of July Movement's successful guerrilla warfare campaign against the Batista dictatorship. He returned in 1961 and by 1964 had visited every Latin American country besides Paraguay. For Debray, Latin American guerrilla movements held powerful appeal and political importance. Che Guevara's writings especially influenced Debray's ideas about revolution. Three fundamental conclusions that Guevara derived from the Cuban Revolution particularly influenced Debray: that popular forces can win against an army, revolutionary conditions can be created, and rural areas are more conducive for revolutionary battles within the Americas. Though Marx had predicted that revolution would take place in urban areas, within Latin America, the countryside seemed to be the best place to incite battles for national liberation.[25]

Influenced greatly by the Cuban Revolution, in the mid-1960s Debray wrote articles such as "Castroism: The Long March in Latin America," which was targeted primarily to US and European audiences. In these works, Debray looked to Cuba and analyzed the potential for revolution within Latin America. Fidelism, according to Debray, was not necessarily a new ideology, but a "regeneration of Marxism and Leninism in Latin American conditions and according to the historic traditions of each country." Debray tried to understand why Cuba's revolutionary example had spread less dramatically in South America. He blamed the divisions within South America (largely the fault of the US) as well as what he deemed the insularity of some South American people and nations. Indeed, Cuba had brought about a massive transformation in Latin American politics, but it also inspired many countries to rein-vigorate their oppression of the left.[26]

In January 1966, Debray returned to Cuba and trained with guer-rillas. In 1967, he wrote *Revolution in the Revolution?*, which was pub-lished in France, the US, Cuba, and England. The work fared well, with three hundred thousand copies published in Cuba. In this work, Debray stressed the importance of the specificity of the Latin American expe-rience as well as small, extremely disciplined guerrilla groups. Debray believed that the role of the guerrilla group constituted more than armed struggle; it also could act as a model of a future, counter society. "Lib-erated zones" could become laboratories for "agrarian reform, peasant congresses, levying of taxes, revolutionary tribunals, and the discipline of collective life."[27] *Revolution in the Revolution?* demonstrated Debray's belief in the centrality of armed struggle in order to foment revolution. Though Debray had been writing about revolution in Latin America for years, his arrest in Bolivia exposed him to worldwide leftist prominence in 1967. Debray had been traveling as a journalist when the Bolivian gov-ernment jailed him and sentenced him to thirty years in prison (he was released in three).

Debray supported the Tupamaros and their part in advancing urban armed struggle in Latin America. As he had claimed in other writings about Latin America, it was the historic conditions and the specificity of each area that should influence and shape the struggle for liberation. The Tupamaros understood the significance of the largely urban Uruguayan population. Debray argued that the Tupamaros represented, "The only armed revolutionary movement in Latin America who knew how, or was able, to attack on all fronts (and not only at one point or one side) and to neutralize the bourgeois and anti-national dictatorship, questioning its very survival."[28] Thus, Debray viewed the Tupamaros as purveyors of new forms of socialist revolution. For Debray, the Tupamaros and their use of urban guerrilla warfare offered an excellent example of how the historical, social, political, and cultural conditions of a country (Uru-guay) should influence armed struggle.[29] Instead of relying on armchair discussions and rhetoric about liberation, the Tupamaros took actions that revealed their political ideology.[30]

At the same time, Debray also admitted that the group lacked a precise ideology, a public program, and a true commander. However, Debray viewed these issues as possibly positive aspects of the group. Ac-cording to Debray, the Tupamaros demonstrated that their unique revolutionary hero was not an individual but the group itself. In this way, Debray believed that the group moved away from egotistical displays of personal glory that plagued leftist organizations throughout the world. Even the press appointed leader of the group, Raúl Sendic, claimed that he simply played a combatant role similar to the other Tupamaros.[31] The Tupamaros claimed, "The leadership is collective. There are no sacred cows."[32] Debray applauded that the Tupamaros did not (publicly) support rigid hierarchies and stressed that the group was not impersonal, rigid, or puritanical. The idea of not having a central organization or commander appealed to leftists as it offered an easily followed romantic model.[33] According to Debray, the Tupamaros further deviated from other "inferior" revolutionary groups that exhibited pompousness and childishness in both rhetoric and action. These faux revolutionaries, who lived throughout North America, Latin America, and Europe, often posed under pictures of Che or Mao in order to give their groups revolutionary credibility. After the Cuban Revolution, many leftist groups in Latin America attempted to emulate Che's and Fidel's success but with superficiality and mere caricature. According to Debray, these movements only illustrated the personal vanity of their middle-class members. In contrast, most members of the Tupamaros ignored notions of personal glory and instead created an organization where fellow militants greeted one another as equals.[34] Unlike the elitist groups that Debray maligned but did not specifically name, the Tupamaros successfully reached out to and garnered support from labor unions, university students, popular movements, traditional parties, and members of the church. Debray believed that by including "the people," the Tupamaros altered the dichotomy between combatants and noncombatants. The movement needed the people's involvement in the revolution— from workers who could not leave their jobs, to housewives, intellectuals, and the "petit-bourgeoisie."[35] Debray argued that these varying types of people supported the Tupamaros but did not actively join the organization.

According to Debray, the Tupamaros, in contradistinction to other inferior clandestine guerrilla movements, appreciated and needed the force of the people in their struggle for liberation. Therefore, because of their continual planned actions and alliance with the majority of the people, Debray viewed the Tupamaros as offering an international example of revolutionary maturity.[36] Debray failed to note, however, that the Tupamaros had trouble connecting with some factions of the labor movement and other factions of the left. While they won the approval of the Sendic-led UTAA and the workers of Frigorifico Fray Bentos, they did not penetrate the trade-union movement or the Uruguayan Communist Party as easily.[37] Thus, when describing the Tupamaros, Debray ignored or seemed unaware of fragmentation within the Uruguayan left. For Debray, the Tupamaros' discretion in targets and actions undeniably proved a high level of prudence and exemplified important political goals the majority of Uruguayan supported.[38]

Beyond their positive standing with Debray and various revolutionary groups in Europe, the influence of the Tupamaros was particularly salient for US radicals. Several US leftist organizations employed the MLN-T's tactics in an attempt to recreate their urban guerrilla warfare practices. One example of the influence of the Tupamaros on US leftist tactics occurred in 1970 when four radicals bombed the Army Mathematics Research Center in Wisconsin and killed one person in protest against US military action throughout the world. The radicals asserted that their actions were a conscious political action of people in solidarity with groups such as the Tupamaros.[39] The White Panther Party (WPP) also derived inspiration from the Tupamaros' strategy of kidnapping government officials in order to bargain for the release of political prisoners. The WPP considered kidnapping Vice President Spiro Agnew and other political figures like Gerald Ford and Senator Robert Griffin in order to gain the release of Black Panther Party leaders such as Bobby Seale and Huey Newton. The group also wanted to use the kidnappings in order to force the United States to withdraw from Vietnam. Thus, the WPP hoped to specifically emulate the style of the Tupamaros by planning to kidnap government officials (though their plans never came to fruition).[40]

The Tupamaros also influenced the Symbionese Liberation Army (SLA), a radical group from California, who achieved most of their infamy after the kidnapping of heiress Patty Hearst in 1974. They used exactly the Tupamaros' so-called Robin Hood tactics and demanded food for the California poor in return for Hearst's release. The Hearst family complied and spent millions of dollars distributing food to impoverished areas, but the SLA ultimately found the type of food offered inadequate. The SLA's tactics mirrored the actions of the Tupamaros who robbed banks and food trucks in order to distribute money and goods to the poor.[41] They also emulated the Tupamaros' notion of a People's Prison, where the SLA tried and convicted those in positions of economic and political power. When kidnapping Hearst, whose family had committed "crimes against the people," the SLA issued a warrant for her arrest and subsequent execution if she resisted. Inspired by the Tupamaros, the SLA contended that its warrant came from the people. The notion of creating a prison as a parallel power was influenced by the Tupamaros and offered a different tribunal structure than the mainstream system leftist groups in both Uruguay and the US deemed unfair. At one point, Hearst herself claimed she was being held as a prisoner of war. Like the Tupamaros, the SLA viewed armed struggle as the only path to true political change and asserted that "guns [should] express the words of freedom."[42]

Another better known organization influenced by the strategy of the Tupamaros was the Weather Underground, a radical faction of Students for a Democratic Society (SDS), which decided to "bring the war home" and attack symbols and institutions of what they deemed "Amerikan injustice."[43] The Weather Underground's statement explaining their first bombing in 1970, penned by leader Bernadine Dohrn, clearly reveals its desire to link with the Tupamaros. According to Dohrn, "Revolutionary violence is the only way. . . . We will never live peaceably under this system. [We are adopting] the classic guerrilla strategy of the Vietcong and the urban guerrilla strategy of the Tupamaros to our own situation here in the most technically advanced country in the world.[44]

By mentioning the Tupamaros during their first bombing, the Weather Underground demonstrated the influence of the MLN-T on their revolutionary actions. Briefly before the group split into different factions, SDS also featured the Tupamaros in their literature urging leftists to "live like them" or emulate the tactics of the group.[45] Obviously versed in the Tupamaros' practice of urban guerrilla warfare, the Weather Underground viewed the group as providing a successful model for revolution in so-called developed countries. The Weather Underground believed that the strategy of the Tupamaros offered an example of how to truly incite revolution in the US. One Weatherwoman said about the excitement of revolutionary life, "It's like riding on top of a wave. Your first realization that you are part of this force, striking down a monster. You read about the Tupes and the Palestine rebels and you identify with them. You are part of the same army."[46] The Weather Underground not only attempted to emulate the tactics of the Tupamaros in their urban warfare strategy of bombing government targets but also by living clandestinely in revolutionary cells.[47]

Beyond hoping to imitate the MLN-T's tactics, some activists in the US left portrayed the revolutionary struggle of the Tupamaros in a romanticized manner, particularly when writing about member and "leader" Raúl Sendic. While Debray stressed that the Tupamaros had no true leader, other admirers pointed to the specific influence of Sendic. However, these admirers also contended that even though Sendic was considered a leader by the press, in reality he had a role in the Tupamaro organization similar to that of his comrades. Once again, Sendic's egalitarian role accentuated the allegedly democratic nature of the group.[48]

An analysis by Robert Cohen in the California based newsletter Alternative Features Service shows obvious admiration for Sendic's reaction to his capture by the Uruguayan government in 1972. Indeed, Sendic had escaped prison before in 1971 and vowed never to let the Uruguayan government stop him or the radical actions of the Tupamaros. Cohen commended Sendic's attempts to fight against overwhelming odds and his faithfulness to his convictions. These descriptions present Sendic as an unfailing inspiration to leftist revolutionaries everywhere. According to the article, admiration for the Tupamaros by US leftists should remain strong, even in times of seeming defeat. Cohen argued that support for the Tupamaros "should not be measured in the glorious moments of Tupamaros victories, but now when the MLN-T has suffered the heaviest setbacks in its history."[49] Cohen posited that Sendic's promise never to surrender to the Uruguayan government represented the Tupamaros' admirable "word of honor." In an attempt to align with the Tupamaros, sympathetic revolutionaries like Cohen often mentioned a common enemy, namely US imperialism. The strong language used to describe the actions of the MLN-T demonstrates the admiration some in the left held for the Tupamaros. US leftists romanticized the Tupamaros and viewed their resilience as an inspiration to all revolutionary movements.

Other publications in solidarity with Uruguay such as the *Uruguay News* (based in New York City) included romantic portrayals of Sendic and depicted him as the best representative of a courageous movement against state repression. In one article, writers at the *Uruguay News* argued, "Despite these conditions, it has become known that these courageous revolutionary leaders, especially Raúl Sendic, still keep their firm values and have expressed their willingness to be sacrificed rather than slow the course of the struggle of freedom in their country."[50] The description presents Sendic as even more heroic than his Tupamaros counterparts, who also demonstrated admirable values in revolution such as self-sacrifice. Much like the AFS bulletin, the *Uruguay News* focuses on Sendic as a martyr-like figure willing to give his life for the revolutionary cause. Overall, however, Sendic was still portrayed as part of a larger group of egalitarian revolutionaries who did not support rigid hierarchies.

More mainstream presses also touted the perceived successes of the Tupamaros. Throughout the 1970s, the *New York Times* referred to the group as the "oldest and best organized urban guerrillas in Latin America"; "spectacularly successful"; "the successful pioneers of urban guerrilla warfare in South America"; and "daring urban guerrillas."[51] Writers of the *New York Times* even asserted that the capture of most of the Tupamaros by 1972 was as crushing to leftist radicals throughout the world as the fall of the Allende regime for communists.[52] The *L.A. Times* referred to the group as "most successful and ablest" of the revolutionary groups in Latin America. They were also seen as leaders in a "spreading fad" of revolution.[53] The *Chicago Tribune* deemed the group "South America's most successful guerrillas."[54] Another article referred to the group as "well financed, well organized and daring."[55]

Even unsympathetic works that referred to the revolutionaries as terrorists, such as Claire Sterling's *The Terror Network: The Secret War of International Terrorism*, argued for the importance of the Tupamaros to left-wing revolutionary groups throughout the world. Sterling considered the Tupamaros so influential that she began her book by telling the so-called history of the Tupamaros, whom she blamed for the demise of democracy in Uruguay. Sterling contends that the Tupamaros offered the initial model for urban guerrilla warfare and were an "instructive case" and "pioneers in the field" of terrorism. The Tupamaros' influence, according to Sterling, spanned to so-called terrorists throughout the globe.[56] The Tupamaros also found their way into popular fiction of the time. In Jon Cleary's famous novel *Peter's Pence*, when the pope is taken hostage his staff blames the ubiquitous communists but also specifically names the Uruguayan Tupamaros as suspects.[57] Thus, despite different representations, both the left and the right touted the Tupamaros as influential revolutionaries.

Beyond the Tupamaros' representation in US newspapers and books, the US government also considered the group a dangerous and significant force. The Tupamaros repeatedly challenged the hegemony of the United States and the Uruguayan government. Along with kidnapping and killing US Agency for International Development (AID) agent Dan

Mitrione, the group bombed US business interests and burned US diplomats' automobiles.[58] Admirers of the Tupamaros deemed the CIA and FBI "children" in comparison to the radical group.[59] Documents declassified by the US government also demonstrate the unease of Congress and others in the government concerning the Tupamaros' level of sophistication and success with high-profile kidnappings. For training purposes, the US government viewed the Tupamaros as an instructive example in order to "acquire knowledge on worldwide terrorist activities."[60] Therefore, studying the Tupamaros' tactics provided an excellent model to help US-sponsored and -trained counterinsurgency groups learn mechanisms to fight against terrorist groups worldwide.[61]

Notions of Technical Superiority

The allegedly technical superiority of the Tupamaros was another reason the group occupied a special position in the imagination of the US left. Alongside Cuba, for the left throughout the world, the Tupamaros represented a "socialist challenge" to the Western Hemisphere.[62] The urban guerrilla warfare strategies of the Tupamaros, along with the organization's dramatic acts of rebellion (such as distributing stolen money to the poor and escaping from prison) impressed those on the left that romanticized revolution. For example, in what many consider their first official act as "Tupamaros," the organization stole a truck during Christmas and distributed food to the hungry. In this action, twenty Tupamaros, holding revolvers and knives, attacked a corporate-owned truck containing chickens and turkeys for a banquet.[63] Referring to themselves as the "junior José Artigas unit" after the hero of Uruguayan independence José Gervasio Artigas, the Tupamaros left a note that read, "Revolutionaries share in the Christmas of the poor and call upon them to form committees in each district to fight against rising prices."[64] From this point on, the Uruguayan leftist press promoted this Robin Hood image, touting the Tupamaros' public relations abilities and sense of humor and their mechanisms of "robbing the rich to give to the poor." The Christmas Eve action garnered a great deal of public sympathy for the group.

With these actions, many in the Uruguayan left felt that the Tupamaros exposed the corruption of an increasingly repressive and socially unjust state. Even Uruguayan authorities admitted their fear of the group's extraordinary ability to organize. This trepidation, in part, derived from the notion that the Tupamaros had infiltrated the ranks of the Uruguayan government and learned details concerning the military.[65] The group appeared to have the ability to obtain voluminous information about the Uruguayan armed forces, including number of officers, private addresses, and schedules. The notion of the Tupamaros' power was so pervasive that a popular joke in Montevideo during the late 1960s claimed that if you wanted to find out the weather forecast, ask a Tupamaros. The Tupamaros further proved the incompetence of police when a psychic revealed she had been hired by the Uruguayan government in an effort to locate the MLN-T's People's Prison. Psychic Maria Zapiola de Sicardi specialized in finding missing objects and people. When asked why she could not find the Tupamaros' People's Prison for the Uruguayan government, Zapiola replied that the interference of too many people disturbed her powers.[66]

For many years, most Uruguayan citizens viewed their country's armed forces as comically ineffective. During the 1950s, Uruguayan soldiers changed their clothes before leaving to go home from work so they would not be mistaken for bus drivers. Uruguayan soldiers did not garner much respect from the people as their primary job consisted of cleaning up littered beaches.[67] The Tupamaros capitalized on the public's dismissive attitude toward the military and police and went out of their way to humiliate the Uruguayan armed forces during the 1960s. Besides their prison breaks, which caused the police a great deal of embarrassment, the Tupamaros would sometimes visit an officer's home and lecture him on how he needed a career change or leave sarcastic "presents." Other times, the Tupamaros would tie family members up and steal items such as weapons and personal documents. In July 1970, MLN-T members broke into four different police officers' homes in one Saturday night. Reports from these actions, however, revealed the same sort of restrained behavior that helped to make the Tupamaros famous. During one attack, the Tupamaros reassured a policemen's family. "Don't worry; we're the Tupamaros." After tying up the family, the Tupamaros explained his motivations: "The police carry out attacks like this against us and other workers."[68] Another Tupamaro told the press, "When we decide to raid the home of a political police agent . . . these actions are aimed not only at supplying ourselves with arms and ammunition. They also serve to undermine the morale of policemen who sooner or later will ask themselves just who the devil they are fighting and what order they are defending."[69]

In another action, a Tupamaro guerrilla left a package containing nearly sixty pounds of dynamite on the doorstep of a Uruguayan Army technician. The Tupamaro, who obviously had a very playful sense of humor, left a note attached to the dynamite that read "Captain Manzino: This material is in bad shape; since it is dangerous to handle it, we have decided to destroy it. We believe you are the best equipped for this task. We are aware of your technical expertise. At any rate, since these boxes were ultimately going to be examined by you, we decided to avoid delays and give them to you."[70] With actions such as these, the Tupamaros hoped to publicly mock the armed forces and expose their weaknesses.

However, by 1972, the Tupamaros ceased ridiculing the Uruguayan armed forces as the state had apprehended the majority of the members of the MLN-T. In just a few years, the Uruguayan armed forces transformed from the butt of jokes into a fiercely repressive apparatus. Scholars have attributed the rapid transformation of Uruguayan government officials from ill-equipped bumblers to methodical torturers in large part to the economic and technical aid of the US government. Evidence indicates that the US helped to professionalize the Uruguayan army in order to promote its anticommunist security agenda. The US government viewed Uruguay as a country of such strategic importance that in the three years leading up to the coup in 1973 it gave 9.5 percent of the total Latin American military budget to the country. In 1970, Uruguay received the second highest military assistance in the entire hemisphere. Most of the funding for Uruguay came through the aforementioned US Agency for International Development (AID).[71]

The US government sponsored thousands of Uruguayan police officers in 276 courses at US facilities, most of which were offered by the International Police Academy (IPA) and the International Police Service School, both in Washington, DC. These schools, which also had links to the CIA, helped to train Uruguayans in counterinsurgency methods and ideologies in order to destroy the left. Training sponsored by the US was ultimately successful; by the early 1970s, IPA graduates occupied the majority of the top posts in Montevideo's police department, and 931 officers had received in-country training by US advisors. While monetary assistance proved important, the foreign training offered to Uruguayan security forces by the US government further enabled them to refine their torture mechanisms. This, combined with coordination between other authoritarian regimes in Brazil, Argentina, Chile, and Paraguay (known as Operation Condor), helped to solidify

Uruguay's place as a nation that perpetuated gross human rights violations during the 1970s.[72]

Before the US intervention, the Uruguayan government was not capable of performing systematic repression like its neighbors in Brazil and Argentina.[73] Despite the significant use of officers and resources, between 1967 and 1970, the police only uncovered eleven underground Tupamaro bases. Of the eleven bases, some were merely hideouts, others ammunition factories, and one a photography shop. The photography shop contained the same equipment used to make ID cards issued by the Uruguayan police. The machines and the paper used to create the fake IDs had ostensibly been obtained from police headquarters. This equipment led some to believe that the Tupamaros helped Che Guevara create the fake Uruguayan passport he used to travel to Bolivia.[74] Because of these discoveries and other humiliations, the Uruguayan armed forces were so insecure about their past incompetence that under the dictatorship it was rumored that they banned the press from publishing pictures of them in certain poses. Reportedly, after the publication of a photograph of General Luis Quierolo smiling, the army sent a note to the press banning them from publishing pictures of army officials smiling.[75]

Another legendary story about the ineptitude of the police involved the various Tupamaros prison breaks. On September 6, 1971, 106 political prisoners escaped from Punta Carretas prison by digging a tunnel from their cells to a nearby house. The Tupamaros emerged from a tunnel into civilian Billy Rial's living room. While Rial looked on in self-described disbelief, the prisoners changed out of their clothes and crashed through a hole knocked into the wall, escaping to another house. In the other house, one woman became fearful of the revolutionaries' invasion. The *Chicago Tribune* reported that a Tupamaro told the frightened woman, "Why don't you knit a little?"

Rial informed the press about the event, "I called the police at 4:30 am but they wouldn't believe me." Finally an officer agreed to call the prison. The officer got back to Rial quickly, assuring him that the prison guards said everything was quiet at Punta Carretas prison.[76] Further humiliating the police, at the entrance of the tunnel, officials found a metal sign similar to street signs made by the city of Montevideo. It said, "MLN-T Traffic Department, please keep to the left." While the Tupamaros made their escape, sympathizers distracted the police on the other side of the city. In a working-class neighborhood in Montevideo known as "the Hill," workers (mostly from meatpacking plants) set buses on fire.

Police and military units who arrived on the Hill were met with spikes on the road and gun fire. One prison guard even told a neighbor, "They told us they were going to leave without firing a shot before the elections and that nobody could stop them. And that's the way it was."[77] Leftist publications in the US reported these incidents with great admiration. One publication even deemed the prisoners escape "one of the most spectacular prison breaks on record."[78] Another radical paper in the US characterized the jail break as demonstrating the Tupamaros' "technical skill and revolutionary love for their comrades and the people."[79] The Uruguayan government perhaps unwittingly promoted the importance and international significance of the Tupamaro prison breaks. After thirty-eight Tupamaras escaped prison in 1971 by crawling out of jail through a tunnel and then the sewer, Uruguay's minister of the interior claimed, "The escape proved the existence of a powerful clandestine army with foreign backing."[80]

The group further taunted officials as they robbed various banks and casinos. The robbery of the San Rafael Casino in the resort town of Punta del Este was the largest hold up in the history of Uruguay and was deemed the "heist of the century."[81] The minister of tourism in Uruguay offered a five-million-peso reward for anyone who could help catch the elusive Tupamaros. Another robbery committed by the Tupamaros turned out to be the biggest bank robbery and jewel heist on record. On Friday the 13th, 1970, four women and five men armed with rifles stole six million dollars in jewels and forty-eight thousand dollars in cash from Uruguay's Bank of the Republic.[82] The previous evening, the Tupamaros had abducted three bank employees in a separate action. A fourth employee was also supposed to be kidnapped, but the Tupamaros allowed him to stay home while he tended to his sick wife. As the robbery took place, an armed MLN-T member waited with the fourth employee and his wife.

The Tupamaro members involved in the robbery used the kidnapped men to convince the nighttime bank guards to let them inside the building. Daniel Camilo Guinovart, a bank employee and reported accomplice of the Tupamaros, also urged the guards to open the doors. Guinovart told the guard, "Let him in, he is my brother." The Tupamaros proceeded to tie up the guards and bank officials. Apparently not concerned with time constraints, it took the commandos nearly three hours to select the most valuable jewels from the bank vault. Guinovart helped the Tupamaros stuff jewelry and money into sacks. As he left with the

Tupamaro robbers, Guinovart reportedly told his bank colleagues, "I am going underground now."[83]

The US leftist press described the profitable bank robberies that involved "elaborate deceptions and disguises." Even when the Tupamaros encountered adversity in their robberies, such as being unable to find the key to a bank vault, the US-based *Liberation News Service* reported that the "cool" group instead took the bank's confidential files.[84] During another robbery, the Tupamaros asked for identification from all of the employees. They called the employees by name and separated them into groups—those belonging to unions and those they deemed "suckers." While some in the group attempted to locate the keys to the bank vault, others explained to the bank workers the objectives of the MLN-T. One man in the group of employees had a large sum of money on him. He assumed the guerrillas would steal his money too, but one Tupamaro told him, "We don't touch the workers money." When a bank employee began to have an anxiety attack, a female Tupamaro took her to the bathroom to calm down.[85]

During another bank robbery, a Tupamaro helped an elderly lady who had fainted from the stress of the situation. On another occasion, before the group bombed the transmission room of the radio station Radio Ariel, they first warned civilians in a nearby house about the explosion.[86] Even police officials had to admit the "wonderful organization, good manner and humane behavior of the Tupamaros."[87] Leftist admirers consistently reported on the kindness of the Tupamaro revolutionaries toward the "people" during their violent actions. One article in the Students for a Democratic Society (SDS) publication *New Left Notes* claimed, "The Tupamaros have achieved the first stages of their strategy without terrorism. They fight with the police only when they are forced. Whenever their raids might hurt civilians, they make a point of protecting them."[88]

Besides the connections forged with civilians during their actions, the missions of the Tupamaros often inspired negative consequences for those they targeted, such as leading businessmen and ranking government figures. The group's successful exposure of corruption helped fuel romantic admiration from the left and others in Uruguay. On Valentine's Day 1969, the Tupamaros broke into the firm Financiera Monty and "expropriated" money, documents, and accounting books. The group turned the stolen information over to the Uruguayan justice system in hopes that they would investigate the shady business practices of

Financiera Monty. The MLN-T made their robbery known to the public through leaflets and gave photocopies of evidence of illegal activities to the Uruguayan press. Consequently, the minister of agriculture had to resign because of his ties with Monty. Later, the archives of Monty were burned. Many claimed this was done in order to stop more damaging information from being revealed to the public. Despite the later destruction of the archives, the Tupamaros action impressed many who saw the group as responsible for exposing corruption and punishing those who deserved to be humiliated. Along with revealing corruption at Monty, in 1970 the Tupamaros also robbed Mailhos Trust, stealing twenty-five thousand sterling pounds, gold bullion, arms, and various documents. Because of the Tupamaros' uncovering of illegal gold bullion, the police arrested a Mailhos primary associate. In order to help the legal case against Mailhos, members of the MLN-T also turned in the stolen records.[89]

The Tupamaros' capture of Pando, a city twenty miles from Montevideo with twenty thousand inhabitants, also pervaded the left's imagination and garnered widespread admiration for the guerrillas. On October 8, 1969, the Tupamaros used a hearse and a number of accompanying cars to create the illusion of a funeral procession driving through the city of Pando. The Tupamaros made their way into the city without arousing suspicion. The coffin inside of the hearse was full of ammunition to use in the raid. Within a short amount of time, MLN-T members retrieved weapons from the coffin, cut telephone wires, shut off the radio, and seized buildings in Pando. They took over the police station and tied up employees as well as attacked three banks. A Cessna plane flew over the city and dropped leaflets, explaining the mission. The invasion took place on the second anniversary of Che Guevara's death and was dedicated to the "immortal hero, Major Che Guevara."[90]

Police officers eventually arrived in air force helicopters and blocked roads to and from Pando. The Tupamaros attempted to escape, but most members were caught or killed in a gun battle. The precise number of Tupamaros that participated in the siege varies depending on the source. The MLN-T claimed that over one hundred participated in the takeover, while police reports asserted only half that number. No matter what the number, the complete occupation of a city by such a small group impressed radicals throughout the world, who saw the Tupamaros' tactics as daring and successful. Therefore, the victory of the mission derived in large part from the propaganda that it garnered for the group. The Tupamaros themselves contended that the seizure of Pando was primarily envisioned as a way to politicize the people.[91]

The Tupamaros attempted to seize another town to create a more rural front in 1971. On the evening of December 30, the Tupamaros took over Paysandú, a town about 250 miles northwest of Montevideo. They occupied the military airport, disarming guards and stealing machine guns and radio transmitters. Tupamaros also took over a calcium quarry on the banks of the Uruguay River and stole explosives and bomb cases. Group members made their way a few miles from Paysandú to the area of Constancia, where they took over the police station. In their Proclamation of Paysandú, the Tupamaros claimed, "This is war and they are going to tremble, because the poor have nothing to lose in this battle except a long hunger, and you, those who have always been rich will sleep restlessly. Because we are going to enter your mansions, your kitchens. . . . You have slapped the people on both cheeks. There is nothing left. Now the humble rise up in arms; and be careful, there are many."

Though this rebellion was squelched by the Uruguayan armed forces, it showed the government that the Tupamaros maintained influence in the more rural areas of the country.[92] In order to commit these audacious acts, according to their admirers, the Tupamaros practiced a higher level of discipline and discretion than other leftist guerrilla movements in Latin America. In an English-language version of the Cuban publication *Prensa Latina*, Prudencio Corres argues that one of the movement's greatest virtues was its "strictest silence." Thus, Corres posits that much of the organization's success derived from the careful compartmentalization of the various cells of Tupamaros. In these groupings, similar to other guerrilla movements, members identified only by their pseudonyms and did not commonly stay in contact with other cells. However, admirers of the Tupamaros contended that had this compartmentalization not worked perfectly, the Tupamaros could easily have been uncovered and defeated. The autonomous structures of each cell allowed for the movement to continue and garnered admiration from leftists throughout the world.[93] Writers for the US-based Alternative Features Service further demonstrated their respect for Tupamaro tactics by referring to the group as "a movement without a head to cut off."[94] Although other guerrilla groups used such strategies, the press presented the Tupamaros as being more successful at clandestine subversion. However, those who romanticized the achievements of underground Tupamaro cells failed to recognize the incompetence of the Uruguayan military and how this allowed for much of the success of the group. Nevertheless, the perception of the Tupamaros' resilience, egalitarianism, and careful organization inspired those on the left who wished to emulate the group's tactics.

This romanticism completely ignored the hierarchal realities of the group. The MLN-T was not as egalitarian in its organizational structures as popular propaganda claimed. While US leftists focused on the superior organization of the group's cells and columns, they usually ignored or were unaware of the hierarchal committees who handled most of the decisions of the Tupamaros. The group contained four rigidly constructed primary units: the cells, the columns, the executive committee, and the national convention. The executive committee appointed each cell a leader and an alternative leader (usually men). The cell remained in contact with the executive committee, usually through the appointed cell leader. Cells loosely banded together to make columns, which also had a leader linked to the executive committee. The Tupamaro executive committee held numerous responsibilities such as approving or rejecting new members after examining a candidate's data. Beyond admitting new members, the executive committee disciplined those who went against the group's policies and ultimately handed down approval of military actions. Members of the executive committee could be replaced only by the national convention (their superiors) or if the committee decided to vote unanimously to replace a member. The national convention held the highest authority within the Tupamaros and had the power to appoint members of the executive committee, change the organization's rules, and if they chose, disband the group.[95]

Thus, the MLN-T was nowhere near as nonhierarchal as popular propaganda claimed. The structure of the Tupamaros relied on masculine ideals of discipline, authority, and hierarchy, similar to the much-maligned Uruguayan dictatorship. In defense of their structure, the Tupamaros argued that they had no time to employ completely democratic tactics while the government worked relentlessly to destroy them. Although the group had no single leader, the leaders of the executive committee and the national convention ultimately made the decisions about the actions of the MLN-T. They communicated these decisions downward to the cells and columns, to places where the majority of the members of the Tupamaros worked for revolution.[96] Therefore, as they clung to masculine centralized authority, the romantic representations of the egalitarian and democratic construction of the Tupamaros overall proved to be false. While the group abandoned the centralized nature of the cells and the executive committee and changed to more autonomous columns by 1967, the authoritarian composition of the MLN-T never significantly transformed.

Furthermore, while other guerrilla groups kidnapped and/or killed foreign officials, the media and leftist groups saw the Tupamaros as better disciplined and organized and able to capture more prominent targets.[97] While some Latin American guerrilla groups often kidnapped and released their victims, they, unlike the Tupamaros, were promptly tracked down by officials. Mexican guerrillas abducted the honorary British consul in Guadalajara but freed him after five days because the Mexican government did not meet their demands to either pay a US$300,000 ransom or set free fifty-one prisoners. Radicals typically freed most kidnapped foreigners after payment, including John Thompson, head of Argentine operations for the Firestone Company ($3 million was paid for his release).[98]

It was the Tupamaros, however, who held important international officials for long periods of time (such as British ambassador Geoffrey Jackson for 245 days). Thanks in part to government incompetence and careful organization of cells, the Tupamaros kept Jackson and others in underground hideouts with little fear of police uncovering them. In fact, the Tupamaros captured Jackson just blocks from the British Embassy in Montevideo. Tupamaro members kept Jackson and other kidnapping victims in what they called the People's Prison. The group argued that the bourgeoisie used jails and so-called justice against the poor in order to destroy them. In contrast, the People's Prisons enforced justice for all civilians and represented a form of parallel power. Holding People's Trials reflected the influence of the inheritance of Uruguayan democracy on the Tupamaros.[99] One Tupamaro explained the importance of kidnappings and the People's Prison, "Kidnappings are, among other things, a demonstration that the Latin American revolution is now capable of creating a jail for its traitors and oppressors, depriving them of liberty as they deprive us of ours, holding them hostage as they hold us."[100] Admirers of the Tupamaros, the US-based Black Panther Party also held "People's Tribunals," including the indictment of Nixon and Rockefeller for murder. The BPP tried and convicted Rockefeller and Nixon for first-degree murder, conspiracy to commit murder, and attempted murder.[101] Like the Tupamaros, the BPP employed their country's tradition of legal process to support their political actions.

The Tupamaros most famous prisoner was USAID agent Dan Mitrione, whom the Tupamaros killed after the Uruguayan government did not meet their demands for the release of 150 imprisoned Tupamaros. Radical leftists throughout the world viewed the killing of Mitrione as a bold action on the part of the Tupamaros. The radical US leftist press reacted to the Tupamaros execution of Mitrione with support for the militants and disdain for the US and Uruguayan governments. In an article titled "Uruguay's Tupes: Mitrione Dies, Whitehouse Cries," an *LNS* journalist in Montevideo reported on the events in Uruguay proceeding the execution of Mitrione. The *LNS* criticized the reactions of the US government, who called Mitrione's murder a "cold blooded crime against a defenseless human being" who was an "example to men everywhere." Uruguayan president Pacheco Areco expressed disbelief in the "inhumane and traitorous episode." According to the radical US leftist press, after Pacheco closed down all government offices, stores, schools, and banks for a day of mourning for Mitrione, no one participated in large mass parades or memorial services in honor of the USAID agent.[102] *LNS* also reported that a Gallup poll conducted by the US embassy in Uruguay found that 20 percent of Uruguayan people were against the execution of Mitrione, 20 percent were in favor, and 60 percent reported having "no opinion."[103] Even the Tupamaros commented on the public's silence and seeming apathy, "Most of the people may not be ready to take part in the struggle, but at least they are not willing to get killed defending a government that harms them."[104]

In an interview with *LNS*, one Tupamaro deemed the killing of Mitrione a "just verdict" as the group had tried the USAID agent and found him guilty. Employing the group's trademark humor, the militant reinforced that the Tupamaros did not want sympathy. He commented, "We don't want the people thinking we are Santa Claus." The *LNS* reporter also asked about negotiations between the Uruguayan government and the Tupamaros for Mitrione, informing the Tupamaro that the US government had responded to the situation by saying, "Today they ask for the liberty of prisoners, tomorrow it will be that the government of Uruguay go to the Antarctic." The Tupamaro cheekily replied to the *LNS* reporter, "We'd never do that. We would send them to Paris, Rome, but never such an inhospitable place as the Antarctic."[105]

Interestingly, theorist and MLN-T champion Abraham Guillén criticized the Tupamaros' execution of Mitrione. He argued that the Tupamaros' People's Prison did not truly benefit the cause of national liberation but instead created a small oppressive state instead of a revolutionary army. Furthermore, Guillén opposed the Tupamaros' detainment of prisoners for such a long period of time. Like others who agreed with the tactical excellence of the Tupamaros, Guillén argued that the kidnappings of Dan Mitrione and Brazilian consul Dias Gomide were overall successful. However, Guillén believed that when the Tupamaros chose to execute Mitrione, they did not accomplish their political goals and ended up looking like assassins in the media. The Tupamaros later admitted their error in killing Mitrione. Tupamaros leader Sendic himself claimed that the Tupamaros did not plan to kill Mitrione, but a communication breakdown occurred after the Uruguayan police captured some of the groups' leaders.[106]

Despite the mixed and often ambivalent feelings of many in Uruguay to the USAID agent's murder, the government issued stamps in commemoration of Mitrione. The mayor of Belo Horizonte, where Mitrione worked as an "advisor" to the Brazilian police, named a street after Mitrione. Frank Sinatra and Jerry Lewis even put together a benefit for Mitrione's widow and nine children.[107] In addition to the responses in the US, Brazil, and Uruguay, European leftist Constantin Costa-Gavras was so impressed by the kidnapping of Mitrione that he dramatized the events in the controversial film *State of Siege* (1972). *State of Siege* represents another way the Tupamaros pervaded the imagination and activism of various types of leftists in the US.

State of Siege

The controversial film *State of Siege* dramatizes the kidnapping of Mitrione (renamed Philip Michael Santore in the film) and his subsequent execution by the Tupamaros. In order to educate the audience about the Tupamaros' goals, the film features several conversations between Tupamaros and Santore. Costa-Gavras interrupts these conversations with scenes of government violence against leftists in Uruguay, the legislative body denouncing the actions of the state, and Uruguayan reporters questioning the government as to the true identity of Santore. In the dialogue scenes, the Tupamaros debate Santore about his ideology and actions. When asked about the police force in the United States, Santore posits that the police are "real men," to which the Tupamaros retort that they do not believe in "real men," only human beings. Thus, the film presents the ideals of the Tupamaros as life affirming and humane in direct contrast with the life-denying actions of Santore/Mitrione and his kind. The film also represents the Tupamaros as an egalitarian group that makes decisions through democratic means such as voting. In the dramatized version of the Tupamaros' decision to execute Santore, the film shows two women voting not to kill the captive and three men affirming their approval of his death. While the gendered vote is somewhat problematic, State of Siege portrays the decision to kill Mitrione as a painstaking one and not something decided at the spur of the moment.

Though the film spends little time developing individual Tupamaro characters, the revolutionaries all appear to be young and fairly attractive. As one reporter for the New York Times wrote, "The Tupamaros we see [in the film] are mostly young, handsome, intensely sincere intellectuals who would like to avoid violence, while the establishment people are either elderly and overfed American puppets or career fanatics."[108] Alternative weekly publication the Village Voice also noted the "virility" of the young male militants and the idealism and beauty of the young Tupamaras in the film.[109] Though Costa-Gavras denied any political posturing, State of Siege undeniably presents the Tupamaros as the civilized and humane characters. In the film, the Tupamaros go to great lengths to make sure that Santore receives an X-ray after he is accidentally shot during the kidnapping. In contrast, the Uruguayan government is shown shooting students and labor union members with machine guns. The film also presents graphic scenes of torture in Brazil such as the shocking of genitals and nipples in front of a group of soldiers and government officials (such as Santore). The film argues that before he arrived in Uruguay, Santore helped the Brazilian dictatorship hone their torture skills.[110] According to the film, Santore, sponsored by the US government, took part in such horrific acts as teaching torture throughout Latin America. Thus, State of Siege demonstrates for the audience why his kidnapping was a viable reaction to a violent and repressive US-supported dictatorship.

State of Siege drummed up so much controversy in the US that the inaugural festival of the American Film Institute (AFI) at Washington's Kennedy Center withdrew the film from its lineup. The AFI's director, George Stevens, argued that showing the film at a memorial to John F. Kennedy would have been in bad taste. He contended that the film "rationalized the act of political assassination." In turn, the coproducer of State of Siege fired back that the AFI censored the film because Stevens had received funds from the Nixon administration. Protestors pointed out that Stevens planned to entertain Nixon in Los Angeles during the week *State of Siege* was to be released. In solidarity with *State of Siege*, several other films withdrew from the festival.

These films included François Truffaut's *Such a Gorgeous Kid Like Me*; *Films from Henry Street*, made by a settlement house in New York; *The Lumière Years*, about the films and drawings of Louis Lumière; *Sambizanga*, a drama about the Angolan war for independence; *New Women, New Films*, a collection of films concerning women; and the musical satire *O Lucky Man*. Ed Emshwiller, creator of two films pulled from the festival, *Choice Chance Woman Dance* and *Relativity*, released a statement explaining the reasons so many filmmakers had removed their movies from the AFI festival in solidarity with *State of Siege*. Emshwiller claimed that the removal of *State of Siege* was a blatant act of censorship and an insult to filmmakers' intelligence and creative integrity. Despite the withdrawal of the film from the festival, the AFI's actions and subsequent accusations of censorship made the film even more popular, particularly with leftist audiences of all types interested in issues concerning US foreign policy.[111]

Two weeks later, the film opened in New York to largely positive reviews from the moderate leftist press and the student press.[112] The film elicited different reactions in viewers; many reported feeling outraged by the corruption, lies, and violence supported by the US government.[113] After the film ended, audiences would sometimes engage in panel discussions or debates about the film. In one panel discussion with Costas-Gavras after the premiere of the film, an activist ran into the aisle and asked the director feverishly, "Tell us! Tell us! What can we do?"[114]

Reporters for the *New York Times* and other publications such as the *Village Voice* as well as everyday citizens became embroiled in the debate concerning the validity of the film's portrayal of the Tupamaros and Mitrione. Reporter Vincent Canby argued that the film overlapped journalism and fiction but ultimately showed the "moral and intellectual" poverty of the world. Canby, like most of the left, appreciated the questions that the film raised. James Loeb, a former ambassador to Peru under President Kennedy, became so enraged by Canby's review that he wrote a letter to the paper in protest against the film. He condemned Canby's and all of the left's supposed "double standards" concerning political morality. Loeb asserted that *State of Siege* ultimately ignored the facts (much like McCarthyism) and that elitist leftist intellectuals justified the violence of the Tupamaros while condemning the actions of the United States. Andrew Sarris echoed a similar concern in an article in the *Village Voice* when he criticized what he perceived as the romanticism of the "voting process" and subsequent assassination of Mitrione. Sarris asserted, "I cannot participate vicariously in the murder of Mitrione."[115] Loeb's letter and Sarris's article articulates an issue in the US left that *State of Siege* and the actions of the Tupamaros brought to the forefront—the "acceptable" uses of violence as a means of political change.[116]

Another debate about the presentation of US foreign policy in *State of Siege* occurred after a former counsel to President Kennedy, Theodore Sorenson, contended that although the film amounted to more than mere propaganda, Mitrione was not as evil as the film simplistically portrayed. Sorensen criticized the film for presenting Mitrione as a "cruel or greedy right winger who knowingly abetted the suppression of human values."[117] Sorenson also feared that the film's romantic portrayal of the Tupamaros would encourage US youth to engage in violent acts in order to incite political change. Sarris of the *Village Voice* echoed similar concerns, arguing, "It's all such a lark to 'expropriate' cars by luring dumb drivers with pretty decoys, and then brandishing guns all over the place."[118]

In response to Sorenson's article, José Yglesias, a writer on Latin American affairs, criticized Sorenson for liking the film but hating what it said about USAID policies in South America. Yglesias, like other leftists, argued that the facts concerning the negative actions of USAID and other US government agencies were "irrefutable." He objected to the notion of the mainstream US press that the Tupamaros committed cold-blooded murder. According to Yglesias, only guilty Americans put themselves in Mitrione's position in the film, which accounted for the outraged reactions. Yglesias argued, "I suppose we can't bear to be told that we're imperialists." [119] Echoing this statement, in the University of Michigan student newspaper the *Michigan Daily*, writer Richard Glatzer claimed, "Only those Americans who feel kindly towards the administration of Greece or the Soviet Union had reason to take offense."[120]

Thus, while officials who participated in the former Kennedy administration took personal offense to *State of Siege*, others in the left such as Yglesias saw the film as an opportunity to teach US citizens about their government's role in Latin America and expose them to the politics of the Tupamaros. Yglesias's letter, of course, inspired reactions from others who did not completely accept the Robin Hood image of the Tupamaros.

One letter to the editor of the *New York Times* stressed that Uruguay was a democracy and that the Tupamaros' "kangaroo courts" failed to follow fair judicial processes.[121] Therefore, *State of Siege* inspired a great deal of debate between those who saw the film as a teaching tool and those who took personal offense to its portrayal of the US government and its agents.

Sorenson's claim that *State of Siege* inspired violent radical activism in the US contained some truth. The movie did influence proviolence leftists, in particular those in the Symbionese Liberation Army. One of the founders of the SLA, Russ Little, professed his admiration for the Tupamaros and especially the film *State of Siege* as inspiring him and others to start a violent organization. Little said that he and others felt that the portrayal of the Tupamaros in the film showed that "those guys got it figured out." Beyond their political message, films such as *State of Siege* brought together members of the SLA for their initial meetings. The politics involved in the film offered an example which the SLA hoped to emulate. SLA members admitted that the kidnapping of Patty Hearst was first envisioned as a prisoner swap as had occurred with Santore and the Tupamaros in *State of Siege*. After realizing that they would not get a prisoner exchange, the SLA moved on to attempting to force the Hearst family to feed the poor (a move also inspired by the Tupamaros).[122]

The influence of the film and the controversy surrounding it escalated so much that even the US government got involved in the debate. Charging the film with defaming Dan Mitrione, a State Department spokesman strongly claimed that no State Department official had taken part in torture or police brutality.[123] Thus, the film's message proved so powerful that even the US government felt the need to comment on its alleged falsehoods.

So what was Dan Mitrione's real role in the Uruguayan dictatorship? Was he involved in practices of torture as the Tupamaros claimed? While the Uruguayan government argued that the murdering of Mitrione only confirmed the "loathsome crimes" and the "homicidal cold bloodedness and absence of any trace of human feeling" of the Tupamaros, others argued that Mitrione had a large part in teaching torture techniques to Uruguayan officials.[124] New data suggests that US advisors, including Mitrione, coordinated and even instructed Uruguayan security forces about torture techniques.[125]

While some of the sources seem dubious, declassified documents corroborate many of the claims. Former CIA agent Philip Agee and

Manuel Hevia Cosculluela (who also worked for the CIA but was a Cuban double agent) have claimed that Dan Mitrione's mission in Uruguay consisted of training police in better, so-called scientific ways to torture people. While these sources may incite some skepticism, others such as *New York Times* reporter A. J. Langguth have also supported the aforementioned accounts.[126] One example of Mitrione's role involves the agent providing the Uruguayan government electric needles of differing thicknesses to replace the "rudimentary" torture needles obtained from Argentina. Corroborating this claim, a 1970 report on human rights abuses in Uruguay denounced the treatment of prisoners and the "use of electric needles" during interrogation. Therefore, the film's portrayal of Mitrione as an agent who taught more sophisticated torture techniques to Uruguayan officials was most likely accurate.[127]

Despite the controversy about the validity of the film's portrayal of US and Latin American relations, *State of Siege* helped bring a message about the invasive nature of US policy in Latin America to an audience that otherwise may not have been familiar with international politics, particularly in relation to a small country like Uruguay. In an interview with *New York Times* reporter Judy Klemesrud, Costa-Gavras asserted that he chose Uruguay and the Tupamaros in part because of his interest in attempts of more powerful governments (such as the US) to repress and control smaller states.[128] Therefore, for Costa-Gavras, the Tupamaros represented a successful liberation movement that emerged in large part because of the harmful and uneven relationship between the US and Uruguay. Through *State of Siege*, audiences learned about the politics of the Tupamaros in an overall positive manner. Costa-Gavras specifically picked the Tupamaros to represent the violent reactions of a left-wing group against an increasingly repressive government. The dramatization of the kidnapping of Mitrione reinforced leftists' romantic notions about the Tupamaros and introduced others to the actions and ideas of the group.

Criticisms of the Tupamaros: Ideology

Not all leftist organizations in the US and elsewhere completely supported the Tupamaros. While few leftists dared to challenge the Tupamaros' military efficacy, some Marxists, particularly of the Moscow line, and some Maoist groups disliked the group's supposed lack of ideological content.[129]

Those who criticized the Tupamaros, however, appeared to be in the minority. While some pro-Soviet leftists existed at the end of the 1960s and the beginning of the 1970s, most young radicals did not view the USSR as an appropriate socialist model.[130] The Cultural Revolution in China, on the other hand, appeared to some as a more creative kind of socialism. Officially, the Cultural Revolution advocated the participation of everyday people and their criticism of those in power, even those in positions of authority in the Communist Party. Furthermore, advocates of the Cultural Revolution purported to create change through ideological and not economic development.[131] This explains, in part, why some Maoist groups expressed doubt over the ideological validity of the Tupamaros.

Pro-Maoist and pro-Moscow critics of the Tupamaros contended that after analysis, the group's philosophy revealed its imprecise and ambiguous nature. The alleged lack of Tupamaro ideology caused some on the left to argue that the Tupamaros' direct action alone could not win over the masses or create a real revolution. The Partido Comunista Uruguayo (PCU) echoed a sentiment similar to that of pro-Moscow and pro-Maoist groups in the US. According to the PCU, the politics of the Tupamaros represented mere vanity and not true revolutionary actions that encouraged the inclusion of the people. They argued that direct action "proposes to substitute action and the experience of the masses for the heroics of one group."[132] Some Uruguayan communists even deemed the Tupamaros a "childish group," a Leninist term for radicalized middle-class young people. Others on the left deemed the Tupamaros a "band of delinquents."[133] Another US Communist Party member criticized the Tupamaros for wanting to participate only in glamorous actions and not the dull and tedious tasks supposedly needed to make a revolution. However, most Tupamaros frequently experienced the banality of day-to-day life. As clandestine revolutionary fighters, they went for weeks and months without contact with others and often had to wait long periods of time between revolutionary attacks.[134]

One pro-Chinese group, in a pamphlet entitled "Tupamaros: Conspiracy or Revolution?," also contended that the middle class Tupamaros remained isolated from the masses.[135] While many of the Tupamaros came from middle-class backgrounds, pro-Tupamaros activists argued that the group successfully raised the consciousness of urban and rural workers. For evidence, they pointed to the frequently reported acts of solidarity from the working class with the Tupamaros such as the political rallies and strikes that featured workers holding pro-Tupamaros signs. In her 1970 work *La Guerrilla Tupamara*, María Esther Gilio interviewed a wide range of Uruguayans to better understand citizens' ideas about the Tupamaros. Gilio's interviews reveal strong support of the working class for the Tupamaros (though there were exceptions) and widespread disillusionment with the government.[136] Gallup polls taken between the years 1967 and 1972 reveal that nearly 40 percent of the population held a "positive" view of the Tupamaros. When broken down by age, 47 percent of young people reported a positive image of the organization. Highly educated, upper-class people also held the most positive view of the Tupamaros.[137]

Many in the public had positive responses to the Tupamaros, specifically to the group's robbery of the San Rafael Casino and the subsequent distribution of the stolen money to casino workers. The Tupamaro released a statement about the mission, "We must make a clear distinction between the bourgeois property and the workers' property. The former, undoubtedly is ill gotten, amassed through exploitation of workers. The latter is a result of personal effort and work. . . . We must maintain complete respect for the property of the workers, small businessmen and small producers."[138]

In an interview with Gilio, a thirty-two-year-old tractor driver said about the Tupamaros, "They don't behave like common robbers." Another worker contended that the Tupamaros stole only from places "where there is too much money." Overall, the working-class people Gilio interviewed believed that the Tupamaros took money only from those who "deserved it." Like in the US, some in Uruguay even idealized the Tupamaros. One seventy-five-year-old man went so far as to deem the group like "the first Christians."[139] Rumors also abounded about both student and worker protestors chanting Tupamaro slogans. One popular story told of health workers who occupied private clinics in order to offer free health care to Uruguayans. They put up signs claiming, "If there is not health care for everybody then there will be health for none." These signs took their inspiration from the aforementioned popular Tupamaro slogan "There will be a country for all or a country for none."

Thus, in the late 1960s, in part because of the actions of the government, the Tupamaros' popularity increased within their own country. Everyday Uruguayans developed a growing disgust at increasingly repressive police controls. This repression varied by class as police usually behaved cordially when searching upper- and middle-class homes but often treated members of the working class with brutality. When working-class suspects were absent from their homes, the police reportedly broke down doors and sometimes even stole items.[140]

Despite garnering a level of support from the Uruguayan people, some leftist groups in the US and Uruguay accused the Tupamaros of conceptualizing merely a nationalistic and not socialist program aimed at liberating the people. The notion that the Tupamaros appeared to fight primarily against the dictatorship and not for the values of socialism emerged as one strong and pervasive criticism. For some strict Marxists, the name of the group supposedly proved their nationalist leanings. The Tupamaros derived their name from Tupac Amaru II, who fought against Spanish colonization in eighteenth-century Peru. Amaru was a mestizo but claimed to be a descendant of the last Inca Empire. He led an indigenous movement to overthrow Spanish colonial rule and reestablish Inca authority. Therefore, some viewed the name of the Tupamaros as a symbol of the group's attempt to link their struggle to the liberation from Spanish and Portuguese colonizers.[141]

Not fully understanding the history of Amaru, however, critics deemed this integration too nationalistic and not internationally Marxist in scope. Pointing to the fact that the Tupamaros represented a solely "nationalistic" group because of their name proved little, especially considering that other left-wing groups in South America named themselves after independence members and leaders, such as the Argentine Montoneros.[142] Other revolutionary groups in Latin America, such as the Nicaraguan Frente Sandinista de Liberación Nacional (FSLN) and the El Salvadorian Frente Farabundo Martí para la Liberación Nacional (FMLN), named their struggles after their country's historical figures for liberation.[143] Furthermore, all these groups named themselves after national figures who had helped their own country.

The Tupamaros deviated from this last pattern by naming their group after a Peruvian figure who led a largely indigenous army. While the Tupamaros focused on urban resistance and were primarily of European descent, they derived their name from a rural figure who helped incite a peasant rebellion. The name Tupamaros suggests the group's flexible ideology and international composition more than any nationalistic leanings. With the name Tupamaro, the MLN-T proclaimed solidarity with Andean peasants rather than the urban, middle-class youths who made up their movement. The group's choice of name adds another layer to the eclectic nature of the ideology and tactics of the Tupamaros.

Supporters of the MLN-T also compared the Tupamaros' present-day struggle with that of General José Gervasio Artigas as both fought for the independence of the Uruguayan people. For Uruguayans, Artigas represented the original heroic struggle for their country's independence. Once a Spanish captain, Artigas deserted his assigned mission and led the fight for Uruguayan independence from its colonial masters. Artigas and his soldiers used rural guerrilla tactics and also engaged in some full-on battles. One incident often remembered in modern Uruguay concerned the sixteen thousand people who marched three hundred miles on foot under the leadership of Artigas.[144] Understanding his important place in the Uruguayan imagination, the Tupamaros co-opted the public's support for Artigas and used his mythology to recruit new members. The Tupamaros and their supporters deemed those who collaborated with or supported the current government "bad Uruguayans."[145] This harkened back to an expression of contempt employed by Artigas for those who identified with the Spanish. In one communiqué, the Tupamaros explained how they viewed themselves as inheritors of Artigas's legacy of rebellion, "This is why we salute those who spontaneously rebel. . . . Anyone is a Tupamaro if he does not merely make demands but disobeys the laws. . . . They were Tupamaros, called bandits by the Spaniards, who joined Artigas' army and drove the foreigners out. Let us drive out the corrupt men and speculators who have taken over the country."[146]

Thus, the Tupamaros hoped that invoking Artigas would inspire "average" Uruguayans to join their organization. In other proclamations, the MLN-T asserted that many in the country realized they "were living through events which were like what had happened before our first independence."[147] Using the history of the sixteen thousand Uruguayans who marched with Artigas, the Tupamaros inspired "common people" by mentioning those "like the people on the eastern march, [who] have left their families and the comforts of home to join underground Uruguay."

By recalling the actions of the past struggle for independence, the Tupamaros hoped to inspire Uruguayan people of all political persuasions to join their movement. In trying to convert possible supporters, the group neutralized some of its Marxist rhetoric and made the struggle of Artigas synonymous with the struggle of the Tupamaros. They argued that their program expressed the Uruguayan historical tradition. Just as Artigas wanted to "use the land to feed the poorest people," the Tupamaros strove to reappropriate land from large estate holders (most of whom were foreign).[148] By using such language, the MLN-T hoped to attract the "nationalist bourgeois" who had lost financial stability in the economic crisis of the 1960s. While this rhetoric had some success in recruiting members, the Tupamaros primarily attracted those with elements of left-wing political orientation. Using nationalistic mythology for inspiration also drew criticism from hard-line Marxists who saw the Tupamaros' political ideology as opportunistic and not entirely devoted to the socialist project.

Beyond the rhetoric concerning Artigas, the Tupamaros emphasized their fight for "liberty, independence, bread and the earth." Sometimes mentioning the socialist state, the group focused on continuing its struggle until it achieved for the people definitive freedom from an increasingly oppressive government. Moreover, the Tupamaros' discourse focused on universal ideas of freedom and independence from tyranny. This rhetoric had as much in common with that of independence movements throughout the world as it did with socialist revolution.[149] The Tupamaros also included elements of anarchist thought in their ideology. They focused on creating radical change through direct participation and followed no definitive blueprint for the future besides that of liberty and justice. In doing so, they continued a long tradition of anarchist activism in Uruguay. Indeed, beginning at the turn of the twentieth century, anarchists dominated the urban labor movement in Uruguay.[150] Therefore, the Tupamaros could be categorized as a socialist, anarchist, or independence movement, or perhaps a combination of the three.

The ideological criterion for joining the group, especially at its inception, seemed more open than for other revolutionary movements of the time. According to the rhetoric of the Tupamaros, their members did not necessarily need a hard-line Marxist ideology but a willingness to give everything for an "Uruguay without repression." The lack of an ideological litmus test for possible members and a desire to include all that hoped to change the situation in Uruguay moved the Tupamaros away from a strict adherence to lofty socialist rhetoric or a desire to indoctrinate and create ideological clones. Instead, the Tupamaros appeared much more concerned with action and the struggle to remove the restraints of the dictatorship.[151] By focusing on one unifying goal, the Tupamaros hoped to unite disparate political views and create a mass party. An unofficial Tupamaro document delineates the ambiguous nature of the group's ideology: "We want the abolition of all property . . . absolute equality between the government and those they rule, both in sacrifice and pay. This, in short, is our program. We do not call it an '-ism.' We are a huge movement whose militants include all sorts of groups from Marxist to Catholic and we do not need an '-ism.'"[152] For most organizations, such ideological differences caused insurmountable problems. However, for members of the Tupamaros, the impulse for action and change absorbed most ideological divisions.[153] One of the group's most popular slogans was simply, "Words divide us."[154]

Even the aforementioned Abraham Guillén found fault with aspects of the organization's strategy and lack of a cohesive ideology. He admitted that the MLN-T followed an ambiguous political line that promised "something of interest to everybody." For example, a bulletin for the organization contained speeches from conservative nationals such as Aparicio Saravia, while other Tupamaros forbade members from criticizing the pro-Moscow communists. Ultimately, like the pro-Moscow and pro-Maoist groups in the US and Uruguay, Guillén believed that the Tupamaros' efficient tactics had been hurt by "mediocre strategy" and "questionable politics." He argued that the Uruguayan government had stayed strong because of the weaknesses of the Tupamaros' revolutionary discourse. Yet, despite these issues, Guillén continued to view the Tupamaros as the greatest "academy" in the world to teach others about urban guerrilla warfare. He believed that the group undeniably taught by actions and not theories. However, Guillén hoped that the Tupamaros' brilliance in tactics could one day be matched by sophistication in politics.[155]

In response to these criticisms, those in the transnational left who wished to counter the attacks against the Tupamaros argued against using "outdated" Soviet Union or Chinese models. The Tupamaros contained flexibility in both their ideology and actions, which some Marxist organizations and individuals viewed as a positive aspect of the group. Supporters of the Tupamaros often pointed to the Cuban Revolution as a positive example of ideological flexibility and revolutionary action. Tupamaro supporters argued that a systematic study of Fidel Castro's ideology during the combat phase of the Cuban Revolution also appeared less "clearly defined" under the lens of a "consistent Marxist analysis."[156] Therefore, these supporters contended that leftists who recognized the groundbreaking events of the Cuban Revolution should not thoughtlessly condemn the actions of the Tupamaros. While those from the Moscow line of Marxists criticized the Tupamaros, they ignored the fact that Latin America created distinctive permutations of revolution for the left.

In his work *Utopia Unarmed: The Latin American Left after the Cold War*, Jorge Castañeda argues that revolutionary groups such as the Tupamaros and others in the Latin American left contain a unique character. He posits that the left in Latin America was and remains varied and that it achieved relevance beyond the rigidity of former Soviet countries. As well as hard-line Marxists, Latin America contained a large movement of the national-populist sector of the left, which had staying power. Furthermore, the Cuban Revolution (particularly at its inception) represented a different kind of revolution, which built on the long revolutionary tradition of Latin America, including Emiliano Zapata in Mexico, José Martí in Cuba itself, Augusto César Sandino in Nicaragua, and many others.[157] Castañeda points out that the majority of revolutionaries in Latin America did not fit into the Marxist conceptualization of revolutionary leaders. The majority of revolutionaries in guerrilla movements like the Tupamaros were educated, intellectual, and middle class.[158] Thus, according to Castañeda, those in North America and elsewhere who criticized the lack of so-called true Marxism in the Tupamaros showed little understanding of the distinctive nature of revolution and revolutionary groups in Latin America.

The Tupamaros seemingly flaunted their ideological ambiguity and flexibility. At different times, they referred to themselves as both Marxists and socialists. Though vague, in their plans the Tupamaros called for the nationalization of banking and exportation as well as land reform by state appropriation of larger land holdings. They applauded the Cuban Revolution and its rejection of the infusion of foreign capital into the country. However, the overall lack of a specific theoretical base seems understandable considering that the Tupamaros eventually encompassed thirty-five different parties of the Uruguayan left.[159] Their group also included Christians, atheists, agnostics, Trotskyites, anarchists, and those from traditional parties in Uruguay.[160] The absence of sectarianism allowed for a different type of unity than that which commonly divided the left. However, this flexibility also left the organization open to criticism from hard-line Marxists who argued for straightforward, cohesive definitions and ideology.

In reflection, members of the Tupamaros claimed that the Tupamaros represented "human life and happiness" and a "feeling instead of a political line."[161] The Tupamaros themselves argued that they came from a mosaic of ideologies but were united by the need to create an apparatus for armed struggle that would subsume all other political efforts. In a 1970 interview, one Tupamaro said about the group's plans for the future, "We don't tie ourselves to schemes. We'll see next year what our attitude is."[162] Another manifesto claimed, "Strategic lines [are relevant] only for the day, month and year in which they are issued. A strategy is formed on the basis of facts and reality changes."[163]

However, the group also demonstrated its awareness of outside criticisms, particularly after its defeat by the government by 1972. In 1973, as part of the self-critique involved in their regrouping, the Tupamaros analyzed their lack of a defined ideology. In response to the lack of a unifying ideology, which they viewed as an integral part of their defeat, the Tupamaros suggested that they should better train members in Marxist theory and the "moral values of the workers."[164] Other ex-Tupamaros reflectively admitted that the organization's "clear lack of strategy" decided the outcome of the conflict between the Tupamaros and the Uruguayan government.[165]

Some in the US and Uruguayan left, particularly from the pro-Maoist and pro-Moscow line, criticized the Tupamaros' lack of a cohesive Marxist ideology and supposed inability to reach the masses. They pointed to the Tupamaros' nationalist rhetoric as strong evidence that the group failed to commit wholly to Marxist revolution. The Tupamaros undeniably employed a nationalist rhetoric, particularly by invoking Artigas in order to recruit the masses, but they also moved away from rigid definitions of who could be a revolutionary and attempted to include activists from a variety of backgrounds. This ideological flexibility reflected a common trend in twentieth-century revolutions throughout Latin America. However, the idea that the Tupamaros lacked a comprehensive ideological base was not the only criticism from members of the left. Pacifist leftists viewed the Tupamaros' practice of violence as an ineffective mechanism to inspire true revolutionary change.

Criticisms of the Tupamaros: Violence

Additional criticisms from the left concerning the Tupamaros included a disavowal of the group's use of violence as a means for revolutionary change. For example, the group Socialist International, which called for leftist reform through electoral means, denounced the undemocratic military regimes of Latin America, the political and economic interference of the US in the region, and the violent tactics of the Tupamaros. Socialist International, based primarily in Europe, was formed in 1951 as a worldwide coalition of labor, democratic socialist, and social democratic organizations. Socialist International supported political parties in Latin America that worked to create "freedom, social justice, and independence" but not those who chose violence as a way to fight for change.[166]

Specifically concerning Uruguay, Socialist International blamed the Uruguayan government for its structural problems and the monopolization of land by what they deemed greedy estate owners. However, they also criticized the Tupamaros who supposedly "put fuel on the fire" of their country's increasing political intolerance.[167] The actions of the Tupamaros, claimed Socialist International, proved contrary to Uruguay's democratic traditions. The criticisms of the Tupamaros derived in part from a larger critique of the "terrorist" left by the Socialist International. The group asserted that the root of violent tactics by the left derived from a reactionary political philosophy. These terrorist actions had nothing in common with true socialism but rather helped to create new inspiration for repression. Socialist International viewed violent political groups such as the Tupamaros as elitist and unconcerned with the majority. Similar to critiques from the proviolence left, the Socialist International portrayed the Tupamaro as predominately middle class and unable to ally with the working class and labor movements.[168]

Not all activist groups that disavowed violence agreed with Socialist International's assessment of the Tupamaros. During the mid-1960s, for some in the pacifist left, the Tupamaros' Robin Hood tactics had method to their perceived madness. Some in the left-leaning pacifist religious community such as activist Eugene Stockwell admitted that the group was "wildly imaginative" and "tightly disciplined." However, by 1971, after the kidnapping and killing of Dan Mitrione and other violent actions, left-leaning religious pacifists criticized the Tupamaros' intensification of violent tactics. Between 1966 and 1971, the Tupamaros killed eleven police officers, mostly in self-defense. Nevertheless, pacifists argued that beginning in the 1970s, the Tupamaros unleashed on the Uruguayan people a "campaign of terror." Arguing along similar lines as the Uruguayan government, some North American activists claimed that the actions of the Tupamaros only incited violence from the state and right-wing groups. For example, in 1972, para-police groups such as the

Juventud Uruguaya de Pie detonated bombs throughout Montevideo, killed presumed communists, and shot at students at the Universidad de la República. The pacifist left condemned these "rightist thugs" as fervently as they did the Tupamaros. They argued that "force was opposed to force, military might to subversion." Thus, to those who opposed violence, participants as well as perpetrators were considered guilty.[169] The criticism of the tactics of the Tupamaros anticipated feminist activist Audre Lorde's later statement concerning how to truly change society: "The master's tools will never dismantle the master's house."[170]

It is important to note that while the Tupamaros asserted the need for violence, they claimed to do so only at the "correct" time and against the "correct" target. The group primarily used violence in self-defense or to protect third parties.[171] In one interview, a Tupamaro explained the group's philosophy about violence, "We follow one basic rule: Do not use violence that is not understood by the people. If the people don't understand it, the government can use it against us."[172] There were exceptions to this claim, however, most notably when members killed rural worker Pascasio Ramón Báez with an injection of Pentothal in order to protect themselves from being discovered by authorities.[173] In the majority of cases, however, the group directed its violent actions toward government officials and not Uruguayan civilians. The Tupamaros claimed that the "very fact of being armed, prepared, equipped, the process of violating bourgeois legality, generates revolutionary awareness, organization and conditions."[174] Therefore, the Tupamaros believed that knowledge of self-defense and readiness for armed confrontation enabled the possibility of true revolutionary change.

After years of their violent actions failing to change the dictatorship's policies, the Tupamaros eventually modified their philosophies concerning the political expediency of violence and considered electoral solutions. In anticipation of the November 1971 elections, seventeen political groups created a coalition named the Frente Amplio or Broad Front. Dominant groups in the Frente Amplio included communists, socialists, and the Christian Democrats.[175] The Tupamaros maintained their tactical differences with the Frente Amplio but endorsed the party for the election of 1971 and eventually joined its ranks. The Tupamaros believed that the Frente Amplio offered one avenue for the mobilization of workers. In supporting the elections, the Tupamaros also argued that the work of the Frente Amplio should not "begin nor end with the elections."[176] The Tupamaros also stated, "We will be patient as long as the process is truly democratic and one of transformation. But if the Frente Amplio becomes bureaucratic, fence straddling and begins the customary political maneuvers . . . we'll go back to armed struggle."[177] Despite their criticisms, the Tupamaros saw the Frente Amplio and traditional political solutions as the most expedient way to end the dictatorship and the repression of the Uruguayan people. Thus, the Tupamaros continued to prove their ideological flexibility by transforming from a group concerned with violent revolutionary practices to supporting a public discourse on human rights and electoral solutions. This, of course, proved to be more politically expedient as the change to a language of human rights also helped to support "concrete goals" of the movement and the eventual triumph of the Frente Amplio, which later integrated former Tupamaros into its party.[178]

DURING THE 1960S AND 1970S, the Tupamaro guerrillas garnered the attention of leftists throughout the world, many of whom imagined the group in an overtly romanticized manner. These admirers perceived the Tupamaros as a fundamentally egalitarian group that performed more successful actions than other Latin American revolutionary movements. Supporters of the Tupamaros argued that unlike most other direct action groups, the MLN-T had outwitted the state and also won the support of the people. However, most on the left failed to recognize that the incompetence of the Uruguayan state allowed for many of the Tupamaros' successes.

Admirers perceived the Tupamaros as consistently successful practitioners of urban guerrilla warfare. Abraham Guillén, the so-called theoretical brain of the Tupamaros, helped to articulate the group's revolutionary development through his descriptions of the practice and theory of urban guerrilla warfare, specifically as it applied to the MLN-T. Supporters also applauded the Tupamaros' allegedly advanced organizational skills, all of which were common in other guerrilla groups but viewed as exemplary in the case of the Tupamaros. Beyond the idea of their perceived successes in organization and urban guerrilla warfare tactics, the film *State of Siege* offers another example of how the Tupamaros pervaded the imagination of the international left. Through its positive portrayal of the Tupamaros, *State of Siege* hoped to justify the group's violent actions.

Despite a great deal of romanticism from the left, some pro-Maoist and pro-Moscow groups criticized a lack of ideological coherence within the Tupamaros. The Tupamaros focused much of their propaganda on nationalist rhetoric and allowed for various political affiliations to join their group. They did not support hard-line Marxist ideology but allowed for a degree of flexibility in their activism, as has been a characteristic of leftist movements in Latin America. Other activists, who expressed pacifist beliefs, criticized the Tupamaros for their advocacy of violence as a means of political change (which the group later rejected for political expediency). Alongside romanticism from many on the left, these debates demonstrate the degree to which the Tupamaros influenced the US left's discourse and actions.

While some US leftists perceived the Tupamaros as successful practitioners of urban guerrilla warfare and hoped to emulate their tactics, the MLN-T and the rest of the Uruguayan left harbored their own complex opinions about politics in the US. The Uruguayan left criticized US foreign policy but also expressed international solidarity with militant movements in the US, specifically members of the Black Panther Party. The next chapter examines the significant influence of the US left, particularly the Black Power movement, on Uruguayan leftist ideology and strategy.

2

Supporting the "Other" America
Leftist Uruguayan Solidarity with US Radicals

> It is difficult for either Latin or North American revolutionaries to
> win alone. . . . Only working together for their common liberation
> can they overcome the prospect of a Latin American Vietnam.
> —Abraham Guillén

BY THE LATE 1960S, an integral part of the political strategy of the
Tupamaros and the majority of the Uruguayan left involved the concept of international revolution and an alliance with radicals throughout the world.[1] The Tupamaros argued that direct violent action helped
weaken US imperialism and also encouraged all of Latin America
to move toward socialism. Because of their country's relatively small
size, the MLN-T advanced the idea that revolution in Uruguay needed
to extend throughout the continent in order for it have any staying
power. International concepts of revolution and solidarity influenced
the Tupamaros as well as the greater Uruguayan left to forge ties with
radical groups, even in the US, the very country whose ruling government they hoped to help destroy.[2] Both the Tupamaros and the Uruguayan left demonstrated particular solidarity and admiration toward
the BPP and civil rights organizations in the US.[3] They viewed the African American struggle as genuinely capable of creating revolutionary
change in the US and perhaps throughout the world. Ironically, while
the predominantly white middle-class Uruguayan left rarely attempted
to align with people of African descent in their own country, the Black
Power movement offered a militant model that the movement hoped to
emulate.[4]

The leading source of the international education of Uruguayan
revolutionaries came from the leftist intellectual newspaper *Marcha*, one
of the only leftist periodicals in Latin America with subscribers throughout the continent.[5] Published in Montevideo, Uruguay, *Marcha*'s articles

informed readers about US politics, foreign policy, and the revolutionary actions of the US left.[6] *Marcha* also provided a forum to debate political issues in Uruguay such as the formation of a leftist front, the Frente Amplio, for the 1971 elections.[7] The newspaper's extensive letters-to-the-editor section also offers insight into issues of importance within the Uruguayan left, many of which concerned the US. Thus, the Tupamaros and the Uruguayan left received a great deal of their knowledge concerning radical happenings in the US from *Marcha*.[8]

In part because of their knowledge of US politics, the Uruguayan left did not simplistically consider the US a land solely of oppressors and imperialists. Instead, they followed the US workers' struggle, the actions of the white left, and particularly the fight of the Black Panther Party during the late 1960s and early 1970s.[9] These groups came to represent the inner rebellion and disintegration of US society. For the Uruguayan left, there were two United States, one of internally oppressed peoples, such as minorities and the working class, and the other of imperialist ruling elites, who caused discord and poverty throughout the world.[10] Looking specifically to the Black Power movement, the primarily white Uruguayan left found similarities in the repressive practices of their respective governments. Publications such as *Marcha* employed the US's treatment of African Americans as one way to critique their own country's disintegrating democracy.[11]

The Uruguayan left empathized with US radicals' criticism of the increasing repression of dissent in the US. Indeed, both groups had grown up with the idea that their nation possessed democratic exceptionalism. In *Left in Transformation*, Vania Markarian writes about the historical tradition of an "inclusive model of democracy" in Uruguay. She contends that this model "upheld social and political equality in the name of liberal ideas of legality, freedom, rationality and progress. These ideas were manifested through a state that intervened in every sphere and established contractual relations with the citizenry." Like in the US, for most of the twentieth century, two traditional political parties dominated Uruguayan politics without any real danger of subversion from radical forces or third parties.[12]

While the proviolence left of the 1960s shunned traditional politics, leftist activists also employed a discourse supporting universal ideas of freedom and justice. Within the US, radical political activism simultaneously entailed both "cooptation and dissent,"[13] meaning that while they criticized US institutions, leftist dissenters often supported

"American" ideals such as liberty and freedom. Similar ideas appeared within the discourse of Uruguayan leftists, even for the Tupamaros who advocated violent action against the ruling state. The MLN-T employed a nationalist rhetoric that advocated universal justice and equality, ideals historically honored by the Uruguayan government.[14] Protests from the Uruguayan left featured protest signs with slogans such as "Liberty or Death" and "Tyrants Tremble." During these rallies, protestors often shouted simply, "Freedom!"[15] The parallels between the Uruguayan and US left's conceptions of democracy and activism inspired solidarity as both groups fought for similar causes and saw themselves as persecuted victims of governments hostile toward the left. As part of this solidarity, many in the Uruguayan left aligned with the oppressed minorities of the "other" US in order to help incite worldwide revolution and the downfall of the imperialist portion of America.

The "Other" America

As the US left moved toward more radical conceptualizations of their country's history by the late 1960s, some suggested that two separate nations existed within the United States. These leftists contended that because African Americans had never truly been included as equal citizens, the US contained a dominant white supremacist nation and an oppressed black colony living within their country's borders.[16] Part of understanding these two separate nations entailed looking at what leftists deemed the "imperialist history of slavery."[17] Radicals vociferously chose which nation they would align with, proclaiming their alliance to the so-called black colony. However, the US was not the only place where radicals supported this idea; sources generated by the Uruguayan left suggest that Uruguayan activists also envisioned the US as two dichotomous nations. Members of both the US and Uruguayan white left allied with the nation of the oppressed black colony in a common fight against US imperialism. They argued that imperialist oppression was perpetrated as much inside the United States as it was through foreign relations. According to the rhetoric of the left in both Uruguay and the US, the colonized black nation shared more in common with the Third World than white US citizens. Therefore, its status as a colony within the US made the black liberation movement a viable alternative to white America and a challenge to US imperialism.[18]

The aforementioned Abraham Guillén echoed the idea of the US containing two separate and opposing nations. In the preface to the US translation of his work, Guillén acknowledged the importance of US revolutionaries and purported to have great confidence in "youths, students, laborers, technicians, intellectuals, women, blacks, Chicanos and Puerto Ricans in the United States."[19] Guillén argued that these groups constituted an internal proletariat of the US Empire, which also dominated Latin America.[20] He presented these groups as natural allies of Latin Americans, whom he deemed the external proletariat. Guillén predicted that when revolutionary forces within the US and Latin America combined, US imperialism would inevitably fall. Therefore, Guillén refused to homogenize all citizens living within the US as compliant with their government's actions.

Instead, Guillén viewed North American revolutionaries and Latin American radicals such as the Tupamaros as dependent upon one another in the battle against US hegemony. He argued that white laborers and urban African Americans needed to reach out to Latin American revolutionaries in order to undermine US power. In turn, he contended that Latin American revolutionaries required the help of white workers and people of color within the US. This revolutionary relationship relied on combined action and solidarity against a common enemy. Because of what he viewed as an inevitable crisis because of revolutionary conditions, Guillén predicted a subsequent continental war fought by the two Americas.[21] The culmination of this battle included a class struggle in the United States with Latin American allies supporting the revolution of the internal proletariat.[22] Thus, Guillén advocated an alliance with the "other" US or the "internal proletariat" in order to destroy the ruling, imperialist portion of the country.

In addition to Guillén's support of revolutionary groups in North America, articles in *Marcha* suggested that the internal proletariat was steadily gaining power in the US. In an article written especially for *Marcha*, sociologist James Petras presents the US government as repressive and imperialistic but also portrays the country as containing an immensely pervasive revolutionary counterculture that subverted authority.[23] The leftist press in Uruguay seemed to welcome social unrest and reported on the proliferation of radical movements in the US, particularly ones that advocated violence as a means of changing society.[24] They presented groups such as the Weather Underground and the BPP as supporting the values of Marxism, idealizing Che, and denouncing their country's imperialism and dehumanization of its people under capitalism. These groups, therefore, appeared to have a good deal in common with Uruguayans who called for radical change in their own society.

The Vietnam War also demonstrated how the US government seemed to be on the verge of collapse.[25] Protests from the "other" US against the war demonstrated how much unrest truly existed within the country. *Marcha* reported that by the end of 1968, the US was in a state of urban guerrilla warfare similar to Uruguay.[26] The publication reported that in 1968 in Detroit, black militants attacked a group of police officers. Since then, thousands of bombs had exploded in the US and a subculture of violent radicals had emerged. The article also listed some of the radical groups and people the US government appeared unable to locate.[27] This included Weatherwoman Bernadine Dohrn, Rap Brown of the Student Non-violent Coordinating Committee (SNCC), Cameron David Bishop (who hoped to sabotage the Department of Defense), and some of the students involved in the bombing at the University of Wisconsin.[28] *Marcha* consistently presented the US government as progressively losing the battle against the people of the "other" America.

Another article claimed that never in the history of the US had opposition to the government been stronger.[29] After the invasion of Cambodia, *Marcha* reported that high schools and universities, a large majority of the middle class, African Americans, and even sectors of Congress all denounced the move.[30] The alleged crisis of imperialism in the US had digressed to the point where divisions had occurred even in the dominant classes. In order to show the extent of this rebellion, *Marcha* published statistics of student opinions demonstrating vast discontent in the US. For example, one published account showed that 41 percent of North American students believed the Vietnam War to be purely imperialistic. Of this same group, 55 percent argued that the US was a fundamentally racist country. These statistics revealed the existence of allies in the US who felt just as discontented with their government as did the people of Uruguay.[31] One *Marcha* article even asserted that because of popular unrest, the US system "could no longer function." Therefore, to the Uruguayan left, the US government represented a failing and repressive force that hoped to squelch radical movements in their own country and throughout the world.[32]

When analyzing the full acquittal of Black Power leader Angela Davis in 1972, *Marcha* painted a picture of a rapidly changing US society and failing economy.[33] For leftists in Uruguay, the freeing of Davis indicated the advancement of the revolutionary cause within North America and represented a triumph for the people of the "other" US. Leftists contended that Davis's campaign for freedom and subsequent release showed the possibilities of successful transnational campaigns and international solidarity. Davis's acquittal further reinforced the idea of a crumbling US political system caused in large part by vast internal problems with African Americans, Chicanos, Puerto Ricans, the student movement, and other radical elements.[34] According to *Marcha*, these internal struggles helped the destruction of imperialism from within and in turn moved the world closer to global socialism.

Furthermore, while Uruguayan leftists expressed great interest in the US civil rights movement, Stokely Carmichael, and other Black Power activists, they seemed to have a particular fascination with the politics of Angela Davis.[35] Considering the overall invisibility of women of African descent in Uruguay, Davis proved to be an interesting choice to represent the US Black Power movement. Focusing her activism on communism, black radicalism, and international feminism, Davis's politics reflected her extremely transnational life. Born in Alabama, Davis left the US South at age fifteen for New York. There she lived with a white family and attended the Little Red School House, a private school, which encouraged her to study Marx and Engel's *Communist Manifesto*. She attended Brandeis University in Massachusetts, studying with famous philosopher Herbert Marcuse, and spent her junior year of college at the Sorbonne in France. As she had lived outside the South and away from the civil rights movement for most of her adult life, Davis had a variant view of race relations than her Black Power counterparts. Once back in the United States, Davis joined SNCC in Los Angeles, which eventually imploded because of what Davis perceived as the sexism of male leadership. Davis then joined the BPP but remained on the fringes of the organization, in part because of gender politics. Davis critiqued the machismo of the organization, asserting, "Revolutionary practice was conceived as quintessentially masculinist." The critique of the "macho posturing" of the proviolence BPP mirrored the later criticisms by female members of sexism within the Tupamaros. Davis believed that black liberation could truly occur only within an international workers movement, which allied with all racially and sexually exploited peoples as well as white workers.

While Davis's political ideology mirrored that of many in the Uruguayan left (besides her focus on gender), it was not until her arrest that the press took full notice of the international radical. Not surprisingly, Uruguayan leftists' articles about and introductions to Davis focused on her communism and black activism, not her feminist politics. Because of the similarities between the imprisonment of African Americans as so-called political prisoners and the ever-worsening repression for those in the left in Uruguay during the early 1970s, the Uruguayan left focused on Davis's prison activism. Thanks in part to the FBI's COINTELPRO program and its effort to undermine liberation movements, over twenty black activists had been assassinated or murdered by police and federal agents.[36] On October 13, 1970, police finally captured Davis in New York City. After her arrest, Davis spent sixteen months in jail, primarily in solitary confinement, before being released on bail. *Marcha* included letters from Davis in prison, translated from the leftist British publication the *Guardian*. The newspaper followed her trial until June 1972, when the state acquitted Davis of all charges of murder, kidnapping, and conspiracy.

According to the articles featured in *Marcha*, Davis was a "youthful" and "beautiful" woman, a symbol of black revolution in the US that had entranced the entire world. One article about the activist highlighted features about her appearance such as her "golden" and "penetrating" eyes. Descriptions of her physical appearance supported a gendered mystique of Davis as a professor, and activist, and an attractive woman.[37] This sexualized characterization is not surprising. The fascination with the appearances of female leaders within the US left occurred frequently during the 1960s and 1970s. For example, Bernadine Dohrn, leader of SDS and the Weather Underground, was praised by leftist men for her "chorus line figure" as well as her ability to mobilize large groups of people. Many men in the radical left desired Dohrn because she "fused the two premium images of the movement: sex queen and street fighter."[38] An article in the Black Liberation Army newspaper *Third World Edition* about "women's roles" in the revolution acknowledged that Davis was a potential revolutionary guerrilla. However, according to the article, Davis did not wear her "crown of femininity based on the self-reliant strong Amazon" as well as Dohrn and Black Panther leader Erika Huggins.[39]

Despite the sexualized manner in which she was perceived by many men in the movement and represented in the countercultural press, Dohrn possessed a great deal of authority in SDS. Accounts from former

Weatherwoman Susan Stern demonstrate the power she felt Dohrn possessed. Stern adored Dohrn because she was one of the few women who seemed to have any sway or privilege in the male-dominated SDS. It was this charisma that helped Dohrn lead what would be the Weather Underground to walk out during the 1969 SDS convention—bringing seven hundred other SDS members with her, chanting, "Power to the people! Ho! Ho! Ho Chi Minh!" Though Dohrn's high ranking in the organization helped change SDS into a platform for the Weather Underground, the three top positions in the new SDS won by the "action faction" clique were given to Mark Rudd, Bill Ayers and Jeffrey Jones, all men.[40]

Dohrn's organization, the Weather Underground, believed that the Panthers' masculinity helped enhance their revolutionary status. Academic and activist Richard Flacks asserted about proviolence groups like the Weather Underground, "As the movement became more militant, many males found it an excellent arena for competitive displays of virility, toughness and physical courage." Soon after their formation in 1969, the Weather Underground began to act as the proverbial political jocks—its members bragged that they hadn't read a book in months, but they could beat up any pig, any time. This anti-intellectualism came from the idea that the Weather Underground wanted to live as the true "working class" by renouncing any sort of knowledge obtained by reading books or attending universities. This renunciation came in large part from the group's stereotyping of the working class and member's guilt about their middle-class past and university education. To eradicate this past, members in the Weather Underground needed to destroy their "honkiness" and "wimpiness": two words that the group, with the help of the Black Panther Party, believed were undeniably linked.[41]

To counteract their privileged backgrounds, white radicals in the Weather Underground hoped to emulate the Black Panther Party. The Weather Underground fervently agreed with the Panthers' belief that African Americans represented a colony living inside the United States. The Black Panther Party, like the Weather Underground, expressed interest in international solidarity against imperialism, which they felt exploited people of color around the world. The Weather Underground believed that earning the respect of the Black Panther Party would legitimize them as true revolutionaries. Also, if the group could prove that they were not wimpy intellectuals, but rather street-fighting warriors, perhaps the working class would join their struggles. The Weather Underground, seemingly almost desperate at times to establish themselves with the Panthers, developed the slogan "John Brown—live like him!" Many in the Black Panther Party, however, were not as receptive. The Panthers' own male chauvinism inspired them to liken members of the Weather Underground to sissies, girls, and little boys. Hence, the discourse between the two organizations was embroiled in sexism, articulated in the Panthers' belief that Weather Underground militants were "sissies" and not sufficiently masculine or tough.

Since their organization's inception in 1969, the Weather Underground had tried desperately to make themselves "tough" like the working-class people they so often stereotyped. Members in the Weather Underground believed that if they learned how to be truly masculine and aggressive it would be easier to fight in the upcoming revolution. Furthermore, the Weather Underground feared that if other revolutionaries, particularly the Panthers, did not accept them as tough, then their radical aspirations would never have any clout. Much to their chagrin, the Weather Underground never did receive approval from the Panthers. In fact, after several harsh statements about the Weather Underground's low-grade masculinity from the Black Panthers, the Weather Underground figured they needed to seek out new allies but had trouble finding them within the New or Old Left or within mainstream America.[42]

Angela Davis, on the other hand, had no problem finding allies within the Uruguayan left. Besides describing her appearance, *Marcha* featured articles supporting Davis's critique of prison conditions in the US. Some in the Uruguayan left likely made connections between Davis's subpar prison conditions and those of arrested leftists in their own country. The imprisonment of Davis incited protests throughout the world. *Marcha* included entreaties from Davis's mentor, Herbert Marcuse, asking for her freedom. In hopes of provoking acts of solidarity from the international left, Marcuse argued that only with the force of world protest would Davis be released from prison. In Marcuse's and others' requests for her freedom, Davis represented not only the struggle of African Americans but that of all oppressed people in the world. For revolutionary Uruguayans, her communist politics made her an excellent symbol for the marginalization of the left as well as a representation of racial injustice. In his *Marcha* article pleading for international solidarity, Marcuse also included Davis's prison address for interested activists to write.[43]

While articles in *Marcha* concerning Davis occurred frequently throughout the early 1970s, some activists did not approve of what they perceived as certain comrades' lack of prioritizing Davis's cause. Varying degrees of devotion to the US civil rights movement existed within the Uruguayan left, causing debate within the university. Some students vehemently criticized the Uruguayan student movement's focus on issues such as the persecution of Jews within the Soviet Union while not focusing enough of their energy on African American civil rights. One activist was so incensed that he wrote a letter to the editor of *Marcha* criticizing his colleagues' focus on Jewish repression in the USSR while radical leftists such as Angela Davis fought for their lives. In his opinion, Uruguayan leftists needed to put their own country first, and if students wanted to focus on international issues, they should fight against the persecution of black power movement leaders such as Davis, who "struggled for the liberation of her people."[44] To some leftists, "preoccupation" with the cause of Jews in the USSR merely showed international Zionism, Yankee imperialism, and a campaign against the Soviet Union and socialism as a whole. In this case and others, members of the Uruguayan left passionately aligned with the "oppressed" portion of the US to show militant, transnational solidarity.

In direct contrast to the "other" US that Uruguayan leftists supported, they vehemently criticized the actions of political leaders from the so-called imperialist portion of the US. The Uruguayan left contended that this repressive contingent of the US harmed people of color, and the working class inside the US as well as hoped to enforce its hegemony throughout Latin America.[45] For example, Uruguayan students and labor organizations reacted passionately to the arrival of President Lyndon Johnson for an Organization of American States (OAS) conference in the beach town of Punta del Este. Students and workers throughout the country staged rallies, street demonstrations, and sit-ins against the arrival of Johnson. The protests indicted Johnson as a murderer of the Vietnamese people and deemed him a supporter of oppression in Latin America and of all people who "fight for liberty." Leaflets handed out by protesters stated, "Uruguay will be crawling with murderers: Johnson, Somoza, Onganía, Leoni, Stroessner and Costa e Silva." Some students attacked the Brazilian and US Embassies in Montevideo, planting bombs and explosives in several vehicles outside. On the outside wall of the Alianza Cultural Uruguay–Estados Unidos (the Uruguay-US Cultural Alliance) protesters left a large painted sign that read, "Go home Johnson, murderer of 250,000 Vietnamese children." Fifty meters offshore from Punta del Este, protestors in a boat hung the flag of the Vietnamese

National Liberation Front along with Uruguay's national flag. Others marched nearly seventy miles from Montevideo to Punta del Este. During the march, protesters stopped in communities and held meetings; waved the flags of Cuba, Vietnam, and Uruguay; and sang revolutionary songs.[46]

The seemingly most maligned representative of the oppressive ruling class within the US was New York senator and would-be vice president Nelson Rockefeller.[47] Rockefeller became an ideal scapegoat for the Uruguayan left after he visited Latin America and subsequently became a fervent champion for anticommunism in the region.[48] For the Uruguayan left, Rockefeller's so-called imperial missions in Latin America made him a fitting figure to inspire Uruguayan resistance.[49] The Uruguayan left, particularly the Tupamaros, reacted violently to Rockefeller's visits to their country. During Rockefeller's June 1969 visit to Uruguay, groups of students barricaded themselves inside the university and high school buildings, defying the shutdown orders of Pacheco's government. The student protestors painted slogans in the school and throughout buildings in Montevideo criticizing "US Imperialism." Two other young leftists were arrested after attempting to bomb Pacheco's home while he met with Rockefeller.[50]

On June 20, 1969, in response to Rockefeller's visit to Uruguay, a group of Tupamaros set fire to a General Motors plant, causing an estimated US$1 million in damage. Despite heightened security measures, four men dressed as police officers broke into the General Motors office and overpowered two security guards before setting the office and six nearby cars on fire. The group left behind leaflets advocating the struggle of the Tupamaros. The next day, the Tupamaros took over a radio station in Montevideo and broadcast a previously recorded message accusing Rockefeller of being an "emissary of imperialism" while criticizing president Pacheco for complying with orders from the International Monetary Fund.[51] Police finally silenced the broadcast by cutting off electricity to part of Montevideo.

The Tupamaros also interrupted radio stations in the resort town of Punta del Este in order to read their manifestos during Rockefeller's speech that same day.[52] The MLN-T reacted with ire to Rockefeller's visit as they believed he demonstrated the shameless intervention of the US government throughout the world. The group also viewed the US as dictating policies to the "worthless" Uruguayan government who blindly obeyed.[53] Therefore, the Uruguayan left posited that both Uruguay and the US had citizens fighting fervently for revolution but also had corrupt governments determined to maintain their hegemony. For the Uruguayan left, the most inspiring revolutionary element within the "other America" was the Black Power movement.

The Uruguayan Left and Black Power

Marcha focused a good deal of their articles in the late 1960s and early 1970s on the Black Power movement in the US. Information in *Marcha* concerning Black Power included editorials, book reviews and translated works originally written in English by African American revolutionaries.[54] *Marcha* featured reprints in Spanish of some of Eldridge Cleaver's and Rap Brown's works as well as George Jackson's letters.[55] When writing about Jackson, *Marcha* presented his death as a murder by the US government.[56] Uruguayan leftists also focused on the response of African American revolutionaries to their mistreatment by the US government and the movement's acts of international solidarity. *Marcha* reported that the Black Power movement understood that its fight coincided with the larger Third World as they fought against the same oppressor—US imperialism. The newspaper supported their contention by including quotes from Black Panther leader Eldridge Cleaver, who argued that African Americans needed to join with millions of other oppressed peoples in what was in reality the same struggle.[57] By including quotes about internationalism, *Marcha* demonstrated for the Uruguayan left that the BPP offered solidarity with the global revolutionary cause.

Marcha also managed to get personal interviews with some African American activists from the US, including Ray Jones, a soldier who deserted during the Vietnam War.[58] Jones, an African American from Michigan, sought asylum in Sweden after he deserted the armed forces as a protest against the Vietnam War and US racism.[59] Blending antiwar activism with the Black Power movement, Jones became a celebrity of sorts for the international left. When *Marcha* reporters asked Jones what he loved and hated, he responded that he loved African Americans but hated white imperialism. Thus, Jones reinforced to *Marcha* readers the notion of two diametrically opposed, warring countries within the United States. The interviewer sympathized with Jones's alliance to the "other" US and pondered whether Jones was a "deserter" or the ultimate "patriot."[60] Ultimate patriot seemed to be the resounding answer from the Uruguayan left. Members of the Uruguayan left linked the Vietnam War to issues of race, poverty, and exploitation.[61]

Further demonstrating the link between the Black Power movements in the US and the Uruguayan left, *Marcha* featured an article from Black Panther leader Stokely Carmichael written exclusively for the Uruguayan publication. By publishing Carmichael's article, Uruguayan leftists showed their solidarity with international revolutionaries in a time of increasingly transnational politics. In this 1969 article, "The Pitfalls of Liberalism," Carmichael explained to his Uruguayan audience that African Americans did not incite the excessive violence and repression perpetuated upon them by the US government. Instead, he argued that African Americans had merely discovered ways to fight back against violent racist oppression. Moreover, Carmichael indicted not only the imperialist regime of the US for its support of rampant racism but also so-called liberals and reformists. Carmichael reminded readers of the absurdity of supporting nonviolence considering the widespread destruction associated with the history of the colonization of the Americas and with US intervention throughout the world. Thus, Carmichael argued the US was never free or democratic, but rather founded on violence. Revolutionary violence intended to destroy an unjust system and replace it with an equitable one, while counterrevolutionary violence merely supported oppression.

As a sort of mediator between both the oppressor and the oppressed, according to Carmichael, white liberals only talked about the problems of racism but refused to take extreme action to solve them. The oppressors denounced violence only when radicals used it against them. Carmichael reported that the US government wanted to use black soldiers to fight in wars against foreign enemies but not arm them for their own liberation. Furthermore, Carmichael condemned liberals and reformists not only in his own country but throughout the world as he viewed them as impeding revolutionary change by maintaining the status quo. To Carmichael, these reformists wanted to change society by working inside the system and petitioning those that already had control. Carmichael argued for the impossibility of speaking about individual liberty in a society "led by fascists." This reflected a criticism of some in the Uruguayan left who contended that the history of Uruguay stunted the ability for its citizens to create new systems of power.[62] Like Carmichael, they argued that only when the masses controlled the political state would true justice and equality exist. To critics of the system, marches, letters, and petitions never accomplished significant change or successfully challenged the state repression.[63] Similar to what Carmichael advocated, the Tupamaros supported organized violence against the government as they believed that other forms of political action, such as elections, had not successfully transformed Uruguay.

The use of violence to fight against repressive governments reinforced many of the current ideas of the Tupamaros and their sympathizers who saw the actions of the MLN-T as justified. According to their supporters, the Tupamaros participated in violence only to fight an unfair system of power.[64] The Tupamaros themselves rationalized their actions by claiming, like Carmichael, that elections and legality were merely facades that attempted to mask the real exploitation that existed within Uruguay's alleged democracy.[65] The idea of revolutionary violence versus state violence would continue to be an important topic for Uruguayans. In the following years, the Uruguayan government publicly denounced the violence of those in the left (particularly the Tupamaros) while continuing to perpetuate repression against its own citizens.[66]

Besides dozens of articles concerning the Black Power movement, the supplemental journal to *Marcha, Cuadernos de Marcha*, devoted an entire issue to the subject of African American politics. A special edition of *Cuadernos de Marcha* entitled "Poder Negro" ("Black Power") sought to trace the roots and goals of the African American civil rights movement and offer insight into a movement that fascinated many Uruguayan leftists. The issue stressed the continuity of the black struggle in the United States and posited that the voice of Stokely Carmichael represented the same voice of African Americans who had rebelled against slavery in the antebellum period.[67] While asserting the essential sameness of Carmichael and slave rebels may appear to homogenize the black struggle, in actuality "Poder Negro" accentuated the multiple types of activism within the civil rights movement.[68] Uruguayan leftists expressed great interest in Black Power but also acknowledged the multifaceted nature of the civil rights movement. "Poder Negro" explored subjects of nonviolence versus violence and integration versus separation. The issue offered a detailed focus on the schisms between the SNCC and the more moderate followers of Martin Luther King, who advocated nonviolent mechanisms for social and political transformation.[69]

The writers of "Poder Negro" also compared the struggle of blacks in the United States to those throughout the Third World. They contended that especially in the Third World, liberation could not occur solely through the unity of class. Therefore, the African American civil rights struggle helped to inform leftist Uruguayans about the complex nature of revolutionary action that prioritized identities other than class. The predominantly white Uruguayan left stressed the need for activism inspired by racial interests as well as class for those in countries on the "eve of revolution." They focused on the need to move beyond territorial borders for a different alliance—those within and outside of the United States who wanted to bring down the ruling government of that nation. The writers of "Poder Negro" felt such an affinity for African American movements that they asserted that the civil rights movement in the United States also represented "our struggle" or the struggle of leftists in Uruguay.[70]

Uruguayan leftists' interpretation of US history in "Poder Negro" conceptualized African American history through a prism of their own experiences. When describing the period of Reconstruction after the Civil War, the writers of "Poder Negro" argued that the North instituted a sort of "military dictatorship" over the South, with the help of blacks.[71] While this may be technically true, the language used the description demonstrates that the writers conceptualized something similar to the repressive forces they lived under at the time. Therefore, as they compared their struggle to the internal colony of African Americans in the US, Uruguayan leftists also translated US history in a culturally and politically understandable way to their readers.

Because of the lack of a common racial identity, the Uruguayan left focused much of their attention on issues of African American labor. The writers of "Poder Negro" fervently condemned the racism of white workers in the US. They pointed out the specific discrimination against black women workers in the US and criticized their sub-par salaries and degrading work. "Poder Negro" particularly indicted the entire white working class in the US as merely another group that participated in African American repression. This terrible treatment, according to the writers of "Poder Negro," explained African Americans' current reticence to ally with white workers.[72]

The condemnation of the experiences of African American workers in the US proved ironic considering the negative situation of black workers in Uruguay. Most Afro-Uruguayans occupied service sector jobs with women working overwhelmingly in domestic service. As recently as 1988, fewer than two hundred Afro-Uruguayans had a college education.[73] This exceptionally low number contrasted with the sixty-one thousand white students enrolled in college in Uruguay in 1988.[74] Therefore, the left in Uruguay condemned the exploitation of black workers in the US but rarely mentioned the plight of Afro-Uruguayans. The Uruguayan left passionately denounced racism in the US and identified similarities between African Americans and Uruguayan citizens as colonized subjects of the US government. However, notions of analogous experiences between blacks in Uruguay and those in the US remained absent from the left's discourse.[75] This absence reflected what many in the Afro-Uruguayan population have argued about the invisibility of the black population in their country's political and social discourse.[76] These critics contend that ignoring the existence of racial differences in Uruguay did not result in equality but rather more subtle forms of racism.[77]

Therefore, the Uruguayan left easily conceptualized the struggle of those of African descent in the US but rarely acknowledged even the presence of black people in their country. In his 2001 essay "The Afro Populations of America's Southern Cone," Romero Jorge Rodríguez writes about the historical refusal of Uruguayans to admit the realities of ethnic differences in their country. He contends that "twenty years ago it would have been inconceivable to admit that the Uruguayan population was composed of a rich mosaic of cultures, and that each of these cultures has evolved according to its own historical specificities."[78] Only recently has any significant discourse about Afro-Uruguayans emerged in the country.[79]

During the 1960s and 1970s, the Uruguayan left's lack of interest in issues of race in their own country mirrored what the rightist Uruguayan government posited about racial relations.[80] Members of both the left and the right often denied the existence of any real racial diversity in their country, especially in comparison to other Latin American countries.[81] For example, in 1975, Uruguayan dictator Juan María Bordaberry argued that no racial problems occurred in his country because indigenous populations were "nonexistent" in Uruguay. Uruguayans' perception of their nation contrasted with those in countries such as Brazil and Cuba who have consistently argued that they support racial equality.[82] Racial equality, however, has never been the reality for Afro-Cuban and Afro-Brazilians. Within Uruguay, the perceived invisibility of people of color also failed to reflect the reality of the situation of Afro-Uruguayans.[83] Therefore, though the Uruguayan leftist press, particularly *Marcha* and other publications, admired the Black Power movement in the US, they overall ignored issues of race in their own country.

Members of the Uruguayan left admired the African American civil rights movements from afar but also interacted with US groups. International issues greatly interested the Black Panther Party, and they reached out to groups and movements throughout the world, including the Uruguayan left. BPP newspapers extensively covered the struggles for liberation in Africa and the developing world. Black Panther leaders visited China (and came back with positive responses), and some party members found sanctuary in Cuba. The Panthers remained so devoted to international solidarity that Panther leader Huey Newton offered for his group to fight in Vietnam for the communist National Liberation Front (his offer was declined).[84] Thus, the BPP understood the importance of forging international connections and gaining support from leftists throughout the world.

The Black Panther Party conceptualized themselves as urban guerrillas. They looked with concern to what they deemed US "fascist satellites" in South America. The group displayed both admiration for and solidarity with guerrilla movements in Latin America, particularly the Tupamaros. In a Black Panther Party newspaper, the group outlined its stance, "It is the duty of the urban guerrilla to smash USA fascism at every opportunity. The guerrilla must seek out and neutralize all the vile lackeys of USA fascism."[85] The BPP had such admiration for the Tupamaros that in their International News Release they claimed, "We are not alone, we have allies everywhere. We support the struggles of all the South and Central American countries against US imperialism and neocolonialism, particularly the dynamic liberation struggle of the Uruguayan people and the Tupamaros. We condemn the US imperialist fascist puppet regime of Jorge Pacheco."[86] Therefore, of all the struggles throughout Latin America, the BPP specifically mentioned that of the Tupamaros as the most "dynamic." The Black Liberation Army (BLA) echoed similar sentiments about the Tupamaros. They argued that the group set the best example for urban guerrillas operating in the United States. The BLA hoped to emulate the tactics of the Tupamaros, claiming that "action is the vanguard and the Guerrilla is the command."[87] Along with the Tupamaros, the BPP also expressed solidarity with labor movements in Uruguay. They applauded student activists for offering solidarity with the "just struggle of the meat packing workers in Uruguay."[88]

Members of the BPP even wrote a letter to the editors of *Marcha*, published in the May 9, 1969, edition of newspaper asking for both monetary support and international solidarity from Uruguayan leftists. The fact that the group reached out to *Marcha* demonstrates the Panthers' awareness of left-wing Uruguayans' support for their cause. Indeed, the BPP must have had some understanding of their important role in Uruguayan leftists' imagination and activism. In order to inspire Uruguayans to send money, the Panthers' letter informed *Marcha* readers about BPP leader Eldridge Cleaver and his recent arrest. Hoping to demonstrate the significance of Cleaver, they compared the activist to Malcolm X and listed his publications and political activism. The BPP turned to Uruguayan leftists to ask for their help in raising fifty thousand dollars for Cleaver's legal resources. The letter even featured the address of the BPP in Oakland, California, in hopes of motivating monetary support.[89] By asking for the support of the Uruguayan left, the Panthers connected with a group that had consistently offered solidarity with and expressed interest in their cause.

While politics represented one way for Uruguayans to form reciprocal exchanges with radicals in the United States, others forged bonds through music.[90] At a July 1967 conference in Cuba featuring protest singers from throughout the world, one observer commented, "Among the Latin Americans, the Uruguayans were particularly able to spell out fresh concepts." Uruguayan folksinger Carlos Molina said, "Protest song must be more than the song of the professional artist. It must be the song of the people. Art is revolutionary." Singer Quintin Cabrera included a message of unity in his work, "Once again, just like before, all America is one. And we put our fists together because that's how it has to be. For already beginning to burn is the consciousness of our people."[91]

During the late 1960s, internationally renowned Uruguayan folksinger and activist Daniel Viglietti became part of this cultural exchange. When Viglietti sang at a benefit for the Center for Cuban Studies in New York City, he was introduced as part of a growing tide of "international solidarity movements that have developed in view of the growing repression and the growing struggle in the whole American continent." While some of Viglietti's songs specifically referred to the Uruguayan struggle, many supported international leftist movements and solidarity.

Viglietti's solidarity, like that of many in the Uruguayan left, focused on people of color. Playing to his US audiences, Viglietti sang the tune "Duerme Negrito" or "Sleep Black Baby," a traditional Latin American folklore song.[92] "Duerme Negrito" centers on a slave woman who works in the fields to support her baby. The woman warns her baby to go to sleep or the "white devil" or "white master" will come. To sing this song for a group of activists in New York City was an interesting choice for Viglietti, who came from a country with a small population of African descent. Like many in the Uruguayan and US left, Viglietti looked to the culture of black resistance in order to inspire current struggles. In another of his songs, Viglietti compared the oppression of Uruguayans to Africans brought to South America during the Atlantic slave trade. He promised, "I want to tear up my map and draw a new map of all mestizos, white and blacks and sketch them arm in arm. We are not the foreigners, the strangers are the others: they are the merchant traders and we are the slaves."

Viglietti also criticized elite white culture in other songs. His song "A Desalambrar" urged leftists to "Tear down the fences! Tear them down! The land is ours. It belongs to Pedro, Maria, Juan and José." Viglietti also warned that if the lyrics bothered anyone, then he must be a "gringo" or an "owner of Uruguay."[93] However, most leftists in the US audience were probably not offended by Viglietti's mention of the white devil and gringos as they saw themselves as part of the revolutionary portion of the United States and not allied with the alleged imperialist portion of the country. Therefore, Viglietti expressed solidarity with the "other" US while still criticizing the country's flaws.

Though he came from a country with a relatively small native population, Viglietti also harkened to the "purity" of the struggle of the native. In his work "America's Song," Viglietti tells his listeners, "Give your hand to the Indian / He will show you the way / He will take you with him. / The Indian's skin will show you the paths you have to follow. / The copper hand will teach you the blood you have to shed." Thus, Viglietti presented the history of the struggle of natives as inspiration for modern left-wing movements. According to Viglietti, native people's histories of resistance throughout the Western Hemisphere offered strength and showed activists "the way." However, Viglietti's admiration focused on an idyllic native past and not current radical struggles such as the occupation of Alcatraz by the American Indian Movement (AIM).[94]

Viglietti was not the only Uruguayan leftist who looked to native people's history of resistance to support current movements. *Marcha* also reinforced such admiration for native people's struggles by featuring articles about the historical repression of American Indians. While the Uruguayan left rarely focused on native struggles in Uruguay or the rest of the Southern Cone, they expressed some interest in the history of the resistance of "Indians" in the US. Reports concerning this particular native population focused on the attempts to force their assimilation to the so-called American way of life. They indicated the awakening of the consciousness of US activists to the plight of Native Americans and the burgeoning American Indian movement within the country. *Marcha* included excerpts from Dee Brown's work on the history of Wounded Knee in order to help Uruguayan activists understand the history of oppression of native peoples and the increasingly vocal AIM.[95] As with their exploration of the history of oppression of African Americans, the Uruguayan left supported an examination of the roots and causes of modern struggles for rights. Reports such as these enabled Uruguayan intellectuals and leftists to learn the history of racial minorities in the US. As with Afro-Uruguayans, the Uruguayan left failed to prioritize native struggles or acknowledge the existence of this population in their country. They focused on the importance of the activism of people of color in the US, while reinforcing the invisibility of people of color in their own country.

Besides the case of Daniel Viglietti, reciprocal connections between the US and Uruguay also occurred with US-born singer Dean Reed (also known as the "Red Elvis"). While Viglietti toured the US and eventually returned to Uruguay, Reed left the United States in 1962 and never again returned to the US for any significant period of time. He visited South America, specifically staying for long durations in Argentina, Peru, and Chile. In Chile, he developed a leftist political consciousness and began to perform free shows in impoverished areas in South America. He lived in Argentina and frequently visited Uruguay until the late 1960s, when he was forced to leave because of the increasingly repressive government. Reed then settled in the former German Democratic Republic, until he committed suicide at the age of forty-seven (the communist government tried to keep his suicide a secret for years for fear of bad press).

Despite his untimely demise, during the 1960s and early 1970s, for many Latin Americans Reed represented dissent against the US government and an alignment with the "other America." His music and exodus from the US was a microcosm of a larger current of US leftist rebellion against the stereotypes of insularity and ignorance of those in the United States. In one *Marcha* article, Reed's interviewer, Cristina Perri Rossi, failed to uncover anything "North American" about the singer besides his accent. This was a compliment as few in the US left hoped to be associated with mainstream "North American" values and ideas. Rossi stressed that Reed's transformation in consciousness came from his political activism in South America. However, Rossi believed that Reed's transformation occurred only because he already possessed an affinity for those in struggle, something that many from the US lacked. Reed appeared to be naturally aligned with the "other America." Thus, the Uruguayan leftist press presented the singer as an example of South Americans successfully teaching their US comrades about leftist activism and in turn opening their consciousness to the poverty and corrupt politics within Latin America.

Prior to Reed's voyage to Latin American in 1962, he identified as a pacifist and a liberal. However, once in Latin America, the singer experienced an "internal evolution" after he witnessed firsthand the initial formation of fascist governments in the Southern Cone, the enormous class differences in the region, and the widespread poverty. Reed held his government responsible for many of the problems in South America and subsequently advocated that the left should focus its attention on more than Vietnam. After all of his travels in South America, the Uruguayan leftist press wanted to know how Reed saw his home country. While the singer had not traveled much to the US in nearly a decade, he believed that changing things in his home country would be very difficult, especially considering the divisions within the civil rights movement. The singer recalled an African American activist leader that refused to interview Reed because he was Caucasian. However, Reed, like many in the Uruguayan left, demonstrated great interest and respect for Angela Davis. In his interview, he named Davis as the most important figure involved in making change within the US. He asserted that Davis contained all of the characteristics of a great leader, but also had three problems impeding her rise to power. She was African American, a communist, and a woman. Surprisingly, Reed made a point to criticize the political and social subjugation of women. The oppression of women within the left puzzled the singer as he viewed them as acutely skilled at understanding injustices of the system. However, Reed also invoked ideas of biology and motherhood as part of the inspiration of women's specific comprehension of humanity.

Reed repeated what many in the Uruguayan left expressed interest in—the increasing repression of any progressive movement or dissent from the left. While the conservative factions of the US asserted that one should either "love" or "leave" the US, Reed argued that revolutionaries did love the US and therefore wanted to change it. The notion of the US left's strong affinity for their country appealed to leftist Uruguayans as they repeated similar rhetoric within their actions. Thus, Reed represented just one of many reciprocal exchanges between activists in Latin America and the United States. While Reed learned from his experiences in the Southern Cone, he also showed those in Uruguay and throughout Latin America the possibilities for rebellion in the "other" America.[96]

In addition to the frequent and usually positive representations of the Black Power movement and the rest of the "other" United States in *Marcha*, the Tupamaros also specifically showed an interest in African American culture and politics as well as US counterculture as a whole.[97]

The Tupamaros and Black Power

Some Tupamaros specifically looked to the Black Power movement for political and cultural inspiration. However, the group revealed little about their genuine political interests and theories; thus analyzing the accounts of MLN-T prisoners exposes information about the group's relationship to the US counterculture. During a conversation with kidnap victim Dan Mitrione, a member of the Tupamaros asked their captive if he had seen the controversial film *Zabriskie Point*. The Tupamaro found the film, which encouraged US countercultural violence, very "interesting." The 1970 film, by Italian director Michelangelo Antonioni, followed the adventures of two disaffected young people, Daria and Mark. The two explore the vacant California desert and philosophize, get into trouble with the police and have sex (the film also controversially included geological features that turned into people participating in an orgy). At the end of the film, in a scathing critique of consumerism, Daria imagines her boss' opulent house being blown up. To a soundtrack provided by the Rolling Stones, Pink Floyd, and the Grateful Dead, Antonioni intermixed apocalyptic and psychedelic imagery. Though the film found an audience with activists, *Zabriskie Point* was widely panned by critics. Roger Ebert commented about the film, "He [Antonioni] has tried to make a serious movie and hasn't even achieved a beach-party level of insight."[98]

Furthermore, just as the Weather Underground knew about the Tupamaros, the MLN-T expressed awareness of the radical US organization. In the same conversation, a Tupamaro and Mitrione discussed the great amount of social unrest within US universities, a topic in which the Tupamaros appeared well versed. As Mitrione spoke of demonstrations and hippies, an unidentified Tupamaro interrupted the captive and asked about the Weather Underground. Though the Tupamaro did not express complete romanticism about the group, he still seemed impressed by the politics of the Weather Underground. He told Mitrione that the Weather Underground at least "make enough noise to be listened to."[99] Therefore, it seems that some Tupamaro members knew of the Weather Underground's tactics and believed that they performed enough violent action to garner the attention of the US government.

In an interview with the US-based newspaper *Prairie Fire*, one Tupamaro expressed great admiration for revolutionaries in North America. The Tupamaro sent a big "abrazo" or hug to US radicals, saying, "You are our great hope, without you there are no limits on the inhumane logic of the men who now control your government."[100] Another document written by the Tupamaros acknowledged with pride the level of "prestige" they enjoyed within US leftist movements. They lamented the many possibilities for solidarity with these US movements that had yet to be fully realized. The Tupamaros argued for the development of a concrete plan to help them ally with the people of the United States. They claimed that in the US there existed "a land that waited" for revolutionary alliances with the MLN-T.[101]

While scholars have traditionally focused on the US left's awareness of other movements, the Tupamaros in turn demonstrated their knowledge of US groups that admired them. However, this relationship did not consist solely of the US left admiring and following Tupamaro tactics. MLN-T members read works written by African American radicals and scholars, particularly those in the Black Power movement.[102] According to captive Geoffrey Jackson, some favorites of the group included James Baldwin and Rap Brown. It was fitting that the Tupamaros expressed interest in Rap Brown, as he had famously found violence as "American as cherry pie."[103]

In addition to reading the works of black activists, the Tupamaros also enjoyed US protest music and musical genres dominated by African American artists. The group who looked after Jackson frequently listened to soul music, which they claimed expressed the inequality of urban life in the US. According to Jackson, his numerous Tupamaro captors also constantly played a recording of an English-language group repetitively chanting "Power to the People." Most likely, the record was the 1971 John Lennon/Plastic Ono Band single "Power to the People." The Tupamaro jailers not only understood the meaning of the words but also joined in the chanting to express solidarity with African American political movements in the US. Chanting "power to the people" was a way to inspire particular Tupamaros and helped to pass the time during their tedious job as jailers.[104] These acts of solidarity offer an example of an affinity not only for Black Power politics but also for African American culture, specifically music and protest songs for some members of the Tupamaros. Therefore, African American culture, particularly music, became very important in the day-to-day lives of the clandestine Tupamaro militants who kept Jackson captive.

The Tupamaros also demonstrated their sensitivity to African American history by their reaction to Jackson's claim that their disguises resembled hoods of the Ku Klux Klan. The Tupamaros associated the hoods with fascism and to the much maligned racist United States. Tupamaro members even willingly took suggestions from their captive as to how not to look like the KKK and ultimately changed their disguises. The readiness of Tupamaro members to alter their jailer disguises at the request of their captive showed sensitivity on the part of the group to the history of the struggles of African Americans as well as a fervent desire to reject the infamous racist organization.[105] The Tupamaros likely learned about the KKK from the Uruguayan leftist press as they educated their readers about the history and activities of the organization.[106] One article described the KKK's activities such as burning crosses and general acts of violence against African Americans.[107] Others condemned the lynching of African Americans and what they viewed as unparalleled racial prejudice within the US.[108] In addition to news articles, Uruguay activist and poet Idea Vlariño wrote passionately about the treatment of African Americans in the US. In the poem "Agradecimiento," she lamented, "Others . . . if they are born black in the United States . . . are killed like dogs."[109] Afeni Shakur, of the New York Panther 21, echoed this sentiment in a US publication, claiming, "When Panthers are shot down like dogs, the people are also shot down like dogs."[110] Therefore, the Uruguayan left presented US society as harmful, perhaps even deadly, for African Americans.

However, while the MLN-T, whose members were primarily of European descent, expressed great solidarity with African Americans, the group included no real program or even rhetoric concerning race and essentially ignored issues concerning people of color within Uruguay. Ironically, though the Tupamaros rarely mentioned racial issues within Uruguay, their name derived from a figure who they believed preached racial unity.[111] Despite their avoidance of racial issues concerning Afro-Uruguayans, the Tupamaros continued to be influenced by the culture and politics of the Black Power movement.

The Tupamaros consumed aspects of African American culture and at the same time denounced US policies. This complex relationship moved beyond dichotomous notions of Latin American left-wing anti-Americanism versus compliance with US policies. Historians have argued that an explanation of the US's influence in Latin America is far too simplistic if scholars focus only on military, economic, and political hegemony.[112] The Uruguayan left's political and cultural solidarity with the "other" United States showed a variant and complicated kind of exchange that did not replicate traditional models of dominance and acquiescence. These contradictions demonstrate the complex nature of US and Latin American relations and prove the difficulty of homogenizing all of Latin America's interactions with the US. As secular, middle-class, and mostly descendants of Europeans, Uruguayans had a different experience with US and European influence and cultural dominance than most of Latin America. In a society already mostly accepting of European influence, consuming US cultural products, whether from the mainstream or the counterculture, did not have a monumental impact on Uruguayan culture as it already existed.[113] For example, two famous groups in Uruguay in the 1960s, Los Shakers and Los Mockers, were modeled after British groups the Beatles and the Rolling Stones. They sang covers of the Beatles and Rolling Stones along with a few of their own songs, all in English.

Most Uruguayans saw their demographic and cultural differences from the rest of Latin America as a positive element that helped to create their exceptional nature. Members of the Tupamaros even contended that Uruguay had more "civilized" traditions and a different history than the rest of Latin America. In a conversation with prisoner Dan Mitrione, one Tupamaro contended that "human life is cheaper [in other Latin American countries] than in Uruguay." The Tupamaro also told Mitrione that the Tupamaros are "smarter" than other radicals because they only kill when absolutely necessary. According to the Tupamaro, other leftist groups in Latin America "indiscriminately kill . . . and shoot and ask questions later."[114] Therefore, the conversation illustrates that some in the

Tupamaros believed that the exceptional nature of Uruguay could also be seen in the MLN-T's tactical superiority and restraint.

Proving the complex nature of the self-conception of cultural and historical superiority, at times the Uruguayan left seemed to ignore their country's predominantly white racial heritage in an attempt to align with African Americans. For example, in a *Marcha* article about controversial African American exhibitions at the Whitney Museum in New York City, the author aligned the Uruguayan left's struggle with that of African Americans. They argued that black US artists confronted similar issues to those any Latin American or colonized artist would face.[115] The article contended that Uruguayans and other Latin Americans, like their black US counterparts, adopted the mannerisms and perceptions of the colonizers' art. Therefore, both African Americans and Uruguayans struggled to create their own unique aesthetic, free of European control and influence.[116] The rarely articulated claim of common European colonization and destruction is fascinating considering that most in Uruguay ethnically represented the so-called colonizer. Thus, while the Uruguayan left usually clung to their country's European traditions, at times they claimed they inhabited part of the Third World in order to ally with African Americans.[117] Viglietti also invoked this common colonized past when he sang "La Senda Esta Trazada" or "The Path Is Set." He claimed, "Spain, England, Portugal too, and now it's the Yankees' turn. / We've been working under the sun for two centuries / Doing nothing else but changing bosses."[118]

While dozens of articles and letters in *Marcha* focused on African American struggles and debated issues concerning Black Power, they rarely paid attention to other minority groups in the US, even those arguably of similar descent as Uruguayans, namely Latinos. In one article about a Chicano protest, *Marcha* writers focused on the disproportionate number of young North Americans of Mexican descent sent to fight in Vietnam, but reported nothing else. While the Uruguayan left expressed sympathy with the protests of Chicanos, it did not identify with those of similar origin and affiliation.

Although the Tupamaros and Uruguayan left expressed little interest in the politics of Latinos, the Young Lords Party, a Puerto Rican nationalist party, prominently featured the Tupamaros in their newspaper *Palante*. The Young Lords appreciated that the Tupamaros did not fight against the "puppets of the pig's but the pig's themselves."[119] They also expressed admiration for the Tupamaros for not "mouthing leftist slogans" but performing admirable and frequent revolutionary acts.[120] Despite the admiration of Latino leftists, the white Uruguayan left seemingly believed that they had more in common with the African American struggle than Latinos in North America.[121]

Thus, just as they decided which ethnic and cultural backgrounds would define them politically, the Uruguayan left selectively decided which elements of US culture they would embrace and which they would denounce. The Tupamaros' enjoyment of African American music and methods of protest as they critiqued US imperialism illustrate this complex relationship. Thus, Tupamaro members supported the politics and culture of the "other" US, that of African descent. The MLN-T proved the importance of culture, movies, and humor in their political actions when they dramatically destroyed a copy of the widely panned 1969 US film *Che!* at a movie theater in Montevideo. The film, which starred Omar Sharif as Che Guevara and Jack Palance as Fidel Castro, portrayed the revolutionaries as psychotic caricatures. The Tupamaros reportedly destroyed the only available copy of *Che!*, which was shown in Montevideo for only two days, by throwing acid on the film. After completely destroying the movie, the Tupamaros wrote political slogans in the theater before they left. Because no other copy of *Che!* existed in Uruguay at the time, the management of the theater had to show the musical *Hello, Dolly!* instead.[122]

Why did the Uruguayan left express specific interest in the Black Power movement in the US? There are several possible answers to the question of motivation, including the fact that like most revolutionaries throughout the world, the Uruguayan left and the BPP fought against a common enemy. However, this admiration went further than a mere alliance against US imperialism. The Tupamaros used the notion of uniting against the "common enemy" of US imperialism with other leftists, including those in Cuba.[123] Members of the Uruguayan left glamorized the struggle of the BPP and its masculinist militancy, which in many ways mirrored the philosophies of the Tupamaros. The Tupamaros viewed Black Power culture and politics as revolutionary and appreciated its mockery of the US establishment and desire to critique "imperialist" America.[124] Both groups accentuated the "cool" or "hip" aspects of the revolution in dress and attitude. However, the Tupamaros took this even further with women often wearing wigs and members dressing in elaborate disguises. One Tupamaro robbery had an all-female group stealing over two hundred wigs from a Montevideo beauty salon.[125] Another mission featured two armed militants on motorcycles shooting at a patrol car.[126]

The Tupamaros' choice of revolutionary pseudonyms also reflected a sort of "coolness" repugnant to the hard-line Communist Party. The influence of US culture emerged in the nicknames of the clandestine left-ist guerrillas in Uruguay. In *7 meses de lucha antisubversiva* (*7 Months of the Anti-subversive Struggle*), published by the Ministry of the Interior in Uruguay, the Uruguayan government detailed the names and arrests of hundreds of left-wing activists. Many of these guerrillas had nicknames that reinforced the hip image of the left in Uruguay. Several women chose more European or US influenced undercover names such as "Laura," "Paula," "Betty," and "Amanda." Other female activists used creative monikers such as "La Gorda Teresa" (or Fat Teresa); "Soledad" (as perhaps homage to Black Power and the Soledad Brothers); "Tania" (in reference to Che's Bolivian companion; "Tania" would later be Patty Hearst's SLA name); and "Dulcina" (or Sweet). Perhaps the most roman-tic nickname of all was Myriam Kayden Montero Stanke's secret handle, "La Rubia Valentina" (or the Blonde Valentina).[127] Valentina is the femi-nine form of the Roman moniker Valentins, which comes from the Latin word "valens," which means strong and healthy.

Men in the Tupamaros also used creative secret names. They ranged from the rather plain "Tom," "Willy," and "Omar," to the dramatic "Spartacus," "Lenin," "Zapata," "Ernesto," "Lucho," and "Gorila," which was an anti-Peronist term. Others were identified by their home coun-try, including "El Brasiliero" (the Brazilian) and "El Ingles" (the English-man). The few women of African descent in the Uruguayan left were often identified as "La Negra"; African men often went by "Negro."[128] The names revolutionaries chose for themselves was another chance to add to the romantic nature of the life of the urban guerrilla in Uruguay.

Besides cultural reasons, another likely motive for the passionate acts of solidarity with African American civil rights was that they pro-vided an outlet for the anger of the Uruguayan left. As the Uruguayan state became increasingly authoritarian by the late 1960s, the frustration that citizens felt for their own government could be channeled through solidarity with African Americans and the student left, who also ex-perienced their own repression by the government.[129] The Uruguayan left likely saw parallels in their own situation when they learned of the imprisonment and persecution of African Americans.[130] While genuine solidarity with African Americans occurred as part of a transnational leftist movement, Black Power and its subsequent repression by the US government offered the Uruguayan left another vehicle to vehemently denounce repressive state apparatuses. For example, in one letter to the editor of *Marcha*, an activist passionately decried a "racist judge" that had treated Black Power leader Bobby Seale and other African Americans unfairly. The letter criticized how the so-called grand democracy of the US no longer facilitated truly impartial trials. The criticism of the US's failing democracy echoed what the Uruguayan left privately and sometimes publicly expressed about their country. Both nations had grandiose claims about democracy but in actuality broke promises to their citizens in the 1960 and 1970s (to varying degrees). In her letter to the editor, the activist also argued for the importance of the Uruguayan people denouncing the alleged farce of justice in the United States. She advocated for Uruguayans to appreciate the significant struggle of the Black Panthers and to denounce their unequal treatment by the judiciary. [131] The question of justice for the incarcerated Panthers, therefore, also mirrored a similar question within the increasingly jailed and interrogated Uruguayan left. The Tupamaros in particular could relate to the Panthers as by 1972 most of the leaders of both groups had been jailed or killed and their movements were foundering. [132]

While not to the same extent, the actions and persecution of the student left in the US also offered Uruguayans another vehicle to criticize their government's treatment of the student left. One article in *Marcha* about the Kent State killings pointed out that US vice president Spiro Agnew referred to student activists as terrorists. Therefore, like in Uruguay, pointing out the radical nature of subversives supposedly justified the unfair treatment and violent tactics of the government. [133] The persecution of the student left in the US mirrored many of the problems within Uruguay. [134] Despite their reputation as a beacon of democracy, the Uruguayan government also presented the student left and the Tupamaros as terrorists and responded to protests with the exertion of violence. [135]

THROUGHOUT THE LATE 1960S and early 1970s, US radicals had an important influence on the politics and culture of the Uruguayan left. This influence was supported in large part by leftist publications, particularly the newspaper *Marcha*. By featuring articles concerning leftist movements in the US, *Marcha* helped to educate the Uruguayan left about the ideas and radical actions of US revolutionaries. The newspaper paid specific attention to the Black Power movement and translated writings by BPP militants into Spanish. Articles in *Marcha* also presented the US as divided into two Americas. One nation included imperialist and oppressive elites, such as Nelson Rockefeller, who perpetrated crimes throughout the world. The "other" US contained students, the working class, and people of color who fought to destroy imperialism and in turn became natural allies of leftist Uruguayans. In large part because of African American revolutionaries, the Uruguayan left presented the repressive part of the US as finally beginning to lose its power.

Thus, the predominantly white left in Uruguay expressed solidarity with the struggle of radicals in the US, particularly the Black Panther Party. Some in the Uruguayan left even argued that the struggle of African Americans represented the same fight the Uruguayan people were involved in. Both supposedly struggled against the same oppressor—US imperialism. Ironically, Uruguayan leftists passionately advocated for better treatment of those of African descent in the US but ignored the marginalization of Afro-Uruguayans in their own country. The fact that the Uruguayan left focused on racial issues in the US and not in Uruguay demonstrates that they too, perhaps unwittingly, supported the invisibility of people of color in their own country. The interest in African American politics stemmed, in part, from the movement offering another outlet for Uruguayan leftists to express their anger toward an increasingly repressive Uruguayan government. The Uruguayan left found parallels in the treatment of radicals by the US government and their own government's jailing of members of the left.

While Uruguayan leftists expressed solidarity with radicals in the US, North American activists also worked on behalf of Uruguayans, particularly after the official institution of the dictatorship in 1973. In order to protest the Uruguayan dictatorship, various types of political strategies emerged. This included letter-writing campaigns and petitions initiated by human rights groups as well as leftist solidarity movements focused on fighting both the dictatorship and the capitalist system. The next chapter explores the specific types of solidarity offered to Uruguayans during the dictatorship and the gendered nature of these interactions.

3

Solidarity and Reciprocal Connections
Uruguayan and US Activists

We must realize that borders exist only on maps.
—Group for the Support of the Uruguayan Resistance (GARU).

IN A 1972 ARTICLE about human rights violations in Uruguay, activist and missionary Eugene Stockwell lamented transnational organizations' lack of concern for the "small" country. He pondered, "Does anybody care about the nation's plight? Are human rights violations less precious in Uruguay than elsewhere? How far must repression go before our 'global village' recognizes that such a cancer, even in little Uruguay affects us all?"[1] Indeed, in 1972 few international activists prioritized denouncing the steady decline of democracy in Uruguay. However, after the official coup in 1973, new and disturbing information emerged about the dictatorship, inspiring a proliferation of international human rights activism concerning Uruguay.[2] Amnesty International expressed particular concern for the erosion of human rights in Uruguay and by the mid- to late 1970s made the country one of its primary foci. At an Amnesty International press conference held in Mexico City in 1976, members reported that Uruguay ranked number one in the world for torture.[3] Besides Amnesty International, in 1979 alone the Human Rights Commission of the UN, the European Parliament, the OAS, the Inter-parliamentary Union, the World Council of Churches, and the International Labor Organization all denounced human rights violations in Uruguay.[4] In March 1980, the Human Rights Commission of the UN listed nine countries that consistently violated human rights; Uruguay was among them.[5] In turn, the Tupamaros and others in the Uruguayan left knew of the international support their jailed comrades received throughout the world and remained hopeful that international denunciations would help their cause. In an unpublished letter about police brutality in their country, the Tupamaros attempted to upset authorities by declaring that international organizations knew of and denounced the gross human rights violations perpetuated by their government.[6]

At its peak the number of political prisoners in Uruguay totaled over six thousand with nearly two thousand Tupamaros jailed. The Uruguayan government arrested people for having Marxist ideals, belonging to trade unions, or merely criticizing the government.[7] Because of the dire human rights situation in Uruguay, many groups focused on condemning government repression rather than offering leftist solidarity. These groups employed statistics and anecdotes concerning torture and used a language of human rights in their activities concerning Uruguay.[8] They petitioned, wrote letters, and worked within every available legal channel to raise international awareness about torture and other human rights violations.[9] While some groups focused on human rights violations and attempted to remain more apolitical, others openly expressed left-wing sentiments while condemning Uruguay's harsh treatment of political prisoners.[10] Uruguayan exiles made up a large part of these groups; they allied with other leftist North Americans to criticize their country's government.[11] Leftist organizations used various strategies in their attempts to offer solidarity to the Uruguayan people. Some condemned the capitalistic nature of the dictatorship as well as its ties with US "imperialism" and apartheid in South Africa.[12] Denouncing the economic, diplomatic, and social relationship between Uruguay and South Africa gave leftists an opportunity to denounce human rights violations in both countries as well as speak out against racism.

Within these various forms of activism, some leftists in the US forged genuine reciprocal connections with Uruguayans. These groups did not behave overtly paternalistically with their Latin American comrades and sometimes created genuine connections. However, most US groups failed to offer solidarity specifically to women prisoners or examine gendered experiences under the dictatorship. In contrast to the majority of solidarity groups concerning Uruguay, one transnational feminist organization, Women's International Resource Exchange (WIRE), made connections with the family of an incarcerated Tupamara, Yessie Macchi.[13] Macchi and her family initiated contact with WIRE in hopes of inspiring international solidarity to help Yessie's cause. Therefore, various types of solidarity groups emerged in the US during the 1970s and 1980s with different priorities concerning Uruguay.

Human Rights Activism

By the mid-1970s, human rights groups in the US fervently denounced the mistreatment of Uruguayan citizens by their government. These groups varied in size and interests, but all fought against gross human rights violations in Uruguay. Groups and committees expressing solidarity with the Uruguayan people could be found in London, Brussels, Cologne, Barcelona, Geneva, Marseilles, Strasbourg, Milan, Tel Aviv, Zurich, Paris, Berlin, and Stockholm.[14] In the US, a handful of transnational groups presented themselves as most concerned with general human rights violations in Uruguay. One such group was the New York–based Committee in Solidarity with the Uruguayan People (CSUP), which later opened offices in Washington, DC, and Boston.[15] The CSUP promoted the release of Uruguayan political prisoners and raised public awareness primarily through the publication of materials about the situation in Uruguay. They encouraged letter-writing campaigns to the Uruguayan and US governments, human rights groups, and media outlets, showing the group understood the importance of international networking and transnational alliances. They also used their position as US citizens to put pressure on the dictatorship by exposing its tactics. However, the CSUP did not merely argue for the importance of US public opinion or present their organization as paternalistically helping Uruguayans. They also declared their international solidarity with the Uruguayan people.[16]

Most newsletters distributed by the CSUP described Uruguay in order to familiarize activists with the historical and geographical details of the country. CSUP's *Uruguay Newsletter"* commonly presented a brief history of the country and located it on a map.[17] However, while activists may not have initially been familiar with particulars concerning Uruguay, this does not mean that they knew nothing of the country's political situation. For example, Amnesty International alone collected over 360,000 signatures from seventy countries in its campaign against political repression in Uruguay.[18] When describing Uruguay's history, the CSUP's materials touted the country's former reputation as a beacon of democracy and liberty. The authors of the newsletter stressed how much the once democratic country had changed and offered statistics about the rising number of political prisoners in Uruguay.

The CSUP also forged connections with groups of exiled Uruguayans such as the Grupo de Convergencia Democrática en Uruguay (CDU). The CDU, made up of different religious, political and social groups hoped to restore Uruguayan democracy by working not only with citizens in their own country but also with international groups such as the CSUP. The CDU argued for the importance of developing relationships with democratic groups and governments throughout the world that supported the freedom of the Uruguayan people. The CDU also emerged in part to put pressure on the Uruguayan government to create a reasonable "time table" for the return to democracy. In turn, the US based CSUP included documents from the CDU in their newsletters and also received information about the situation in Uruguay from the group.[19] Thus, the incorporation of the CDU's materials demonstrated willingness on the part of some US groups to collaborate with and include the voices of Uruguayan activists.[20]

During the mid-1970s, groups similar to the CSUP also emerged in Canada, such as the Toronto-based Committee for the Defense of Human Rights in Uruguay (CDHRU).[21] Like the CSUP, the CDHRU did not focus their activism on leftist solidarity but rather used letter-writing campaigns and created pamphlets and newsletters to raise awareness about the dire human rights situation in Uruguay. For example, in an effort to free Uruguay's political prisoners, CDHRU leader Professor Kenneth J. Golby of York University in Toronto wrote to the president of Uruguay, Juan María Bordaberry, about the inhumane treatment of prisoners (many of whom were Tupamaros). Listing the names of seventeen prisoners, including Tupamaro leader Raúl Sendic, Golby contended that reliable sources such as the International Red Cross reported the methodical torture of prisoners.[22] Golby also compared Uruguayan prison conditions with that of Nazi concentration camps.[23] The professor invoked the history of Uruguay in his appeal to Bordaberry, arguing that "torture and dehumanization are not worthy of a nation with a history like that of Uruguay."[24] Thus, Golby used Uruguay's historical reputation as a shining example of democracy in Latin America as a means to shame Bordaberry and the Uruguayan government's actions.

Proving that the influence of international opinion may have initially carried some clout with the Uruguayan president, Bordaberry responded to Golby's letter within a few weeks. Bordaberry's response demonstrates the influence of international movements in the early years of the dictatorship, if not necessarily to change policy but to garner the attention of leaders concerned with Uruguay's global image. If anything, the president of Uruguay understood the power of transnational activists' publicity and their possible connections with Uruguayan leftists, particularly those affiliated with the university such as Golby. The Uruguayan government responded in large part because it could not afford to ignore the vociferous denunciations of human rights groups.

In his response to Golby, Bordaberry admitted that he usually did not reply to the campaigns of international groups because they commonly only wished to propagate world communism.[25] By taking this stance, Bordaberry hid behind a simplistic Cold War refrain that any dissent or criticism of a government should be discounted as mere communist conspiracy. In his letter to Golby, Bordaberry also contends that the arrests of people whom he called subversives (from a movement he never specifically names) have been wrongly represented in so-called international propaganda. According to Bordaberry, these subversive betrayers sold out to foreign interests.[26] Bordaberry even goes so far as to argue that the Tupamaros received funding from communist organizations and support groups throughout the world while the Uruguayan government had no outside assistance. In an attempt to control the press concerning the Tupamaros, the Uruguayan government forbade the use of the word "Tupamaro." The government allowed the press to refer to the Tupamaros only as subversives, criminals, prisoners, etc. The press eventually became so frightened of the new censorship laws that they began to refer to the Tupamaros as the "unmentionables."[27]

Furthermore, according to Bordaberry, because of the middle-class status of many Uruguayans and their supposed racial purity (Bordaberry stressed that the population descended from the first Spanish colonists or from other European immigrants), Uruguay did not deserve the attacks from the Tupamaros.[28] Bordaberry's government took issue with any ethnic diversity in Uruguay and attempted to render Afro-Uruguayans completely invisible in the country. Within a year of his letter to Golby, Bordaberry's government arranged the removal of Afro-Uruguayans from their homes in the center of Montevideo. Romero Jorge Rodríguez argues that the relocation of Afro-Uruguayans into abandoned warehouses and factories on the fringe of the city had little to do with the unsafe conditions of buildings they inhabited. Instead, he postulates that the underlying motive of the dictatorship was to separate groups of those of Afro-Uruguayan descent and prevent the influence of their culture in Montevideo.[29]

While Bordaberry dispensed untruths in his letter to Golby, the fact that he responded at all demonstrates that during the 1970s the Uruguayan government hoped to protect its reputation and fight against the influence of international activists.[30] Bordaberry's letter to Golby, which was widely published in Latin America, also inspired some moderate left-wing Uruguayan activists to reach out to North Americans. For example, in 1975 Frente Amplio senator Zelmar Michelini sent a letter to Professor Golby refuting Bordaberry's claims.[31] Michelini, originally a Colorado Party minister and senator, later renounced the Uruguayan dictatorship's actions and participated in the founding of the Frente Amplio.[32]

During his lifetime, Michelini connected with numerous international activists, including Professor Golby. A little less than a year before he was murdered, Michelini wrote to Golby criticizing Bordaberry's letter. The senator assured Golby that he was not being used in a communist campaign but rather committed to fighting for a just cause.[33] Michelini also wrote to Golby about specific mechanisms of torture and included descriptions in his letters. Like the CSUP's incorporation of its correspondence with the Uruguayan CDU, Golby's group later used some of Michelini's testimony and descriptions in their newsletter revealing the human rights abuses in Uruguay.[34] Invoking ideas of universal human rights and solidarity, in one of his letters Michelini also applauded Golby for being an activist who "reacts to the suffering and persecution of another human being anywhere in the world as if it were [his] own."[35] Thus, Michelini demonstrated obvious respect for Golby because of his willingness to speak out against injustice and forge international ties with those in Latin America. This exchange represented an instance of reciprocal bonds forged between activists committed to changing and challenging the dictatorship in Uruguay.

A day before the June 27, 1973, coup in Uruguay, Michelini fled to Buenos Aires, Argentina. From exile, he began a campaign of transnational opposition to the Uruguayan dictatorship. Vania Markarian refers to Michelini as joining "with international actors who could help discredit the Uruguayan regime before the broadest audience possible." By the mid-1970s, Michelini hoped to visit Washington, DC, to denounce the human rights violations in his country. However, thanks to coordination between the Uruguayan and Argentine governments, Michelini's passport was suspended.[36] On the evening of May 18, 1976, Argentine soldiers kidnapped Michelini. One of Michelini's contacts in the US, scholar and activist Louise Popkin, called the US State Department and international organizations to report the events.[37] Unfortunately, the State Department did nothing to help. A few days later, Michelini's body appeared along with the president of the Uruguayan Chamber of Deputies, Héctor Gutiérrez Ruiz, and two former Tupamaros. Since regimes in Argentina and Uruguay usually targeted lesser known figures for murder, the reasons for Michelini's assassination prove complex. Most likely, the Uruguayan government's fear of the consequences of Michelini's international associations with human rights advocates caused his murder. However, human rights activism did not represent the only way international activists expressed solidarity toward Uruguayans. Some groups focused specifically on leftist issues and formed transnational coalitions to further their political agendas.

Leftist Solidarity with Uruguay

Demonstrating the nuances within international solidarity organizations, some US groups denounced the Uruguayan dictatorship and also focused their activism on leftist politics. For example, the New York branch of the Committee for the Defense of Political Prisoners in Uruguay (which later changed its name to the Uruguay Information Group) focused on issues of labor and leftist activism. The group's bulletin, *Uruguay News*, begun in 1977, printed articles in both Spanish and English. The primary issues of the organization included the desire to end torture in Uruguay; free political prisoners; restore civil liberties; legalize the Uruguayan labor union Convención Nacional de Trabajadores (CNT); prosecute responsible parties for repression of citizens; and form a government that represented what they called the popular forces.[38] Therefore, the Uruguayan Information Group moved beyond primarily focusing on human rights activism and also hoped to advance leftist politics.

Uruguay News examined the effects of the dictatorship on the working class in Uruguay. The bulletin offered a forum to attack Uruguayan "de-nationalization" or the support of private ownership in industry, a concern for many in the left. According to the *Uruguay News*, the dictatorship planned to sell the country to foreign interests, as evidenced by a full-page ad taken out in the *New York Times* by the Uruguayan government. The ad reassured interested parties that US investments were secure in Uruguay. To those at the *Uruguay News*, courting the financial investments of US businesses accentuated that the Uruguayan dictatorship supported economic liberalism.[39] By linking US foreign investments to the Uruguayan dictatorship, US leftists discovered another angle to critique increasing worldwide economic liberalization. The *Uruguay News* also reported on more than US economic influence as they uncovered cases of alleged CIA participation in the dictatorship.[40]

The aforementioned Chicago Area Group on Latin America (CAGLA) also claimed to uncover the influence of US corporations in Uruguay by listing the numerous companies found in the country. This list included an explanation of what the corporations manufactured and offered in Uruguay.[41] Concerned activists could thus read about which companies had infiltrated Uruguay and subsequently critique neoliberal economic policies in Latin America. Thus, US groups fighting for human rights in Uruguay also used the struggle to condemn their own government's foreign and economic policies. These criticisms demonstrate the multifaceted forms of activism and mechanisms of solidarity within the US left concerning Uruguay.

During the period of the dictatorship (1973–1985) the controversial "Chicago Boys" model inspired Uruguay's economic policy. The government halted import barriers and cut national production. The government also increased military spending and courted foreign investment. The *Chicago Tribune* reported that the Uruguayan government spent anywhere from 1 to 1.5 billion dollars on defense from 1973 to 1983. At the time of the coup in 1973, Uruguay contained three foreign-owned banks. A decade later there were nineteen foreign-owned banks, and the unemployment rate was close to 25 percent.[42]

Beyond criticizing the Uruguayan dictatorship's links with the US, international solidarity organizations also compared Uruguayan prisons and the dictatorship to other repressive regimes such as the one in South Africa. Grouping these governments together gave US activists the opportunity to fight against racism as well as critique the Uruguayan dictatorship. For example, when former Uruguayan senator Wilson Ferreira Aldunate traveled to the US in order to garner support against the dictatorship, he referred to the Uruguayan government as totalitarian and disavowed its identification with South Africa.[43] *Granma* indicted the increasingly cozy relationship between South Africa and Uruguay, claiming, "This growing intimacy represents a danger for the peoples of the Southern Cones of Africa and Latin America and a new obstacle for world peace."[44]

Groups such as the New York Circus, a Christian organization that provided educational materials for progressive activists in the US, criticized Uruguay's ties with South Africa. The organization reported that the Uruguayan dictatorship found friends in the "most tyrannical and repressive governments in the world" such as South Africa and Rhodesia. They also argued that while the United Nations and world opinion condemned apartheid, the Uruguayan dictatorship had strengthened its bonds with the government of South Africa. The New York Circus reported that after the 1973 coup in Uruguay, South Africa deposited large amounts of money in Uruguay's Central Bank. Therefore, according to the New York Circus, the dictatorship not only repressed its people but allowed itself to be bought by the racist regime of South Africa. Beyond economic relationships, members of the New York Circus argued that Montevideo's strategic position made it an asset in the global scheme for the alignment of strong anticommunist governments, which they argued often tolerated torture and apartheid.[45] Therefore, leftist solidarity groups linked the racist policies of South Africa to Uruguay in order to demonstrate the depravity of both regimes. This strategy stressed the corruption of the Uruguayan dictatorship and also provided a mechanism to critique racism. Once again, however, while leftists vehemently criticized South Africa's policies, they failed to examine issues of race in Uruguay. Thus, members of the Uruguayan and US left identified with the struggles of people of African descent everywhere but within Uruguay.

With the help of Uruguayan exiles, the regime's association with South Africa received further international condemnation. One group, the Uruguayan Association against Racism and Apartheid (UAARU) based in Geneva, Switzerland, argued that Uruguay's ties with South Africa ran counter to the Uruguayan people's "anti-racist traditions."[46] While this particular group of Uruguayan exiles still ignored the oppression of Afro-Uruguayans, they also deviated from the usual rhetoric by at least acknowledging Uruguay's multiracial composition. Thus, the UAARA represented one of the few activists groups abroad or within Uruguay that acknowledged the diversity of the country.

The UAARA reported that the South African government began courting Uruguay as an ally for tactical, economic, diplomatic, and social reasons as early as 1966. The group also noted that both the South African and Uruguayan governments purported to reject discrimination in support of apartheid, which supposedly respected racial differences. Therefore, Uruguay emphasized their rejection of racism and touted the familiar refrain that no such social problems existed in Uruguay. The UAARA reported that propaganda within Uruguay presented the South

African government as a victim, unjustly persecuted by international human rights groups. Because of their "unfair" persecution by international organizations, both Uruguay and South Africa claimed to be at the mercy of terrorists and behaved accordingly to maintain internal security. Thus, the governments of South Africa and Uruguay argued that any criticisms against them derived solely from subversive forces that lacked any understanding of the real situation in their respective countries.[47]

The UAARA also contended that the relationship between South Africa and Uruguay was so influential that it altered Uruguay's voting patterns within the United Nations. The positions that Uruguay took within the UN demonstrated that they hoped to (somewhat) distance themselves from South Africa. However, the UAARA insisted that the Uruguayan government also found ways to continue to ally itself with South Africa. When Uruguay's sentiments deviated from the majority, which condemned South Africa, it abstained from voting or did not participate instead of casting a negative vote. Therefore, the Uruguayan government slyly supported South Africa without completely discrediting itself by flagrantly allying with the much maligned regime.[48]

In a pamphlet about the Uruguayan dictatorship and its ties to South Africa, the UAARA further pointed out the similarities between the two countries by referring to South African prime minister B. J. Vorster's speech to the Uruguayan people. In his speech, Vorster assured Uruguayans, "Our cooperation can be developed at all levels because we are the same kind of men."[49] Thus, as part of their denunciations of the Uruguayan dictatorship, international leftist groups pointed to the country's close ties with the racist regime of South Africa. Criticizing the relationship between Uruguay and South Africa demonstrated one of the ways activists showed their solidarity with Uruguayan resistance and also supported other elements of progressive politics. However, while international leftists somewhat examined issues of race within their activism concerning Uruguay, they usually ignored or stereotyped the gendered experiences of female political prisoners. Some exceptions to this sexist treatment existed, such as that of the feminist organization Women's International Resource Exchange (WIRE), which prioritized the campaigns of female political prisoners.

Gender and Solidarity

While some in the US left offered solidarity to Uruguayans through various political strategies, leftist Uruguayans also sought connections with activists in the United States, even relatively obscure feminist organizations. One such example of this is found in an eleven-page letter written in 1984 to US feminist Bobbye Ortiz by Yvelise Macchi, who pleaded for international help for the release of her sister Yessie, an imprisoned Tupamara.[50] Yvelise Macchi hoped that contacting Ortiz's New York–based organization, WIRE, could help garner support for her sister's cause. As a transnational group that claimed to combine anti-imperialist activism with feminism, WIRE deviated from the focus of most organizations concerned with human rights in Uruguay. This may have been one reason Macchi's family reached out to WIRE, as they believed the group would prioritize a campaign to free the Tupamara.[51]

WIRE, founded in 1979 by feminist Bobbye Ortiz, tackled the issue of white, Western feminist supremacy by vowing to dissolve the supposed connection between feminism and imperialism. WIRE's 1984 statement of purpose posits, "It is our conviction that authentic feminism implies a commitment not only to ourselves and our sisters in this country, but also to our sisters globally, especially in the Third World."[52] This global solidarity movement focused much of its attention on women's issues in Latin America and had specific roots in a transnational feminist solidarity organization called Action for Women in Chile (AFWIC).

AFWIC was created after the overthrow of the socialist Salvador Allende government by General Augusto Pinochet on September 11, 1973. The group, officially formed in November 1974 in New York, comprised both Latin American and US feminists. Though AFWIC prioritized attacking the dictatorship in Chile, they also promoted anti-imperialism within the women's movement and hoped to stop the gender-specific abuses of female Chilean political prisoners. After four years of working with AFWIC, Ortiz realized that she had learned sufficient organizational lessons to enable her to create WIRE, also based in New York. At its inception, WIRE's nine-member collective reprinted materials about women in the so-called Third World, some of which were written by women in nonindustrialized countries.[53] Though primarily written in English for their North American feminist audience, WIRE produced and reproduced materials about Latin American feminism and Latin American women's lives.[54] A fall 1982 WIRE catalog featured a quote from Saralee Hamilton of the Nationwide Women's Program of the American Friends Service Committee. Writing about how WIRE's publications influenced her group's activism, Hamilton noted, "We rely on WIRE to provide a continuing source of invaluable connection with the indigenous voices of Third World Women in struggles on every continent. The timeliness and accessibility of WIRE's material challenges and enables North American feminists to operate from a truly global perspective."[55] This illustrates that WIRE helped to offer some North American feminists a more nuanced international perspective.

Primarily through books and pamphlets, WIRE illuminated aspects of Latin American women's lives for US feminists. At a time when US feminists wanted to reach out in solidarity to feminists in the nonindustrial world and conceptualize feminism from a less West-centric perspective, WIRE offered a forum to explore Latin American women's experiences.[56] Thus, WIRE sought to end imperialism and forge transnational connections and understanding between women worldwide.[57] Therefore, it is understandable that Macchi reached out to WIRE as it defined itself as an anti-imperialist, international women's organization that focused a great deal of its activism on Latin America.

In the letter to WIRE, Yvelise Macchi presented a detailed synopsis of her sister Yessie's experiences during her twelve years of imprisonment. Yvelise wrote to Ortiz in order to appeal to her "solidarity, requesting your help to obtain her freedom."[58] Though the letter was dated August 30, 1984, and Uruguay was progressing toward democracy, Yessie remained imprisoned under standards that violated human rights codes. In her letter, Yvelise stressed the arbitrary nature of Yessie's detention and the deterioration of her health while in prison. Believing that US pressure and opinion could influence the Uruguayan government, Yvelise appealed to Ortiz and WIRE to support a campaign to sponsor Yessie's freedom. Yvelise included in her request the names and addresses of military authorities, political leaders, and newspapers for Ortiz and the members of WIRE to contact.

As an international solidarity organization that focused on Latin America, WIRE members probably already knew something about Yessie and her role in the Tupamaros. Yessie was somewhat well known in more radical leftist circles in North America. For example, a *Latin America and Empire Report* entitled "Women in Struggle," published in 1972 by the North American Congress on Latin America (NACLA), featured Macchi on the cover. The NACLA report described Macchi as a

Tupamaro leader and argued that she represented one of many types of struggle in which Latin American women participated.[59] While NACLA referred to Yessie Macchi as a Tupamaro leader, ironically most publications consistently featured the top leaders of the Tupamaros as: Raúl Sendic, José Mujica Cordano, Adolfo Wassen Alaniz, Eleuterio Huidobro, Maurice Rosencoff, Julio Marenales, or other men.[60] Most international solidarity publications focused on the importance of freeing male leaders, but rarely women.[61] One bulletin released by the Comité de Información sobre la Represión en Uruguay contained a list of arrested Tupamaro leaders and had the portraits of important members such as Sendic, Mujica, and Huidobro along with descriptions of their jobs, political affiliations, and number of children. In this particular bulletin, eight arrested Tupamaro women, in a similar situation to their male counterparts, had only their names listed. While these women fought and got arrested just as the identified men, the Tupamaras did not receive a description or portrait, just their names with a sketch of barbed wire beneath. Yessie was considered of such low standing that the bulletin writers misspelled her name as "Dessie."[62]

Most international solidarity groups generally discounted the significance of the contributions of Tupamaras or supported traditional gender constructions of female political prisoners. For example, the Toronto-based organization Grupo de Apoyo a la Resistencia Uruguay (GARU) or Group for the Support of the Uruguayan Resistance focused primarily on leftist resistance and presented female political prisoners in a specifically gendered way. GARU's activism focused primarily on issues of class and the Uruguayan economy. Most of GARU's members were exiles from Uruguay who immigrated to North America in order to escape the dictatorship.[63] The group printed materials in both Spanish and English for Uruguayan exiles and the greater North American public. GARU's bilingual publication *Banda Oriental* helped to create a diverse audience throughout the Western Hemisphere. With this publication, exiles hoped to disseminate information about as many groups as possible, particularly other Latin American organizations.[64]

Therefore, despite blaming Uruguay's problems on what they called imperialist powers, GARU understood that people in the US, Canada, and Europe also actively sought solidarity with Latin American leftists.[65] Along with groups in the United States and Canada, GARU called for Latin Americans to put aside their differences in order to unite against repression and imperialism. Using a language steeped in transnationalism, GARU's members argued that borders existed only on maps. These borders and divisions allowed imperialism and national oligarchies to dominate (which in turn created dictatorships throughout South America). Therefore, the group believed that if they remained divided from other Latin American organizations, they could never triumph against the perceived enemy (imperialist-supported dictatorships). Using Marxist rhetoric, GARU members argued that the dominant classes ultimately forced them out of their homes and into other countries. These members reported that they planned to return to their homes as soon as the dictatorship ended. Therefore, members of GARU had a vested interest in seeing the quick cessation of the dictatorship.[66]

While on the surface most of the language in GARU's *Banda Oriental* concerning resistance and conditions under torture appears gender neutral, closer analysis reveals the gendered nature of the representation of women prisoners. For example, general sections concerning the "Situation in the Prisons" in actuality referred only to male prisoners. *Banda* reported that Uruguayan jails deprived male political prisoners of food and tobacco and limited visits with parents, wives, children, and siblings. Another smaller section analyzed the situation of women prisoners and focused on very different deprivations for women prisoners than those of their male counterparts (food and tobacco). The GARU bulletin lamented that for female prisoners, "photos of children or engagement rings are prohibited."[67] Therefore, while most of the materials concerning the Uruguayan resistance movement superficially made no distinctions between women and men prisoners, reports of female prisoners focused on traditional ideas of what should be significant to women—motherhood and marriage. Thus, *Banda* presented traditionally feminine items as more important to women than food or other essential materials.

The gendered presentation of male and female prisoners occurred in other materials about human rights violations in Uruguay. Another bulletin about women's treatment in prison reported that visitors to women's prisons shockingly had the same restrictions as those visiting male prisoners. The focus of women's prison experiences, however, remained on motherhood. The bulletin reported that mothers could not hand their children anything during visits. For instance, one mother who dared to give her sick child a handkerchief to blow his nose was sentenced to solitary confinement and lost visits with him. This anecdote demonstrated for the reader another way the Uruguayan government treated prisoners cruelly. Though the treatment of women prisoners was undeniably horrible, once again, solidarity groups focused on different issues of importance for male and female prisoners. In leftist presses of all types, the pain of incarcerated mothers appeared to be much more significant than that of fathers in prison who rarely saw their children.[68] The notion of a mother being separated from her child always reinforced the brutality of the dictatorship. One story concerning imprisoned activist Victoria Barcelo claimed that she lived in "double torment" because of the uncertainty of the fate of her children.[69] Others such as prisoner Rita Ibarburu were portrayed in the leftist media as "sensitive, tender, giving and constant" and offering encouragement to her comrades through song.[70]

The leftist press also defined many incarcerated women by their relationships with male activists. For example, the English-language version of the Cuban newspaper *Granma* referred to Hilda Delacroix, an activist who was imprisoned for eight months, as "the wife of communist leader Juan Hose Ormachea."[71] Mirta Ercilia Fernandez, a Tupamara who escaped from prison, was referred to as "the widow of Tupamaro guerrilla Fernán Pucurull." Rosa Maria Aguirre, who died while giving birth in prison, was identified merely as the "wife of a Tupamaro guerrilla."[72]

In contrast to GARU and other leftist solidarity groups, as an "anti-imperialist" feminist organization, WIRE did not support stereotypical images of Latin American women or discount the specific experiences of female political prisoners. Unlike most groups involved with issues of international solidarity, WIRE prioritized the campaigns of imprisoned political women. While there was general knowledge of Yessie's situation in the US activist community, most campaigns for Uruguayan prisoners often placed more importance on the imprisonment of male Tupamaro leaders. Despite most organizations' focus on male prisoners, even after twelve years, Yvelise continued to fight for her sister's freedom and reached out to sources she hoped would influence the Uruguayan government's decisions.[73]

In order to educate WIRE members on Yessie's prison conditions, Yvelise did not employ common statistics concerning human rights, gendered language, or lofty political rhetoric. Instead, she included a biography and personal letters from the Tupamara to her family. The biography sent to WIRE revealed that in 1977 Yessie gave birth to her daughter Paloma while in jail. The father was Yessie's companion and fellow political prisoner Mario Walter Soto, who died of cancer while imprisoned in 1980. What this letter to WIRE did not reveal, however, was the situation concerning how Yessie became pregnant while in prison. Thanks to facilitation by certain prison guards, Yessie and Mario had secret rendezvous while incarcerated.[74] When the Uruguayan government found out about these meetings, guards threatened violence on Yessie in order to make her lose the baby. However, Yessie claimed she would inform international organizations of the Uruguayan government's plan to terminate her pregnancy, which in turn intimidated officials into allowing Yessie to carry her baby to term. Petitions from international organizations also enabled Paloma to remain with her mother for eight months in prison until she was handed over to her maternal grandparents.[75] In contrast, threatening to involve international organizations would not have carried the same weight in countries like Chile and especially Argentina, which murdered imprisoned mothers and/or took their children away.[76]

Included in the packet to WIRE was also what Yessie wrote about Paloma's life without her parents. She lamented the separation from her daughter, writing, "We cannot offer her a rose colored world nor an easy life, nor even a normal family. We cannot save her from her quota of tears and sorrows, nor from the wounds of a warm heart. We can only offer her this handful of tenderness and a long look, so that she will know for whom and by whom she lives." Therefore, in her plea to WIRE, Yvelise included excerpts from Yessie's letters to her family to demonstrate the inhumanity of her sister's situation. Including Yessie's statements about her daughter, her day-to-day life in prison, and her inner thoughts differed from previous solidarity campaigns that focused on more generalized accounts of prison life. Yessie's letters eloquently convey the despair of separation from her loved ones and musings on loneliness. By including Yessie's letters and offering a specific character study of her sister, Yvelise appealed to the sensitivity and humanity of activists in the United States. Thus, Macchi's family's campaign for her freedom focused on interpersonal relationships and the importance of reuniting loved ones.

However, the materials Yvelise included in her plea to WIRE contained a surprisingly genderless tone as they focused on the bonds of families, not specifically mothers. The letters ignore the usual stereotypes of a mother's natural need to be with her children and instead suggested that both men and women require contact with their loved ones. Yvelise's campaign for her sister did not rely on essentialist ideas about women's natural roles as mothers. While Yessie's role as a mother was included in her biography, most of Yessie's letters focus on her own emotional and existentialist struggles in prison.[77]

The creative composition of Yvelise's letter and campaign for Yessie's freedom seem appropriate considering the unusual life of the Tupamara. Macchi did not live a common life restrained by the usual gendered constructions of her time and culture. As a child she lived with her family in the United States for three and a half years, and as a young teenager she became politicized by the leftist tracts and books she read.[78] She also lived in Cuba for some time in the late 1960s, where she joined with radical groups and learned about armed combat. The well-traveled and well-read Yessie escaped twice from imprisonment, once in the famous operation "Estrella."[79]

Unfortunately, North American and other international campaigns for Yessie throughout the 1970s and early 1980s failed to win her freedom. Yessie was finally released along with 250 other political prisoners after the official end of the dictatorship in 1985.[80] There are several possible reasons for the Uruguayan government's reticence to release Yessie along with other political prisoners throughout the early 1980s. Yessie had received revolutionary training in Cuba, outwitted officials, conceived a child while in prison, and escaped incarceration several times. Most of all, however, she challenged patriarchal authority as one of the press-appointed female "leaders" of the Tupamaros who continually disobeyed Uruguayan authorities. Despite the insistence of the Uruguayan government on keeping Yessie imprisoned, her family continued to fight for her freedom by looking to international organizations. The Macchi family's connections with activists in the United States, such as the feminist group WIRE, demonstrate the ways Uruguayans reached out to US activists in search of solidarity.

Other groups and individuals in Uruguay also reached out to the US radical left for political solidarity. In 1972, the Comunidad del Sur (Community of the South), a sixteen-year-old intentional community on the outskirts of Montevideo, asked the US-based publication *Liberation News Service* for help against the increasingly repressive Bordaberry regime. The Comunidad del Sur contained forty adults and children who helped run a modern graphic arts factory and print shop. The community was also known in Uruguay for its experiments with collective education and psychiatry. After three years of harassment, in 1972 the Uruguayan government finally shut down the offices of the Comunidad del Sur. The Uruguayan government arrested most of the group and charged members with running clandestine presses and distributing information and arms in order to subvert the government. *LNS* reported that only five adults remained in the group after the arrests. The remaining five members struggled to take care of the twenty children living on the commune. The women from Comunidad del Sur reached out to *LNS* because they believed that massive international pressure would influence Uruguayan officials. They asked activists in the US to send letters and telegrams to the minister of the interior. The remaining and nameless women also asked for letters and "desperately needed money" to be sent to them.[81] Like Yessie's sister, the women from Comunidad del Sur demonstrated a belief in the importance of US activists denouncing human rights violations. Their plea to the audience of an obscure publication in the US also demonstrates another example of leftists in Uruguay reaching out to the US for help both politically and financially.

Another instance of activists in Uruguay reaching out more specifically to feminists in the US is the collaboration between El Grupo de Estudios sobre la Condición de la Mujer en Uruguay (GRECMU) and feminists from the Centro de la Tribuna Internacional de la Mujer (CTIM) in New York City. GRECMU, one of the most well-known feminist organizations in Uruguay, emerged in 1979 as a discussion group about Uruguayan women and labor. The group analyzed issues of women's labor not solely from a socialist perspective but from an individual, feminist one. In one statement, GRECMU argued that the struggle for gender equality consisted of an individual, collective, and interior process.[82] GRECMU named their bulletin *La Cacerola* or "the casserole" because of its correspondence with the daily work and lives of women and as a homage to activism under the dictatorship. As people protested the government's repression, the "cacerola" or casserole became a symbol of national liberation. During the dictatorship, "Caceroleos" consisted of citizens' nightly bashing of pots and pans.[83] GRECMU members argued that it was no coincidence that a traditional symbol of female oppression transformed into a sign of resistance during the dictatorship. They claimed that under authoritarian rule the private space of the home became a site where everyone, no matter what gender, could collectively participate in rebellion against repression.[84]

With an office in New York, CTIM published the bulletin *La Tribuna* three times a year and offered the publication free to women from what they called the "Third World."[85] The collaboration of the CTIM and GRECMU occurred primarily through letters. Together the groups created a manual of techniques to facilitate consciousness-raising groups for women in Uruguay. By integrating each other's suggestions, US and

Uruguayan feminists participated in a reciprocal exchange and created feminist activities that incorporated ideas from both groups. Therefore, while Uruguayan feminists used some of the techniques North American feminists employed, they also advocated seeing their society as distinct in order to avoid generalizations about women's experiences. The collaboration of these groups proved to be truly transnational as their combined publication was produced by the International Development Research Center in Ottawa, Canada.[86]

In order to achieve what they deemed "reflection" and to cultivate "knowledge" in women's groups, the transnational collaboration called for exercises such as analyzing the current reality of Uruguayan women and imagining an ideal future. Other exercises included "La Caja de Pandora" or Pandora's Box, where women identified obstacles and problems for Uruguayan women, wrote them down, and placed them in a box. The manual instructed participants to find common themes in the box and discuss their merit and possible solutions.[87] Many of the activities involved using art supplies for creative projects and group work in order to foster discussion and raise consciousness in communities of women. The results of the activities in practice within Uruguayan feminist groups proved diverse. Some women demanded more time for projects and called for more profundity and longer discussions. Overall, however, Uruguayan feminists found the exercises enriching to their repertoire of activist techniques.[88] This exchange demonstrates another important instance of connections between activists in Uruguay and lesser-known feminist groups in the United States.

BEFORE 1973, FEW HUMAN rights organizations focused on Uruguay's declining democracy. However, after the official dissolution of rights guaranteed by the Uruguayan constitution and the illegal imprisonment of thousands of dissidents, international groups focused their attention on the situation of human rights in Uruguay. Because of gross human rights violations in the country, many groups such as the US-based CSUP and the Toronto-based CDHRU specifically challenged the Uruguayan government's treatment of prisoners. These campaigns used letter writing and petitions in order to show their disapproval of the situation in Uruguay and initially garnered the attention of the dictatorship. For example, a letter from CDHRU member Kenneth Golby protesting the treatment of Uruguayan prisoners received a response from President Bordaberry. Bordaberry's widely published response inspired activists in Uruguay such as Zelmar Michelini to reach out to North Americans in order to inform them of what they felt was the real situation of political prisoners in their country. Through these reciprocal connections, North American human rights groups listened to the concerns of Uruguayan activists. They rarely adopted paternalistic language and attempted to include the voices of Uruguayans in their materials for US activists.

Other North American activists focused on leftist solidarity with Uruguayans. Leftist solidarity publications also included the voices of various groups in order to move beyond what they saw as arbitrary national borders formed by imperialist powers. In doing so, these groups consciously created transnational campaigns for Uruguay's freedom. Many of these groups also contained large numbers of Uruguayan exiles who hoped to forge ties with North Americans in order to bring international attention to the situation in their country. Leftist solidarity groups also used creative comparisons in their denunciations and linked the Uruguayan dictatorship with US imperialism and racist South Africa. These relationships supposedly demonstrated the corruption of the Uruguayan dictatorship. However, these groups rarely included the specific voices of women or looked at gendered experiences in prison. If reports from the left included any information about female prisoners, they often relied on traditional ideas of women as wives and mothers and focused primarily on gender-specific deprivations.

Another leftist solidarity group, the anti-imperialist feminist WIRE, established connections with the family of one Tupamara prisoner, Yessie Macchi. When writing to WIRE, Macchi's family used creative materials to inspire members' activism and solidarity. Like the Uruguayan intentional community Comunidad del Sur, Macchi's family believed that groups in the United States had the ability to influence and perhaps lessen the Uruguayan state's policies of repression. As a Tupamara, however, international solidarity groups did not prioritize Macchi's situation as much as they did that of her male counterparts. Macchi and other female prisoners were rarely seen as leaders in the movement. Beyond her gendered experiences with international solidarity movements, Yessie's treatment in the Tupamaros and as a prisoner was markedly different because of her gender. Despite rhetoric claiming otherwise, the role of women in the Tupamaros often proved contradictory. The next chapter explores the rhetoric of equality within the Tupamaros and the quotidian realities for female militants within the group.

4

"A Pistol in Her Hand"
Sexual Liberation and Gender in the Tupamaros and the Greater Uruguayan Left

Never has a woman been more equal to a man
than when she is standing with a pistol in her hand.
—Tupamaro slogan

ON A SUNNY JANUARY morning in 1971, British ambassador Geoffrey Jackson rode to his embassy in Montevideo, Uruguay, to meet with a visiting businessman. Just a few moments before he arrived at the British Embassy, a red van emerged from a side street and rammed into Jackson's vehicle. To Jackson's horror, when his driver, Hugo, got out of the car to survey the damage, a young man ran from the van and struck the driver over the head. Seconds after Hugo was knocked unconscious, urban guerrillas holding machine guns surrounded Jackson. Even a seemingly innocent bystander pulled out a gun that had been concealed in a fruit basket.[1] After shooting into Jackson's car, four young guerrillas brazenly climbed in, blindfolded Jackson and injected him with tranquilizers. After a bumpy car ride and a subsequent forced descent into what seemed like an underground fortress, Jackson's kidnappers finally removed his blindfold. Obviously amused, one of the numerous masked men and women who surrounded Jackson asked him in English, "And who do you think we are?" Jackson, who had heard stories about his controversial kidnappers replied, "We all know that." The captors wanted more. "But say so," they insisted, "say so, use the word." Jackson paused then finally answered, "Of course . . . the Tupamaros."[2]

For over half a year Jackson lived in a small dank underground cell that the Tupamaros deemed the People's Prison. During this time, Jackson met dozens of gun-wielding male and female revolutionaries. In a memoir about his experiences as a prisoner of the Tupamaros, Jackson most consistently and disdainfully mentions the Tupamaras who guarded his cell. For the very traditional Jackson, beyond merely guarding his cell, the Tupamaras' extensive training in guns and other weaponry deviated from proper notions of feminine behavior. The relatively high number of women involved in the Tupamaros as well as their participation in violent acts such as kidnapping and bank robberies give the impression that the group consistently supported gender equality. However, day–to-day realities for female militants in the Tupamaros proved to be much more complex than Jackson's simplistic assessments. Phallocentric ideas concerning "proper" masculine revolutionary behavior within the MLN-T often coexisted alongside notions of gender liberation.

Despite the Tupamaros' support of new roles for women, during the 1960s and 1970s most of the Uruguayan left ignored or disparaged women's liberation as the concern of the so-called bourgeois middle class.[3] When Uruguayan women did participate politically, the majority of the left presented their activism as pacifist and innately tied to their husbands and children. Even an article from a US leftist newspaper describing Uruguayan women protestors claimed that "thousands of women have marched through the street in support of their husbands."[4] In contrast to this characterization, the Tupamaros offered a place for politicized women as individuals and even a program for their participation. The Tupamaros contained a relatively high number of women combatants who took part in armed robberies and other missions that required them to handle and use weapons.[5] By 1972, in large because of a political program that consciously recruited women, the organization reportedly contained more than 25 percent female members.[6]

On the surface, the Tupamaros' supported equality between men and women in both ideology and everyday relations. Descriptions of women's place in the Tupamaros critiqued the very notion of differences in the "revolutionary roles" of men and women. Thus, in their rhetoric, the Tupamaros contended that female militants held so much sway that the group could not properly function without the contributions of women.[7] Admirers of the Tupamaros reinforced the notion that the group supported women's equality. In 1970, Tupamaro sympathizer and author Alain Labrousse argued that Tupamaras acted as armed commanders and sometimes led cells. Most importantly, female militants in the MLN-T never inhabited solely supporting roles.[8] Therefore, the Tupamaros allegedly offered women a place for militancy without prejudice.[9]

The MLN-T contended that one of the most important obstacles to the revolution did not come from the ruling class, but rather from women not utilizing their full revolutionary potential. Part of the practice of the Tupamaros' revolutionary rhetoric included sharing all tasks equally without a gendered division of labor. Therefore, the group claimed never to give assignments based on gender and encouraged women to fulfill combatant roles.[10] Unlike some militant groups in Latin America such as the Nicaraguan Sandinistas, the MLN-T never romanticized motherhood or women's domestic life.[11]

In her work *Mothers of Heroes and Martyrs: Gender Identity Politics in Nicaragua 1979–1999*, Lorraine Bayard de Volo analyzes the role of Nicaraguan motherhood in the Sandinista revolution. Bayard de Volo argues that while invoking concepts of motherhood succeeded in organizing women into the public sphere of revolution, more importantly, mobilizing motherhood offered an acceptable means of female participation.[12] Bayard de Volo asserts that the Sandinista movement remained unthreatening to the existing gender order by encouraging personal, emotional positions for female militants instead of focusing on the political. As one Sandinista woman said, "We are mothers, not politicians. We want peace."[13]

Bayard de Volo claims that "combative motherhood" was the most common ideology employed in order to rally Nicaraguan women's activism. During battle, as well as after the revolution, notions of the revolutionary woman almost always intertwined with the maternal idea of the protector. A woman needed to protect her children *and* the nation's children. One Sandinista revolutionary contended, "When attacked we must defend them [children], like a lioness defends her cubs."[14] Thus, the Sandinistas used the cultural construction of women as natural protectors of life to recruit women into the military and other revolutionary activities.

The concept of the defense of children through combat led to some "extraordinarily juxtaposed images." Several Nicaraguan artists reproduced the most famous image of this kind, a photograph of a young woman with an AK-47 and a baby suckling at her breast. One neighborhood Sandinista Defense Committee featured the picture with the slogan "The woman of the SDC, tender in love, fierce in battle." Therefore, a woman could be fierce in battle as long as she remained tender in love. The promise that the militant woman would above all else maintain her femininity enabled her to carry an AK-47 without threatening the conventional masculine order.[15]

In contradistinction, the Tupamaros believed that as long as society forced women to perform domestic duties, women would never achieve autonomy. Women needed liberation from domesticity, which only occurred through the demolition of the gendered division of labor. Departing from the notion that motherhood inspired Latin American women's activism, the so-called theoretical brain of the Tupamaros, Abraham Guillén, deemed the life of a mother "petty, tedious and sterile."[16]

Beyond ending the gender division of domestic labor, the Tupamaros also stressed the equality of the revolutionary contributions made by women and men. Therefore, notions of gender parity proved significant in the revolutionary rhetoric of the Tupamaros.[17] Some scholars have even suggested that the Tupamaros represented one of the few guerrilla organizations during the early 1970s to develop a detailed ideology concerning revolutionary women.[18] Stressing the importance of women's role and advocating their revolutionary equality departed from common ideas of the time about the proper role of politically active Uruguayan women. For example, an article published in *Marcha* about activist women in Uruguay asserted that until they organized out of economic necessity in 1970, women preferred to live in a "small world" of domestic chores and rearing children. According to the article, scarcity and need, not political consciousness, inspired the women of Uruguay to abandon their perpetual state of "limbo."[19] In contrast, within the MLN-T, young women organized for their own interests and for the liberation of Uruguay, not because of their maternal instincts or necessity.[20]

Marcha's portrayal of women's lack of interest in politics before 1970 was not completely accurate. For example, a 1968 Gallup Uruguay survey of Montevideo found that 45 percent of women and 54 percent of men talked about politics at least occasionally. This percentage contrasted with other countries in Latin America such as Mexico, where 55 percent of men and only 25 percent of women talked about politics at least occasionally. However, of the women who did discuss politics in Montevideo, 80 percent did so with family members, compared with 59 percent of men who did. Women who discussed politics were also more likely than men to restrict their discussions of the issues with friends in the private realm.[21]

Therefore, the Tupamaros undeniably opened a political space for Uruguayan women and deviated from traditional constructions of women as passive, maternal, and nonviolent. This contrasted with the greater part of the Uruguayan left who usually clung to ideas of motherhood and pacifism.[22] However, despite their rejection of traditional constructions of femininity, the Tupamaros also at times denied women the opportunity to define their own roles in the organization. Group members' rigid views on maternity and romantic relationships (both seen as distractions from the cause), perhaps unwittingly marginalized female combatants.

Whether in clandestine revolutionary cells or in prison, issues of sexuality also had an enormous impact on the treatment of female members of the Tupamaros. These conflicting constructions and expectations created a complex gendered world for the Tupamara to navigate with both her comrades and Uruguayan prison officials. While by no means radically so, the Tupamaros proved to be more sexually liberated than mainstream Uruguayan society, which supported expressions of sexuality primarily inside of marriage for women. Sexual mores in the MLN-T supported heterosexual sex before marriage but primarily within monogamous relationships. Despite containing some slightly more liberated views about sexuality, the MLN-T often ignored or marginalized aspects of women's sexuality, specifically concerning reproduction. Many Tupamaro members argued that pregnancy ruined female combatants' chances of achieving true revolutionary status.[23]

Such stringent restrictions against motherhood inevitably inspired a demographic difference in the composition of the membership of the Tupamaros. A study performed by the human rights organization Servicio Paz y Justicia (SERPAJ) demonstrates that at the time of their arrest, 62 percent of militant men were married compared with only 29 percent of women. Furthermore, "housewife" was the occupation of only 2 percent of politically active incarcerated women. Other occupations for female militants included professional (the highest at 35 percent), administrator (24 percent), full-time activist (13 percent) and student (12 percent). When compared to their male counterparts, double the number of militant women listed their occupation as "professional" at the time of their arrest. Furthermore, at the time of their arrest, more women lived alone than men. Thirty-two percent of male revolutionaries lived as part of a couple with children, three times more than females. Because more men lived with their partners, a greater number of women lived in political groupings of activists than men. Furthermore, 73 percent of incarcerated female militants reported to have no children as compared with 51 percent of men.[24] These statistics counter the notion that women join revolutionary groups primarily because of familial obligations or maternal inspiration. Maxine Molyneux writes about this argument concerning women's political interests, "Women it is argued, are animated by emotion, by values which are altruistic: women's love and care for others is not based on rational self-interest but on other, moral, imperatives."[25] The demographics and ideology of the Tupamaros complicate this commonly held notion.

These statistics both diverge and contrast with the experiences of women in other revolutionary movements in Latin America. In her book *Women and Guerrilla Movements: Nicaragua, El Salvador, Chiapas, Cuba*, Karen Kampwirth asks what attracted women to revolution and activism in Nicaragua, El Salvador, and Chiapas. Kampwirth analyzes structural changes, ideological and organizational changes, political factors, and personal factors. Over the course of ten years (1990–2000) Kampwirth interviewed 205 social movement activists. The highest number of interviewees (76) came from Nicaragua.[26]

Kampwirth argues that a combination of many factors mobilized women into the Sandinista army. In contrast to the largely secular Tupamaros, Kampwirth finds that Liberation Theology played a role in the mobilization of Nicaraguan women into revolutionary action. Interviews with Nicaraguan women reinforce this inspiration for activism. Dorotea Wilson, among many other interviewees, pointed to their "religious life as being critical in initiating them into political life."[27] Statistically, women born into families with histories of resistance during the Sandino era were more likely to participate in the Sandinista movement. Family networks offered an opportunity for recruitment and a greater sense of trust. Furthermore, because the Sandinistas recruited heavily from the student population, combatant Sandinista women were usually educated. Like the Tupamaros, many female militants in Nicaragua came from the middle or upper class.[28] Kampwirth also discovered that women in the Sandinistas turned out to be more "urban" and "educated" than the average FSLN man. Kampwirth's findings reflect the demographics of the Tupamaros, who contained more educated females than educated males. As with the Tupamaros, being "urban," "educated," and "young" allowed for larger freedoms for women, which in turn enabled them to participate in the Sandinista revolution. This however, did not guarantee militant women leadership roles.[29]

The perception of leadership roles within the Uruguayan left also had a specific gendered character. At the time of their arrest, 19 percent of leftist men believed they maintained "leadership positions" in the group, while 11 percent of women reported the same. Self reporting from prison indicates that a few leftist women believed that they held significant roles in their groups. Therefore, while the MLN-T ultimately excluded women from leadership roles, a few Tupamaras asserted their power in the revolution. However, these women remained in the minority. Stereotypes within the Uruguayan left about political women were common, despite women's participation.[30]

The specific sexual marginalization of women culminated in popular stereotypes about Tupamaras within the MLN-T and more broadly in the Uruguayan left. These stereotypes focused on sexuality and provided politically active women with two characterizations—that of promiscuous provocateur or asexual butch.[31] Both choices limited the full participation of female combatants and reinforced sexual stereotypes. In addition, once in prison, pregnant Tupamaras experienced serious punishment for what the Uruguayan state perceived as their liberated sexuality and deviance from socially constructed gender norms. It is interesting to note that men also experienced feminization as a form of punishment from guards and state officials. This gendered torment proved to be one of the most humiliating ways to torture a male prisoner as it threatened his masculinity and honor.[32]

Women's Role in the Greater Uruguayan Left

During the 1960s and 1970s, most politically active Uruguayan women focused on denouncing the treatment of political prisoners and on the deteriorating economic conditions of the country. At a 1979 international conference about women in exile, one Uruguayan feminist argued, "We cannot say there exists [in our country] a widespread movement for women's liberation, fighting against specific conditions of oppression under which women live."[33] Uruguayan women's organizations of the time, such as the Movimiento Nacional Femenino por la Justicia y La Paz (the National Women's Movement for Justice and Peace) focused on humanitarian issues and not directly on feminism.[34] The Movimiento Femenino found inspiration to organize after the police murder of Universidad de la República student Liber Arce in 1968. The Movimiento Femenino claimed to integrate all classes of women, housewives and workers as well as those from various political parties and religions. Most members of the movement, however, came from middle-class backgrounds and were middle-aged.[35]

The Movimiento Femenino's first public act was a sit-in they claimed was influenced by the US civil rights movement. The leader of the organization, Lil Gonella de Chouy Terra, commented on how seeing a group of women protesting, the majority of them housewives, initially confounded Uruguayan police. The state did not know how to punish the subversion of the women of the Movimiento Femenino. As housewives and mothers, group members defied any stereotypes that the Uruguayan government associated with radical activism.[36] Completely pacifist in their mechanisms of protest, members of the Movimiento Femenino advocated for matters of traditional feminine importance. Indeed, group leader Chouy Terra described politicized women in a somewhat essentialist manner. She claimed that women needed emotional inspiration to motivate their activism, such as the defense of their husband and children.[37]

A celebration of International Women's Day in 1972 demonstrates the variant paths leftist Uruguayan women pursued concerning political activism. Descriptions in *Marcha* of International Women's Day stressed that the celebration supported peace and the struggle against fascism. The organizer of the event, Chouy Terra, contended that the protest called for peace, economic justice, liberty of expression, and the defense of national sovereignty. Along with the struggle against fascism, those participating in the International Women's Day celebration also hoped to consolidate the activism of female workers. Although the plans for the protest called for an alliance of women workers throughout the country, the celebration ignored mentioning specific gender issues.[38]

When asked by *Marcha* reporters why the event had to consist only of women, organizer Chouy Terra argued that the problems within Uruguay affected all citizens, but women experienced such issues more severely. Marchers protested specifically against scarcity and militarization, problems that led to increased violence against women. While the organizer implied women's supposedly natural attraction to pacifism, she also argued that society constructed Uruguayan women, like their counterparts throughout the world, to passively accept their situations and be confined to the home. Chouy Terra's focus on pacifism versus passivism echoed the argument of some feminists who distinguished between traditionally feminine traits such as passivism, which implies inactive suffering, and instead opted for pacifism, defined as peacemaking or agreement making.[39] To these activists, pacifism did not mean tacit acceptance, but rather resistance that refused to use the tool of the oppressor: violence. While Chouy Terra critiqued the notion that women "naturally" belonged in the home, she and other organizers insisted on the politics of compromise and argued against creating political divisions between men and women.[40] Therefore, the Movimiento Femenino struggled not to appear too radical or demanding. Examples of signs from the march consisted of requests such as "For the Peace of the Country," "National Sovereignty," and "End the Scarcity."[41] Despite the group's desire to avoid any confrontation with the greater left or the police, the very public tactics of the Movimiento Femenino deviated from previous mechanisms of "correct" female political participation in Uruguay.

Proving the complexity of issues of gender in the Uruguayan left, women within autonomous political parties often focused their activism on the importance of women's roles as wives and mothers. For example, in a statement concerning their activism, El Comité Nacional Femenino del Frente Izquierda (National Women's Committee of the Leftist Front) focused on exposing human rights violations in the country, expressing solidarity with the families of political prisoners and the fight against imperialism.[42] Thus, the National Women's Committee focused less of their attention on specific women's issues and more on the nation as a whole. Similarly, the Congresso Nacional Femenino del Partido Demócrata Cristiano or the National Women's Congress of the Christian Democratic Party (PDC) attempted to inspire women's participation without speaking directly to them as autonomous political actors. To encourage women's activism, the group appealed to the future of Uruguay's children. They reminded women of the impoverished elderly population as well as the need for the education of all classes and sufficient medical assistance for every citizen.[43] According to the feminine branch of the PDC, these issues mattered most to women as they naturally supported the common good for every citizen in Uruguayan society, especially the downtrodden.

Like other political parties of the Uruguayan left, the Frente Amplio also presented gender politics in an overall traditional manner. For example, Frente Amplio–sponsored pamphlets encouraging women to vote in the 1971 elections assumed that all women voted based on the interests of their family and children. Even a childless woman had some ties to motherhood and domesticity as she too followed her "inherent" feminine interests. The party reinforced this idea by featuring pictures in their pamphlets of smiling women of all ages holding and caressing babies. According to the Frente, women's suffering should inspire them to join the struggle and support their brothers and/or spouses. Thus, the Frente tied women's political participation with that of their male relatives. Not competent enough to vote for their own interests, the Frente assumed women would vote on behalf of children, brothers, or husbands.[44]

Other pamphlets designed to court women's votes centered on health care, education, and improving the lives of children. The 1971 Frente presidential candidate Líber Seregni promised women voters public clinics specifically designed to help mothers and infants, medical assistance to rural areas, and cheaper medicines and guaranteed education for all Uruguayan children. The Frente also hoped to appeal to women by pledging to build more schools and create sports facilities for children.[45] Once again, the campaign assumed that all women's political aspirations derived from a desire to improve the lives of children. Thus, almost all of the issues on which the Frente focused harkened to a supposed ethic of caring in Uruguayan women.

The marketing campaign of the Frente's platform for women rarely focused on economic issues. When the group spoke to women about economics, instead of analyzing structural problems, they blamed Uruguay's economic difficulties not only on unemployment but the disintegration of the family. The Frente's solution for combating the disintegration of the Uruguayan family ambiguously focused on creating conditions that helped to reunite the family unit. It is unclear what these specific conditions were, but the Frente obviously thought this promise held great appeal to women. In fact, the Frente argued to women voters that their ultimate goal was the happiness of the family.[46]

When trying to recruit male voters, the party took an entirely different track. It did not look to the family, but to larger issues of economic justice and opposition to the increasingly repressive state. In other general Frente declarations, the concerns of the family and children proved nonexistent. To the larger "masculine" left, the Frente combated repression and the illegal imprisonment of dissenters, fought for an end to poverty through social welfare, and appealed to workers and students. In their general politics, the Frente brought attention to changing the economic structures of Uruguay and developing what they deemed an anti-imperialist country.[47] These issues obviously mattered to Uruguayan women as many joined the Tupamaros, a group that never ascribed importance to children and families.

Despite an overall traditional marketing campaign, the Frente's appeal to female voters also contained priorities concerning women's rights. First, the campaign lamented that thousands of students of both sexes lacked education. By doing so, the party acknowledged the importance of education for women. Even more unexpected, however, was the organization's inclusion of a vaguely feminist proposal to inspire women voters. The Frente claimed that under Seregni's government, women would be integrated into the community and liberated from the drudgery of daily domestic work. Unlike their other, more ambiguous campaign promises, the Frente put forth a solution to help ease women's domestic drudgeries. They argued for the creation of public laundries and government-sponsored services to cut down on the large amount of housework for women.[48]

Featuring these promises in the Frente's 1971 campaign demonstrates the pervasiveness of feminist politics within the Uruguayan left. Even though some, such as writer Carina Perelli, have argued against the existence of any feminist consciousness in Uruguay in the 1970s, the inclusion of such campaign promises demonstrates at the very least an awareness of feminist issues.[49] The critique of women's domestic drudgery reflected what the Tupamaros asserted about constructed feminine roles. However, the Frente blended traditional ideas of maternity and a feminine ethic of caring with a promise to help ease women's domestic chores and integrate women into society. Unlike the Tupamaros, the Frente acknowledged political women's roles as wives and mothers. This tactic proved somewhat successful in inspiring female participation as the Frente eventually garnered enough support to inspire the march of a reported hundred thousand Uruguayan women in 1980.[50]

Because of the focus on motherhood in leftist Uruguayan politics, in an essay about women's activism, Carina Perelli argued that Uruguayan women's political activism lacked even the consciousness of "being resistant." In reference to political women's role in Uruguay, Perelli argues, "Women in general did not resist because they wanted to change the society they knew, with all its gender and class inequalities; on the contrary, they wanted to restore the good old Uruguay which they had been comfortable."[51] While Perelli posits that politically active women in Uruguay had little consciousness, in actuality, large groups of women fervently denounced injustice in ways much more public than they had in the past. Beginning in the 1960s, leftist women's participation proved multifaceted as they forged different political paths. As Maxine Molyneux writes in *Women's Movements in International Perspective: Latin America and Beyond*, "Women have been an active, if not always acknowledged, force in most of the political upheavals associated with modernity, as members of trade unions, political parties, reform and revolutionary organizations and nationalist movements.[52]" These forms of activism may have important meaning for women as individuals but are linked to more universalist messages and/or to national independence. Molyneux refers to this type of organizing as "directed mobilizations." Within the Uruguayan left and the Tupamaros, women were mobilized to achieve a certain goal, such as supporting a political party or overthrowing an authoritarian regime. In these types of mobilizations, women's "interests" are not usually at the forefront, just as gender identity does not constitute women's only identity.[53]

Many Uruguayan women's public activities also influenced later movements that deemed themselves feminist. Therefore, only rigid definitions of liberation and feminism exclude Uruguayan women as so-called conscious political actors. Historian Karen Offen has argued for two distinct but sometimes overlapping trends in feminist thought and practice—"relational" and "individualistic" feminism. While individualistic feminism (more prominent in the United States) focuses less on the community and emphasizes the similarities between men and women, relational or maternal feminism (popular in Latin America) highlights women's differences from men, particularly their role as mothers.[54]

Besides activist women who espoused pacifism and women within leftist parties, female militants in the MLN-T exhibited radical political ideologies and actions in comparison to the traditional gender constructions of Uruguayan society. Therefore, Perelli's narrow assumptions about women's supposedly limited political role in the left during the 1960s and 1970s also ignore the Tupamaras, who consistently challenged common constructions of femininity in Uruguayan society. Even Perelli admitted that she and other Uruguayan girls conceptualized the Tupamaras as a new role model for the younger generation. Perelli recalls the excitement of growing up in Uruguay at the height of Tupamaro popularity, "[I remember] the mute admiration many of us felt for those mythical older sisters who braved bullets to bring about a new order. They incarnated a new way of being a woman, not bound by the limits of a household with a husband, children, family obligations, or by the routine of schooling, a job and bills. They seemed so free to us, we who were searching.[55]

Thus, of all women, the Tupamaras deviated most from the norms of the left and greater Uruguayan society, which usually focused on women's roles as wives and mothers. Women joined the Tupamaros not because of familial obligations, but for the same reasons as men; to fight against the disintegration of freedom in Uruguay. The Tupamara became such a mythical symbol that the aforementioned Uruguayan folk singer Daniel Viglietti wrote a song about her entitled "Muchacha."[56] In "Muchacha" or "Girl," Viglietti sang of a young woman guerrilla fighter. When the Uruguayan government outlawed the word "Tupamaro," numerous words replaced it, including "muchacha."[57] The "muchacha" represented the female counterpart to Che's "New Man." In his song, Viglietti referred to the revolutionary Tupamara as a "complete woman," "compañera," and "guerrilla fighter." Besides Viglietti's reference to the guerrilla fighter's hair, he ignores the Tupamara's appearance and chooses to focus on her revolutionary attributes. He applauds her bravery and "completeness" as a woman. Therefore, in Viglietti's song, a real woman is a revolutionary fighter, not solely a maternal being. While Viglietti did not sing much about women specifically, when he sang about the Tupamaras, he used the same reverent characterization that he did for male guerrilla fighters.[58]

Therefore, while by no means completely equal in their treatment of women, the Tupamaros offered a different kind of political option for women that did not exist in most of the greater Uruguayan left. Even those from countries with supposedly more liberal gender constructions conceptualized the Tupamaros' treatment of women as unique.[59] The radical and at times contradictory political role for militant women proved to be so intriguing that prisoners of the Tupamaros, such as captive Geoffrey Jackson, wrote extensively about female MLN-T members with interest and sometimes disdain.

Geoffrey Jackson and the Tupamaras

While many in the left viewed the Tupamaros as an exemplary revolutionary organization that supported egalitarian gender roles, other sources emerged during the 1970s that demonstrated a much more complicated picture of the group. In his 1973 autobiographical account, *Surviving the Long Night*, former British ambassador and onetime Tupamaro prisoner Geoffrey Jackson offers details about the MLN-T's attitude toward women's liberation and the group's quotidian gender constructions. Unwittingly, through his chauvinistic descriptions and fascination with various Tupamaras, Jackson offers a gendered account of the Tupamaros that provides valuable insight into the group's gender structures. Though not meant to be an account about gender, Jackson repeatedly expressed an almost obsessive interest in the role of female combatants in the Tupamaros.[60]

While held in the Tupamaros' People's Prison for nearly 250 days, Jackson observed the complex relations between male and female Tupamaros. Jackson's descriptions of his experiences obviously contain biases, political and other types, yet they offer an insight into the nature of gender relations in the Tupamaros beyond the rhetoric they espoused. Above all, Jackson's account reveals the contradictions that occurred within the group concerning gender, something corroborated later by interviews with Tupamaras.[61] Jackson's account demonstrates that the group strove for gender equality but also marginalized women in their day-to-day interactions and ultimately supported a militaristic, masculine ideology concerning violence and interpersonal relationships.

An interesting example of gender relations within the Tupamaros comes from Jackson's description of the eventual reassignment of a female guard. While imprisoned for nearly a year, Jackson was guarded by both male and female Tupamaros twenty-four hours a day. Jackson had a variety of interactions with female guards during this imprisonment. Like their male counterparts, some were tough (to Jackson's horror) and some showed him kindness (which he in turn perceived in a gendered manner). Unlike their female counterparts, Tupamaro men who displayed kindness did not receive an indictment of innate femininity from Jackson. According to Jackson, some female guards were self-conscious about their status as militants and compensated by being overly aggressive toward Jackson and sometimes other Tupamaros. However, Jackson's own notions about proper feminine behavior obviously influenced the ambassador to judge the women harshly. Most of the Tupamara guards behaved similarly to their male counterparts—some showed Jackson kindness or indifference, and a few treated him cruelly.[62]

Most of Jackson's female guards displayed what he described as modesty, but to his horror one particular guard frequently spoke obscenities with her male cohorts. According to Jackson, the guard was also completely unselfconscious as she urinated in front of Jackson and her male comrades. While the female guard merely used the same facilities as the male Tupamaros, Jackson viewed her actions as overtly sexual and "lost his temper" over this allegedly unfeminine guard. The prisoner lodged a formal complaint with his captors, and the group subsequently replaced the Tupamara with a man. While the Tupamara merely used the same facilities as her male comrades and cursed with as much intensity as they did, the Tupamaros acquiesced to Jackson's complaint about her conduct.[63] Perhaps the Tupamaros hoped to avoid friction with the prisoner, or the reassignment of the female guard could indicate that the group expected Tupamaras not to mimic all stereotypically masculine traits such as bawdiness, rowdy behavior, and cursing.

Besides his issues with the rowdy female guard, Jackson observed the gender division of labor in the People's Prison. While popular rhetoric ignored the idea of a gender division of labor within the revolutionary group, the quotidian realities of Tupamaro guards often reified traditional gender roles. Women sewed clothes and other items when needed and usually prepared Jackson's meals.[64] Jackson also contended that the one outstanding moment where women's liberation was acknowledged by MLN-T members occurred after the prisoner jokingly drew a picture of a beauty contest for Miss Comrade.[65] In Jackson's picture, female militants donned bikinis and the aforementioned pointed jailer hoods. In response, one Tupamara dismissed beauty competitions as meat markets and humiliating for both women and the Tupamaros.[66] One male captor, purportedly "addicted" to women's liberation, contended that women and men only achieved true equality when they each held a .45 pistol. According to Jackson, the principal time that the Tupamaros embodied their rhetoric of equality occurred when women and men assembled and used weapons together. Jackson noted with shock that young women adeptly assembled and disassembled weapons with the same precision as their male counterparts.[67] Therefore, according to Jackson and some Tupamaro members, only when Tupamaras "took up the gun" could they achieve equality. Newspaper writer Maruja Echegoyen, who interviewed Geoffrey Jackson while he was in the People's Prison, conveyed similar observations about the Tupamaros. Echegoyen noted with surprise about the Tupamaras guarding Jackson, "Even the women are spare in their conversation and completely at ease." Women still, however, prepared all the food when Echegoyen visited the People's Prison.[68]

Jackson's account reveals that in most ways the MLN-T successfully integrated women into the organization. Tupamaro cell leaders gave several different female militants the responsibility of guarding Jackson and taught both women and men how to handle weapons. Therefore, from Jackson's account it seems that less overt instances of gender inequality proved more common in the Tupamaros, such as the sexual division of labor and perhaps the reassignment of the "unfeminine" guard. Jackson's examples offer insight into the contradictory treatment of women within the group. Tellingly, many of his observations reflect what some Tupamaras later criticized about their experiences in the MLN-T.

The Role of Women in the Tupamaros

Although chauvinistic in his descriptions about the role of women in the Tupamaros, Jackson's contention about the less-than-equal treatment of female militants has been corroborated by testimonies from some Tupamaras. While the organization opened new spaces for women, it often disallowed women to speak for themselves about their place in the revolution.[69] The ignorance of women's marginalization partially derived from the fact that Tupamaro members thought of Uruguay as a nation more intellectually and socially aligned with Europe than with other countries in Latin America. Citing the history of Uruguayan democracy, MLN-T members argued that Uruguayan women already occupied an advanced place in society, more so than other women in South America. Because of these nationalistic ideas, the Tupamaros presented Uruguay as the most politically, culturally, and ideologically advanced country in Latin America. Furthermore, a paper written by Latin American leftists about the history of Uruguay asserted that before the dictatorship, the country had been an example of democratic institutions and liberal ideas, leading all of Latin America in cultural and social matters.[70] Once again, notions about Uruguay's exceptional nature influenced political discourse, this time concerning the allegedly superior role of women in the country. When the Tupamaros mentioned women's subjugation, only rarely did they acknowledge that the oppression of women came from more than the reproduction of class domination within the home.[71] Thus, in part because of their belief in Uruguayan exceptionalism, the Tupamaros failed to offer a comprehensive critique of women's marginalization in cultural and social spheres.

According to former Tupamaras, the group devalued the realm of the feminine as they encouraged women to take on socially constructed masculine traits of aggression and emotional control in order to demonstrate true political validity. A well-known saying about gender within the MLN-T was "Never has a woman been more equal to a man than when she is standing with a pistol in her hand."[72] Thus, women's equality derived from an external element, in this case a pistol, and not from deserving acceptance or fighting for change. While some measure of equality prevailed in the alleged sameness of revolutionary contributions, the group also limited women by continuing to place restrictions on their self-expression. The MLN-T avoided critiquing socially constructed traits of masculinity as these practices supported their pro-violence ideology and behavior. Therefore, criticisms of gender construction focused on obliterating constructions only of femininity and never masculinity. However, the revolutionary and masculine "New Man" also paradoxically appropriated traditionally feminine traits such as sacrifice, suffering, and austere discipline.[73]

In reference to the role of female militants, the Tupamaros argued that women made excellent service team members. These jobs ranged from the photographer, who took photos for fake passports and identity cards, to medical professionals responsible for the health of combatants. Service actions also included finding meeting and hiding places, buying food, and obtaining arms and other needed supplies.[74] Besides populating service teams, most female members also received military instruction. The Tupamaros valued their female members as combatants in large part because they realized that women had the ability to obtain easier entrance into certain places. Therefore, according to the Tupamaros, women's accessibility best demonstrated their propensity to be good soldiers. Because mainstream Uruguayan society stereotyped women as innocuous and nonviolent, Tupamaras infiltrated neighborhoods and secure buildings with ease. The "innocent" appearance of Tupamaras also allowed for the transmission of messages and objects such as weapons in purses and bags. Using disguises to make their appearance like that of everyday women, female militants easily tricked officials.

Thus, in the few instances that the MLN-T specifically described the importance of the Tupamaras, they usually focused on how Uruguayan stereotypes allowed female combatants more access to target areas than their male counterparts. While women did participate in violent actions, focusing on access discounted the other contributions of the Tupamaras and greatly reduced the possibility for leadership roles in the organization. According to the Tupamaros, women brought meticulous care to already existing plans but rarely crafted strategy in the group. The MLN-T also purported to admire women's patience and silence in the armed struggle.[75] Though the group intended to compliment female militants, they inadvertently reinforced stereotypes of women as neat, patient, and compromising. While female militants were technically equal to men in battle, the MLN-T failed to admire women's combat or leadership skills, instead focusing on the more innocuous contributions of Tupamaras.

Some feminist critics have argued that the few women who received leadership roles in the MLN-T obtained them in large part because of their romantic linkages to male Tupamaros.[76] If a Tupamara had a boyfriend or husband within the operation, their relationship often overshadowed any individual identity of the Tupamara. For example, group members commonly referred to one Tupamara as "the companion of Manchin" (her boyfriend). When the Tupamara got pregnant, she did not want to stop fighting as she firmly believed in the cause of the MLN-T. However, when her pregnancy became visible, her boyfriend told the cell leader, "You send her to me in services" (another unit). Acquiescing to the demands of Manchin, group leaders subsequently removed the Tupamara from the military sector without ever consulting her. The female combatant went through her pregnancy alone as her boyfriend performed many dangerous actions for the organization.

According to another Tupamara, pregnant militants ultimately underwent displacement from their cells, and the group banned pregnant women from the military sector after their fourth month of pregnancy. The group also forbade certain tasks dealing with combat even months after a woman had given birth. Within the Tupamaros, maternity represented a serious career obstacle for the female militant. Some Tupamaras reported feeling deep disappointment at being forced to stop their revolutionary activities once they had children. The notion of maternity as an impediment, however, changed when the pregnant woman involved turned out to be a Tupamaro's wife or girlfriend. The MLN-T encouraged so-called average women to reproduce as every child symbolized another potential revolutionary. The group never questioned if fatherhood presented an obstacle to Tupamaro men and their ability to serve their cells.[77] Therefore, while the Tupamara broke down the traditional model of Uruguayan womanhood, some former members have argued that the group did not allow women to create any new set of values to replace it.

However, for others in the left, the MLN-T represented a group committed to egalitarian relations between male and female combatants.[78] Furthermore, some Tupamaras argued that in comparison with other Uruguayan leftist movements, the MLN-T proved to be more committed to egalitarian relations between men and women. The Tupamaras who claimed to experience no sexism within the group also often maligned feminism. These Tupamaras characterized feminism as a revolt against domestic tasks such as child rearing, cooking, and housework.[79] As independent, middle-class professionals who considered themselves already "liberated," these Tupamaras failed to see how feminism affected their lives. They also viewed the feminist movement as containing middle-class "snobs," who were unable to present a radical enough solution to the problem of women's societal, political, and economic marginalization.[80] Weather Underground leader Bernadine Dohrn expressed a similar sentiment about the role of feminism in militant leftist movements: "Most of the women's groups are bourgeois, unconscious or unconcerned with class struggle and the exploitation of working women. . . . Instead of integrating . . . these women are flailing in their own middle-class images . . . their direction leads to a middle class single issue movement—and this at a time when the black liberation movement is polarizing the country, when national wars of liberation are waging the most advanced assaults on US imperialism, when the growth of the movement is at a critical stage!"[81]

While Tupamaras rejected the label of feminism, most subverted gender norms as they refused to inhabit traditional feminine roles as defined by their society.[82] Instead of adhering to traditional gender roles, Tupamaras strove to cultivate their studies and participate in political activism. Many Tupamaras reported that they hoped joining an armed struggle would save them from a life of cooking, cleaning, and raising children. Thus, many Tupamaras rejected adhering to societal norms in their personal lives, but on a political level they did not prioritize the gendered transformation of society as a whole.[83]

Stereotypes and Sexuality

Despite the Tupamaras' challenge to the notion of the passive and nonviolent Uruguayan woman, the Tupamaros also harbored stereotypes about female militants. While the group usually presented these stereotypes in a humorous manner, they still limited women's full participation and propensity to be taken seriously as militants. Stereotypes within the group concerning the Tupamara functioned in a dichotomy—the sexless, masculine female soldier and the promiscuous, beautiful combatant. In the "drill sergeant" stereotype, an ugly and authoritarian woman was usually represented as a person of African descent. This *Negra* (black woman) often owned a motorcycle and was asexual. Ironically, the stereotype of the Negra proved to be one of the only ways that the Tupamaros actually acknowledged the existence of racial diversity in their country. However, this negative representation differed greatly from the MLN-T's portrayal of the masculine Black Power movement in the US. While the group supported black male revolutionaries (particularly in the US) and applauded their militant use of violence, they also reinforced stereotypes of black female militants (within Uruguay). Within the Tupamaros, the female militant of African descent was not as romanticized as her male counterparts. This gendered racial stereotype demonstrates another layer of the Tupamaros' complicated relationship with race.

The other side of the gendered stereotype of female militants derived from the James Bond image of political women as sexualized provocateurs. Within the popular myth of the group, this sly and gorgeous militant radiated such beauty that she distracted the police so guerrillas could commit their covert actions. This attractive woman, whose mythology ostensibly came from James Bond films, was also sexually promiscuous and usually blonde.[84] While denouncing some aspects of US culture and politics, some male Tupamaros enjoyed the imperial West's James Bond films so much that they appropriated the films' representation of women. This particular cultural reference had an influence on the group's mythology concerning the role of female guerrillas.[85] Members of the Tupamaros even admitted that they liked and admired James Bond films during an interrogation session with captive Dan Mitrione.[86] In response to the influence of James Bond in the group, some Tupamaras argued that the stereotypes of the femme fatale supported bourgeois attributes of women but cleverly placed them in the context of serving the revolution.[87] Within this representation, women remained sexual objects and reinforced the same stereotypes of the greater Uruguayan society, but at the service of an important cause.

Alongside the Tupamaros, the greater Uruguayan left also reinforced dichotomous stereotypes about sexually ambiguous or promiscuous politically active women. An article in *Marcha* about the role of women in politics in Montevideo described female political activist Elsa Fernández and initially focuses on her masculine appearance. The writer deemed Fernández as not pretty but a "severe" beauty with a well-defined face, firm chin, and short hair with sideburns. *Marcha* reported that Fernández also wore men's clothing—a black jacket, black pants, and red sweater.[88] Therefore, the *Marcha* article focused on the female activist's appearance and not her politics. The preoccupation with the appearance and sexuality of politically active women also occurred with the few women who achieved positions of power in the country such as Senator Alba Roballo. Many on the right and left conceptualized Roballo as simultaneously a "whore" and a masculine "lesbian." In the 1960s, Roballo had served as a minister of culture in the Colorado Party before moving to the Frente Amplio in 1971. Nicknamed "La Negra," Roballo was the first female minister in Uruguay but soon had her title removed by President Pacheco Areco in 1968. At various times, Roballo represented both sides of the aforementioned stereotypes—that of a lascivious sexual predator and then conversely, an asexual militant.[89]

During the 1960s and 1970s, Roballo was one of the few women with some political power in Uruguay and spoke openly about the treatment of women in both the left and the right. She argued that Uruguayan men rarely recognized the value of their female counterparts and politically excluded them (Roballo experienced this firsthand). Even in the General Assembly, colleagues addressed Roballo "Señora" and not "Senator," her rightful title and appropriate in that context. While Roballo acknowledged that women's liberation and especially the Black Power movement had influenced the Uruguayan student left, she argued that the Uruguayan system of government excluded women and completely ignored people of color. Despite all of her outspokenness, Roballo continued to believe that women's activism would only begin once their husbands, children, and friends disappeared or faced incarceration. Unwittingly, Roballo also reinforced the stereotype of women committing to politics only in order to protect their families, particularly their children.[90] Therefore, the Tupamaros and the greater Uruguayan left often limited women's political participation by relying on simplistic and binary stereotypes about female activists.

These stereotypes had parallels within US revolutionary movements.[91] Both the radical and the mainstream US media seemed to support two primary stereotypes about female militants, to varying degrees.

The first was the nonthreatening "Housekeeper," who joined the group because of relationships, versus the power-wielding "Amazon." Both types of women were considered dangerous but differed in their motivation and the amount of power they possessed within their organizations. The "Housekeeper" stereotype maintained her femininity and was easily manipulated, while the "Amazon" held power over the men in her group. The idea of the hypermasculine "Amazon woman" has often been used to describe militant leftist women in the United States. These "Amazons" purportedly contained "a cold rage about them that even the most alienated of men seem quite incapable of emulating."[92] Furthermore, so-called terrorist experts claim that the Amazon woman longed to keep her position of power so desperately that she would do anything to keep command—including "killing children" to maintain status and gain the approval and respect of the men. Analysis of most radical groups, such as the Weather Underground, however, demonstrates that women seldom occupied leadership positions, much less controlled the entire group.

According to both the mainstream press and some in the US left, other female militants merely played relational roles in their groups. Though most US male and female radicals came to revolutionary politics through a romantic, friend, or familial affiliation, women have been consistently portrayed as the ones manipulated into the group. Similar to the descriptions within the Tupamaros of women having access to certain places because of their gender, the "Housekeeper" may innocently push her "baby" in a pram, but in reality she harbors a bomb. The Housekeeper secures her "feminine," peripheral role by stressing her status as wife, girlfriend, and perhaps mother.

Similar to the stereotypes about women in the Tupamaros, the characterization of militant women in the US—as Amazon or Housekeeper—resulted in a very simplistic, binary view of activists. Even leftists and feminists such as Robin Morgan and Jane Alpert reiterated the idea that female militants acted merely as pawns of controlling men. Robin Morgan labeled women in the Weather Underground as "Manson Killers" because she believed they committed violent crimes only to gain male approval.[93]

Similar to US stereotypes, some female members felt that the MLN-T offered them two options: to mimic the masculine image of the guerrilla for the politico-military fight or to play the role of sexualized provocateur used to distract the police. Most often, however, denouncing the feminine and taking on masculine traits proved to be the political choice offered to female militants. One Tupamara recalled of her role in the group, "You were required to adhere to masculine values, to de-feminize yourself in all areas, to repress traditional values but without anything more: without creating, without searching within yourself, your body or your emotions for new values."[94] Within such narrowly defined notions of proper female militant behavior, the Tupamara had difficulties constructing her own role within the group. Literary scholar Saldaña-Portillo has contended that this type of "revolutionary universalism" absorbs all differences and in turn makes the promise of true equality impossible.[95]

This idea also permeated proviolence groups in the US such as the Weather Underground. According to the Weather Underground document "Honky Tonk Women," if one wanted to view truly revolutionary, emancipated women, US radicals should look to the Third World. "Honky Tonk Women" contended that Vietnamese women earned their equality not by creating their own movement, but by "picking up the gun" to destroy the US. Though the document did halfheartedly acknowledge that men must change, it stressed that women should not expect them to do so until a communist revolution occurred. According to the Weather Underground, any other issues besides communist revolution were merely selfish, white, middle-class concerns.[96]

In the early 1970s, the socialist feminist group Bread and Roses wrote an indictment of the promasculine rhetoric and action of the Weather Underground. Even though they too had revolutionary tactics and beliefs, Bread and Roses disapproved of the Weather Underground's idea of a "woman of steel" or a "street fighting woman." The group contended that ideas in the Weather Underground's document "Honky Tonk Women" offered an insufficient plan for women's liberation. According to the Weather Underground, learning to be a "street fighting woman" would earn women the respect of men and thus subsequently end male chauvinism. Bread and Roses critiqued the notion that women should embrace machismo as the one true method of social change. The idea of the "street fighting woman" reeked of "me-too" politics. It promised women if they acted "masculine" enough, perhaps they too could be included. Women needed to jump on the aggressive, authoritarian bandwagon if they wanted to be considered anywhere near equal to men. Bread and Roses found the idea of women having to earn their equality through socially constructed macho behavior offensive and sexist.[97]

However, Tupamaras' experiences as female militants contained instances of both subjugation and liberation. The reality of militant women was complex and never solely oppressive or emancipating. The complexity of gender constructions and the change in traditional roles for women also affected the realm of sexuality and pleasure. The Tupamaros and the greater Uruguayan left hoped to support freer lifestyles concerning relations between men and women.[98] Although the Tupamaros support of sex before marriage may have been somewhat more open-minded when compared with the greater Uruguayan society, their beliefs still remained nowhere near radical. Even political prisoner Geoffrey Jackson deemed the Tupamaros' attitude toward sexuality "prudish."[99] According to Jackson, his captors had informed him that sexual promiscuity, along with excessive drug and alcohol use, only harmed the revolution.[100] Thus, members of the MLN-T and the Uruguayan left primarily supported only heterosexual expressions of affection and usually in monogamous pairings. Many militants' characterization of marriage as a confining institution reflected the ideas of turn of the century Uruguayan anarchists as much as 1960s countercultural ideas of "free love." Uruguayan anarchists and the Tupamaros both argued for the importance of sexual expression outside of marriage, but primarily in the confines of heterosexual, serial monogamy. Therefore, for both the Tupamaros and turn-of-the-century Uruguayan anarchists, in order to avoid a traditional and stifling marriage, women and men coupled because of shared attraction and love.[101]

During the 1960s and early 1970s, some in the Uruguayan left openly professed a disdain for matrimony, which deviated from mainstream ideas about proper sexual relationships. These activists hoped that in the future, society would not be based on the institution of the family, but on free relations between men and women. They participated in sexual relationships outside of marriage based on what they deemed "friendship" "affection" and "mutual understanding." Thus, some younger members of the Uruguayan left believed in sex before marriage but advocated monogamous relationships instead of sexual promiscuity. In one interview with *Marcha*, male leftists also overall expressed positive views of women as partners in love and in the struggle against the dictatorship. One leftist student even argued that women struggled against the same system as men and that any person with a developed consciousness, male or female should practice political militancy. While the interview ignored women's individual voices, young leftist men also argued that women contributed greatly to the revolutionary struggle within Uruguay.[102] The Tupamaros mirrored the ideas of the young Uruguayan left as the group supported sexual expression between monogamous heterosexual couples. These standards, however, applied more to Tupamaros than Tupamaras, whose romantic attachments seemed to be judged harsher than that of their male counterparts. The Tupamaros' views on female sexuality in some ways paralleled gender and sexuality taboos within the larger Uruguayan society. One Tupamara reported that the group rarely discussed contraception and only at a superficial level. Male Tupamaros expected women to take responsibility for preventing pregnancies, and women who did not assume responsibility for birth control were judged irresponsible by the group.[103]

In contrast to the Tupamaros, a limited number of leftist groups expressed more countercultural ideas about sexuality. The feminist faction of the Partido Socialista de los Trabajadores (PST) represented a group that supported a more open discourse about sexuality in Uruguay.[104] The PST moved away from other socialist groups of the time by attempting to integrate specific feminist issues into leftist politics. Uruguayan feminists of the PST criticized the left for accepting the "double exploitation" of women, but ultimately postponing their liberation until after profound changes in social structures (as the Tupamaros advocated).[105] The group fervently blamed unions and political organizations for continuing to place women's liberation at the bottom of their political lists. For the PST, telling women to "wait for change" merely reinforced traditional feminine stereotypes of women as self-sacrificing and always patient.[106]

While most of Uruguayan society during the 1970s and early 1980s marginalized homosexuals, the PST's feminist platform called for an end to discrimination against gays and lesbians in employment, in everyday life, and in receiving custody of children.[107] In contrast to the PST feminist platform, most Latin American groups with a Marxist base such as the Tupamaros did not openly support the rights of homosexuals or place it as priority in their activism. The PST's stance on homosexual rights demonstrated revolutionary ideas and concepts rarely discussed within the Uruguayan left during the 1970s. Besides including homosexual rights in their platform, the PST also expressed very emphatic support for reproductive rights. The group called for free abortions, an end to forced sterilization, better information about methods of birth control, comprehensive sexual education, and an end to the societal sexual double standard for men and women.[108] The demands of the feminist branch of the PST proved radical in comparison to the activism of the majority of Uruguayan socialists.

Other groups of the early 1980s, such as the aforementioned GRECMU and other feminist groups also hoped to redefine sexuality for Uruguayan women as more than a reproductive function. They openly discussed the sexual double standard, sexual violence, and pleasure. According to GRECMU members, the Uruguayan media commonly portrayed Uruguayan women as maternal figures or conversely as sexual objects for the consumption of men. These feminist groups attempted to educate women about their bodies and even featured diagrams and definitions concerning female sexuality. Some of these included explanations about the clitoris, estrogen, and sexual dysfunction.[109] They criticized Uruguayan society for teaching women that their sexual organs were "dirty," which in turn inhibited their quest for sexual pleasure. By featuring criticisms of societal constructions of sexuality, feminists argued for sexual freedom in a way very different than the Tupamaros and the rest of the Uruguayan left. According to GRECMU, women's free use of her body derived from her own definitions of pleasure, not because of others' denunciations of the bourgeois sexual practices of the middle class. Liberal feminists' support for women's sexual pleasure moved beyond allowing for serial monogamy or heterosexual relationships based on mutual attraction. Instead, these groups argued that female sexual power and pleasure should be defined individually, by women.[110]

Despite the less than radical sexual practices of the group, Tupamaras' deviations from conventional modes of feminine participation provoked an extreme reaction from those in positions of authority in Uruguay.[111] Once she was imprisoned, a Tupamara's undeniable deviance from proper Uruguayan constructions of femininity inspired her captors' brutality to contain a specifically gendered character.

Femininity and Masculinity in Prison

Of the two thousand imprisoned Tupamaros, 450, or nearly 25 percent were women.[112] The treatment of these women contained such a gendered character that government reports from within Uruguay as early as 1970 found that "especially harmful torture methods were applied to women."[113] Guards seemed to especially fear the Tupamaras and claimed that they could be more dangerous than male militants because of their supposed lack of femininity and violent tendencies. Guards and state officials argued that the Tupamara deserved her punishment as she was not a "real" woman. According to one interrogator, because the Tupamara had attempted to enter the masculine realm of politics, she deserved to be treated as a "man" by her captors.[114] However, ultimately, government officials treated female and male Tupamaros very differently. The torture of women contained a specifically gendered character as guards punished female militants for their gender subversion, especially if the militant was pregnant. Women's treatment in prison proved to be so different from men's that a member of Uruguay's military personnel wrote a letter to Amnesty International in 1976 denouncing the actions of his government. The official argued that, "Women are a subject apart: officers, sub-officers and the troops gloated when young female prisoners arrived. Some even would come on their days off to participate in the interrogations. I have personally been present for the worse aberrations committed with women in front of other prisoners by several interrogators. Many of the women detained were there to learn the whereabouts of husbands or fathers or sons, there was no accusation against them."[115]

Therefore, officials subjected women to especially vicious torture, often of a sexual nature. One survey from SERPAJ found that seven percent of both male and female prisoners reported being raped. Within these assaults, torturers often inserted mutilating devices into the vagina or anus.[116] However, even SERPAJ asserted that rape statistics for prisoners were probably higher because of the difficulties of talking about sexual assault. Furthermore, the survey excluded forms of sexual abuse usually perpetrated against women such as fondling or non-penetrative harassment. Guards' disgust for the feminine also translated into women prisoners suffering extra humiliation during menstruation. Several political prisoners reported that menstruating women suffered particular outbursts of rage from male guards. One female prisoner attributed this anger to macho ideologies. She recalled, "It looked as if they got especially enraged because they could not accept the fact that a woman was doing things improper for her sex."[117]

For imprisoned pregnant Tupamaras, torture took on a gendered characteristic. In order to address the problem of incarcerated pregnant combatants, the MLN-T developed two positions. One was that the imprisoned Tupamara must disclose the pregnancy to the government in order to lessen the severity of torture. This proved to be an essentially futile suggestion since pregnant Tupamaras often received even harsher treatments than men. On the other side of the debate, MLN-T members contended that women should never benefit from special treatment in comparison with their comrades. Either way, the debate about pregnant Tupamaras rendered women invisible as it offered them little freedom in deciding what to disclose to their torturers.[118]

Besides degradation within the group about a woman's pregnancy, government officials also generally chastised pregnant Tupamaras for expecting a child while belonging to a militant group. For these officials, the most important aspects of Uruguayan women's lives should be family, obtaining economic security, and reproduction. To show their disgust at Tupamaras' gender subversion, interrogators constantly asked one pregnant militant how she could rank her child and family second to a "man's war." Government officials also assumed that unmarried, pregnant Tupamaras must be sexually promiscuous. Interrogators told one Tupamara who was in her third month of pregnancy that it was the ideal month to "get fucked" by her captors. Uruguayan officials also frequently touched the Tupamara's stomach, claiming they planned to kill the child by kicking the militant. After the frequent abuse the Tupamara lost her child.[119]

Testimonies of female political prisoners during the Southern Cone dictatorships of the 1960s through 1980s further demonstrate the humiliating gendered nature of torture and imprisonment. In her essay, "Surviving beyond Fear: Women and Torture in Latin America," Ximena Bunster-Burotto argues that military regimes, such as Uruguay's, specifically exhibited gender differences in torture in order to secure the "privileged status of masculinity."[120] More than any other patriarchal institution, the authoritarian state strives to perpetuate the values of masculinity, the military, and power.[121] Undoubtedly, Uruguayan torturers employed attacks specifically designed to degrade women, most commonly through violent sexual attacks.[122] According to prison officials, Tupamaras had dared to introduce themselves to the political world of men and in turn deserved punishment. Thus, just as the Tupamaros broke from traditional models of the left, the role of women in the group also deviated from the societal mold of the passive Uruguayan woman.

Uruguayan interrogators employed sexual violence against female political prisoners as a means of control and to exert masculine authority. Once in prison, some women reported having cigarettes extinguished on their breasts by interrogators. One prisoner, Sara Youtchak, had her breasts completely covered in cigarette burns.[123] Reports also illustrate the ubiquity of rape in interrogation sessions. Soldiers subjected young women in particular to habitual rape. In one case, a pregnant prisoner was raped by twenty-five different men, causing her to miscarry. Interrogators also brought in the fathers of young women prisoners to witness the torture and sometimes rape of their daughters.[124] One Uruguayan prisoner wrote to his wife, "All of the girls who were in the prison were raped by the Uruguayan military right in front of their relatives."[125] This degradation and humiliation fit into a larger framework of patriarchal relations in Uruguay. Through these sexual assaults, female prisoners lost their dignity and socially constructed notions of purity. In turn, fathers could do nothing to protect their daughter's honor. The government also sometimes had uncooperative prisoners' female relatives brought into prison. Interrogators sexually assaulted wives and daughters in front of their lovers, husbands, or fathers in order to manipulate information out of the prisoner.[126]

Along with their gendered torture, imprisoned Tupamaras also often felt marginalized by the MLN-T, especially when compared with their incarcerated male counterparts. For example, activities within the men's prison seemed to be inspired by crudeness and sexism. One group member reported that in Punta Carretas prison, during recess, Tupamaro political prisoners often played soccer games that contained a specifically chauvinistic quality. During their games, the male prisoners named one team the "Proletarian Penis" which played against a team called the "Bourgeoisie Vagina." While the political prisoners associated the despised bourgeoisie with the female anatomy, Tupamaro men referred to their sexual organs as proletariat. Beyond the obvious connotations of the superiority of the male anatomy, the two teams played against each other in a battle of not only the sexes, but of classes.[127]

Even while incarcerated, male MLN-T members participated in writing theoretical and tactical political tracts and maintained close contact with outside revolutionaries. In contrast, the Tupamaros rarely asked women to participate in the creation of theory and strategy while incarcerated. One Tupamara reported that incarcerated militant women's political position and practical experiences seemed to matter little to the group. While female militants had limited influence from prison, in Punta Carretas men's prison, the Tupamaros maintained political and administrative structures in groups named the C-1 and the C-2. The C-1 group created strategies, debated national and international politics, and kept in contact with the executive committee whenever possible. The C-2 presided over activities in prison such as study groups and physical exercise. Incarcerated male leaders also made important tactical decisions from prison. For instance, leaders at Punta Carretas concocted the "Cacao Plan" which focused on bombing "bourgeois" buildings (it ultimately failed). After a debate with members outside of jail, incarcerated male leaders also decided that the group would support the electoral campaign of the Frente Amplio. On the other hand, women's prisons had little formal structure or opportunity for leadership. Instead of participating in political decisions, imprisoned Tupamaras usually exercised and studied literature.[128]

Even when the mainstream Uruguayan press named Lucia Topolansky the "leader" in the kidnapping of Geoffrey Jackson, Cuba's state newspaper *Granma* downplayed her role in the action. In one article, *Granma* claimed that the police asserted Topolansky's importance in the kidnapping only after capturing her. The inept police only wanted to assure the public they had arrested someone important to the group and therefore made Topolansky a leader.[129]

While female Tupamaros performed prison breaks, some former members argued that most of their escapes functioned as actions of propaganda for the MLN-T. According to some Tupamaras, female militants' escapes ultimately had little influence or importance within the group on either a political or military level. These Tupamaras reported feeling useless within the MLN-T, even after their imprisonment and torture because of their association with the organization. Though women's prison breaks inspired propaganda touting the power and technical superiority of the Tupamaros, the liberation of the men's prisons produced positive press and also the freedom of important revolutionaries. Thus, some former Tupamaras claim that the organization saw male prison escapes as important recoveries of valuable members who contributed to the fight for the liberation of Uruguay.[130]

Women's prison escapes also had international implications, which perhaps misrepresented the true nature of these seemingly gendered actions. For example, in the Marxist *Red Papers* periodical, published in the US, a special issue about women's fight for liberation featured the Tupamara jailbreak. According to the *Red Papers*, the freeing of the Tupamaras demonstrated the ability of socialism to also prioritize women's rights. Choosing March 8, International Women's Day, as the day to stage the jailbreak supposedly showed the MLN-T's commitment to women's rights. According to a reprint from *Granma* in the *Red Papers*, the coordination of Operation Dove demonstrated flawless planning by the group as female prisoners overpowered a guard during Sunday mass. Waiting to take the escaped female prisoners was an ambulance, two taxi cabs, three private cars, and a fake police car.[131]

To the international left, the female militants' escape demonstrated another example of the tactical superiority of the Tupamaros. Choosing to free the prisoners on International Women's Day brought another gendered level of consciousness to the Tupamaros' actions. To MLN-T supporters, the action solidified the notion that the group prioritized women's rights. To capitalize on the positive press, after Operation Dove an MLN-T bulletin published the escaped female combatants' photos and wrote, "It's true, one cannot accomplish the revolution without them." However, according to the testimony of one Tupamara, the fact that the group freed the prisoners on March 8 turned out to be purely coincidental. She claims that only later did the Tupamaros learn that March 8 was International Women's Day.[132] The MLN-T subsequently used this fact to bolster their international propaganda, which was ultimately successful as the international press asserted the tactical superiority of the group as well as their focus on women's rights. Therefore, according to some Tupamaras, women's prison escapes focused on increasing positive propaganda for the organization, particularly the jailbreak that occurred on International Women's Day.

The Tupamaros and Homosexuality

For the Tupamaros, other Tupamara prison breaks revealed the existence of homosexual predators inside of the inhuman prison system of Uruguay. Instead of mentioning the frequent sexual assaults perpetrated on female prisoners by male guards, in an explanation of Operation Estrella, another mission liberating Tupamaras from prison, the Tupamaros chided the angry lesbian guards that manhandled and molested female militants.[133] While most likely same-sex abuse occurred, the MLN-T demonstrated an ignorance or perhaps apathy concerning the rampant sexual assault women experienced in prison. Furthermore, when describing the conditions of men's prisons, the Uruguayan left not only denounced sub-par nutrition and medical care but also pointed to the militants' exposure to homosexuals in prison. Indeed, two-thirds of political prisoners were confined in prisons that placed them with the regular prison population.[134]

One article in *Marcha* concerning political prisoners contended that "homosexuality [in prison] creates daily problems of all types."[135] The Uruguayan left criticized prison authorities for not searching for intelligent solutions to the problems of so-called deviants in prison. Assuming that no political activist could also identify as homosexual, the article lamented that prison authorities placed homosexual prisoners in cells with political prisoners. These placements provoked situations that ended in violence (in which homosexuals were to blame). To prove their point, the article cited the case of a young prisoner who cut an "active" homosexual with a piece of glass from a window. Prison authorities placed the young man in solitary confinement for years, and he returned from his punishment with severe mental illnesses. Thus, the Uruguayan left presented prisons as dangerous places for Tupamaros and other political prisoners not only because of human rights violations but because of predatory homosexuals. The sympathy for the youth who stabbed the homosexual inmate demonstrated the deeply rooted disdain many in the left had for gays and lesbians.[136]

According to another article in *Marcha*, male prisoners had their natural sexual instincts squelched by solitude and a lack of interaction with the other sex. In turn, prisoners turned to masturbation and other practices deemed deviant (such as homosexuality). The writers of the article argued that men needed to propagate the species and prison stifled these desires, which led to violent, deviant behavior. Therefore, prison supposedly destroyed the morals of inmates and supported onanism and pederasty. Exposure to these sexual practices demonstrated another violation of human rights within prisons in Uruguay. Sympathy for the sexual life only of male prisoners reinforced traditional ideas about gender as well as supported homophobia.[137]

When men experienced gendered humiliation in prison, it was most likely because of state sponsored torturers, not predatory homosexuals. During interrogations, officials applied electric current to prisoners' testicles and feminized their victims by taunting them about their manhood and the size of their penises. Guards referred to male prisoners in feminine derogatory terms such as "the putrid bitch." They also degraded the looks of male prisoners and particularly commented on their weight. During frequent confiscations of items in male prisoners' rooms guards attempted to emasculate prisoners with sexualized insults. Reports indicate that some guards would look at pictures of male prisoners' wives or girlfriends and ask, "How many is she fucking now, this whore?"[138]

Psychological torment had a specifically gendered character as it focused on questioning the honor of prisoners' wives and girlfriends. Similar to the rapes of female family members in front of incarcerated males, these acts aimed to destroy the male prisoner by emasculating him. Through their treatment as "passives" in prison, literary critic Jean Franco argues that male political prisoners inadvertently gained insight into the daily subjugation experienced by women.[139] Male prisoners began to understand how it felt to constantly be cognizant of the body, to be taunted and abused and to find comfort in daily activities such as laundry or talking with friends. While incarcerated men experienced what some women did on a daily basis in greater Uruguayan society, once outside of prison they rarely reflected in their political consciousness any change concerning gender constructions.

Outside of prison, the Tupamaros viewed both homosexuality and its association with the feminine as negative and counter revolutionary. The MLN-T's ideas about homosexuality proved to be similar to their rightist military enemies. Like the Uruguayan military, overall the Tupamaros supported the polarization of masculine/feminine and active/passive, with feminine and passive as synonymous.[140] The Tupamaros considered "passivity" in both males and females undesirable and harmful to the revolution. Thus, the Tupamaros, like the Uruguayan armed forces, ultimately excluded those who supported what they deemed open sexual deviations. During the 1960s and 1970s, many in the Uruguayan left believed that homosexuality was a bourgeois vice or in the best-case scenario a sickness or mental illness.[141] For its part, besides exclusion of homosexuals from the military, the Uruguayan dictatorship enforced a social science curriculum for students in the 1970s that taught that homosexuality, along with abortion and student revolt, represented deviation and a loss of morality.[142]

In comparison to the Tupamaros, the greater Uruguayan society did not fare much better in its treatment of homosexuals. While Uruguay never passed any official laws condemning homosexuality during the twentieth century, it never attempted to protect homosexuals either.[143] Ultimately, homosexuality, like nonwhiteness, seemed to be invisible in Uruguayan society. As late as the 1980s, gays and lesbians reported that publicly no language even existed to interpret their sexuality. Uruguayan society, therefore, often ignored homosexuality and especially the reality of homosexual desire. Homosexuals in Uruguay reported living a double life and lying about their sexuality in order to keep their jobs and families. In contrast to reports about Uruguay's open-minded politics, many homosexuals of the 1970s and 1980s attested to the conservative nature of Uruguay and its supposedly traditional people.[144] Therefore, Uruguayan homosexuals expressed little hope for change in a country that contained what they deemed "conservatives" and "oppressors."

Some activist gays and lesbians in Uruguay refuted the assumption from many in the left that homosexuality represented a symptom of the so-called decadence of society. Instead, they attributed hunger, unemployment, and torture to decadent society, not to sexual orientation.[145] Other homosexual students and activists blamed the legacy of colonialism in Uruguay for the repression of homosexuals. Like the greater Uruguayan left, these activists linked their struggle to the subjugation of indigenous peoples and those of African descent throughout the world. Some Uruguayan homosexuals viewed their experiences and categorization as "other" as similar to the repression of blacks in Africa and the United States. They argued that such othering by the state served to justify both racial and sexual violence. Once again, another segment of Uruguayan activists created parallels with their experiences and the civil rights struggle in the United States. According to these homosexual activists, repressive governments, like the Uruguayan dictatorship and the US government, attempted to create a place where all citizens acted the same and supported a similar vision of the world.[146]

Some homosexual activists saw the transition to democracy in the 1980s as an opportunity to fight for inclusion in the emerging state. These activists never denied what they saw as Uruguay's prejudicial mentality concerning homosexuality but also hoped that the emerging Uruguayan democracy could create rights for sexual minorities. Uruguay's homosexual activists especially looked to the university as a site to rouse activism. During the 1980s and the transition to democracy, the university became a place to debate issues of personal liberty, democracy, and ideas about respect for a plurality of opinions and lifestyles. Despite a hope for homosexuals' inclusion in the new state, the Uruguayan government and many leftist groups failed to prioritize the rights of homosexuals and rarely acknowledged their struggles.[147]

To MANY OF THEIR admirers, the Tupamaros represented a group committed to integrating women into the revolutionary struggle. Undeniably, the MLN-T subverted traditional concepts of women as maternal nurturers and inherently nonviolent. The group also offered a space for deviation from the common construction, even within the Uruguayan left, of women as politically passive. However, while some of the Tupamaros' attitudes toward women demonstrated a progressive stance, overall the group never prioritized women's struggle for liberation on their own terms. For the MLN-T, the participation of women in the fight against the dictatorship automatically implied women's liberation.

The Tupamaros used popular societal stereotypes about women as harmless in order to help them in armed missions. The group especially praised female militants' work on service teams and their ability to gain entrance into places less accessible to men. However, despite somewhat stereotypical representations of the role of Tupamaras, the MLN-T also included women in armed missions and taught them how to handle weapons. As prisoner Geoffrey Jackson observed, only when a Tupamara held a gun did complete differentiation between the sexes cease within the MLN-T. In a sense, the group used guns as a great phallic equalizer.

While the Tupamaros offered a new type of political participation for women, they also expected female militants to "lose" their femininity and especially reject motherhood as their inspiration for revolution. In order to be an accepted member of the Tupamaros, women were encouraged by the group to transform into socially constructed models of the masculine militant. In contrast, many other groups within the Uruguayan left accentuated women's roles as wives and mothers as inspiration for their political participation. However, within either option—embracing femininity and maternity or embracing masculinity—dichotomous gender restrictions confined women's political participation to constructed gender norms. A female militant had the option of embracing her motherhood or femininity as a source of political activism or transforming into a "pseudo-male." However, despite these restrictions, all of the aforementioned groups also offered women a vehicle for political participation and opened a new space for women to articulate their politics, opportunities very limited to them before the 1960s and 1970s.[148] Whether under the banner of motherhood or the cult of masculinity, women publicly protested human rights violations and fought for revolutionary change in Latin America. They contributed to the struggle against repression with undeniable restrictions, but in ways vastly different and much more public than in the past.

Issues of sexuality played a significant part in the treatment of female militants by both their comrades and the Uruguayan state. Despite rhetoric of equality within the MLN-T, female militants experienced double standards concerning their sexuality. If a Tupamara became pregnant, the MLN-T punished the militant by continuing to exclude her from group actions long after the birth. The treatment of male militants, however, remained unchanged even after they became fathers. Furthermore, while the group supported somewhat freer ideas about sexual expression in monogamous relationships than the greater Uruguayan society, the Tupamaros expected women to ultimately take responsibility for the prevention of pregnancy.

The treatment of the incarcerated Tupamara proved to be much harsher than that of her male counterparts and had a specifically sexual character. Female militants' punishment for being gender traitors consisted of sexual harassment and assault, particularly for the pregnant female combatant. Incarcerated Tupamaras' treatment by the MLN-T also succeeded in marginalizing the female militant. Once in prison, male MLN-T members had opportunities to lead missions and produce ideological tracts, while the incarcerated Tupamara usually functioned as an arm of propaganda for the organization.

The state also subjected imprisoned men to gendered forms of torture as guards attempted to feminize them with insults about their appearance and the honor of female relatives and lovers. Beyond torture by the state, the Uruguayan left envisioned prison life as treacherous because of political prisoners' contact with alleged homosexual predators. Even outside of prison, many in the Uruguayan left generally disdained homosexuality or ignored its existence all together.

Just as homosexuality was seen by many in the Uruguayan left as a symptom of an unchecked bourgeoisie, Tupamaros also viewed feminism as secondary to the revolutionary project. By the 1980s, largely in response to marginalization from the Uruguayan left, autonomous feminist groups emerged within Uruguay to fight against gender oppression. These organizations consciously prioritized common gender interests and not class as the primary inspiration for their activism. These feminist groups often went to battle against the Tupamaros and the greater Uruguayan left, especially concerning issues of reproductive rights. In the next, concluding chapter I trace the path of the Tupamaros to electoral solutions.

Conclusion

General strategic lines . . . are subject to modification
with the change of circumstances.
   —Tupamaro manifesto

IN 2009, FORMER TUPAMARO and Frente Amplio member José "El
Pepe" Mujica won the presidency of Uruguay. While it is difficult to
imagine that any Tupamaro who suffered years of imprisonment and
torture could ever obtain a high position of power in the Uruguayan
government, within only a few years of their release from prison, numerous Tupamaros learned to successfully navigate electoral politics.[1]
Calling for democratic solutions to the problems within Uruguay, the
Tupamaros participated in all elections after 1989. In 1994, Mujica, a
founding member of the Tupamaros, became the first MLN-T member
to be elected to the Uruguayan parliament.[2] In 2004, Tabaré Vázquez,
leader of the ruling Frente Amplio coalition, won with an absolute majority, making him the first center-left president in modern Uruguayan
history.

The popularity of the Frente Amplio, which had significant numbers
of Tupamaros in its coalition, disrupted the traditional party politics
of Uruguay. For nearly two hundred years, two traditional parties had
dominated the Uruguayan political scene—the aforementioned Partido
Nacional (formerly known as Blanco) and the Colorado Party. While political opponents of the Frente Amplio criticized the party's inclusion of
the Tupamaros because of their violent past, most Uruguayans ignored
these tactics. In their campaigns, members of the MLN-T reassured the
public of their departure from past political ideologies and tactics. On
an international level, for some critics, the triumph of the Frente Amplio
and the Tupamaros in the twenty-first century represented another example of the alleged socialist takeover of Latin America. Following the
election of Vázquez, political analyst Jaime Yaffé predicted, "Everything

indicates that with the inauguration of Vázquez, we will be in a new country that will put an end to neo-liberal policies to focus attention on social problems and abandon automatic alignment with the United States." [3] Even those that did not condemn the leftward turn in Latin America often lumped together the elections of Hugo Chávez in Venezuela, Luiz Inácio "Lula" da Silva and the Workers' Party in Brazil, Néstor Kirchner in Argentina, Evo Morales in Bolivia, and Vázquez in Uruguay. Latin American historian Jorge Castañeda has attributed all the aforementioned elections to a backlash against free-market reforms, openness to allying with the United States, and the consolidation of democracy.[4] In this way, the multiple players in this Latin American "left wing tsunami," as Castañeda deemed it, all appear to have similar agendas. However, the political actions and ideologies of the Frente Amplio and the Tupamaros did not and do not necessarily reflect a simplistic backlash against the US and neoliberal economic policies. As he campaigned for president during the summer of 2009, Mujica vowed to distance the Uruguayan left from "the stupid ideologies that come from the 1970s. . . . I refer to things like unconditional love of everything that is state-run, scorn for businessmen and intrinsic hate of the United States. I'll shout it if they want: Down with isms! Up with a left that is capable of thinking outside the box! In other words, I am more than completely cured of simplifications, of dividing the world into good and evil, of thinking in black and white. I have repented!"[5]

As a former proviolence guerrilla, Mujica may have left some perplexed when he seemingly rejected Tupamaro ideology. One of the most admired figures of the Tupamaros, Che Guevara, once deemed the United States "the great enemy of mankind."[6] However, after tracing the ideology of the Tupamaros, Mujica's disdain for political simplifications is not surprising. In the late 1960s, in a communiqué released by the MLN-T, members continued to assert the political malleability of their group. They contended, "We do not call it an '-ism.' We are a huge movement whose militants include all sorts of groups from Marxist to Catholic and we do not need an '-ism.'"[7] Therefore, even during the height of the Cold War, the group refused to categorize themselves with specific labels. The group's disdain for confining categories continues to the present day as MLN-T members hope to create a new left, influenced by their own unique experiences as Uruguayan revolutionaries. Considering the complex ideologies and actions of the group over the last fifty years, the Tupamaros' departure from their past beliefs should not come as a surprise. The Tupamaros' lack of a monolithic ideology was and continues to be their unifying ideology.

A Malleable Ideology

The Tupamaros' ability to easily integrate new ideas into their politics derives in part from Uruguay's historical freedom from stringent ideological influences. During colonial times, the Spanish applauded what they deemed the "free" lifestyle within Uruguay. Indigenous peoples, mestizos, pirates and bandits from Brazil and deserters from ships of various nations all contributed to the so-called frontier conditions within the region. Control from Europe proved to be so insignificant that the king of Spain ordered the official creation of the capital city Montevideo in 1726 only after feeling pressure from the encroachment of the Portuguese. Showing the lack of strength of the church in the region, in 1830, Uruguay contained only one hundred Catholic priests for 128,000 inhabitants.[8] Therefore, Uruguay's fringe status during colonial times created a unique society as the state, church, and oligarchic elites never gained a significant amount of power in the country. Thus, no specific or strict mold existed concerning issues of politics, economics, or religion in Uruguay. This "weak colonial legacy" enabled Uruguay's variant state building processes when compared with their Latin American counterparts.[9] By the time the move toward modernization occurred in the late nineteenth century, the common forces throughout Latin America that resisted change and controlled the master political narrative remained feeble. According to Francisco Panizza, the lack of powerful economic elites and church ties to politics allowed Uruguay to take a more democratic, liberal, and politically flexible path than its neighbors.[10]

Surrounded by rhetoric of Uruguay's exceptional liberal democracy, the Tupamaros simultaneously found inspiration from political violence as well as their country's democratic past. Therefore, since their inception, members of the Tupamaros demonstrated a unique ability to integrate multiple and seemingly conflicting ideologies into their politics. This flexibility extended to group members' transformation from proviolence revolutionaries into candidates seeking electoral solutions, largely because of political necessity and expediency. Thus, the Tupamaros embraced electoral politics because it offered a better alternative than the previous repressive dictatorship. Undoubtedly, the trauma Tupamaro members experienced under the dictatorship and their large rates of incarceration challenged group members to rethink previous ideologies and tactics.[11] Some scholars such as Richard Gillespie have argued that for the Tupamaros, "bourgeois democracy has become preferable to bourgeois dictatorship."[12] Embracing the long tradition of Uruguayan democracy gave MLN-T members an opportunity to achieve political prominence and provided a previously unavailable platform from to speak about their hope for the transformation of Uruguayan society as a whole. As early as the 1960s, the group claimed to support a "realistic" approach to gaining power in Uruguay. According to the Tupamaros, this approach could change in a day, month, or year depending on the circumstances in Uruguay.[13]

Besides their ability to navigate democratic politics after their violent past, the actions of the Tupamaros after the transition to democracy demonstrate the immense ideological and political flexibility of the group. The Tupamaros even changed fundamental aspects of their social ideologies. For example, by the twenty-first century, the Tupamaros had altered their ideologies about homosexuality. As my research demonstrates, many Tupamaros and Uruguayan leftists initially adhered to homophobic thinking. Yet by 2007, the Tupamaros reversed their attitude toward homosexuality. That year the ruling Frente Amplio party, which included significant numbers of Tupamaros, affirmed the rights of homosexuals by approving a bill allowing civil unions for homosexual couples. The bill gave homosexual couples who lived together for five years or more the same rights as married couples.[14] By approving this legislation, Uruguay became the first country in Latin America to approve nationwide civil unions. Just as the Tupamaros changed from supporting violence to supporting electoral solutions, the group demonstrated their capabilities for political flexibility concerning homosexual rights.

The Guerrilla as Neoliberal

Although during the 1960s and 1970s the Tupamaros vehemently opposed the infusion of foreign capital into Uruguay, on the campaign trail Mujica promised to continue the Frente Amplio's "investor friendly policies."[15] Therefore, while Castañeda and others homogenized the government of the Frente Amplio with the Chávez regime, Mujica and his party have supported free-market economic policies and pushed for a friendly dialogue with the US. So how did the Tupamaros become supporters of the free-market economy? My research provides clues as to why the Tupamaros would change their position. I posit that the MLN-T demonstrated a willingness to integrate other ideas from abroad, even from the often-maligned United States. The Tupamaros and others in the Uruguayan left chose which facets of US cultural and political ideas they would appropriate or reject for their benefit. Thus, despite anti-US government rhetoric, MLN-T members rarely seemed to thoughtlessly reject an idea or product solely because of its affiliation with the US or capitalism. As one US radical contended, "Uruguay is possibly more like the US than any other Latin American country."[16] As my research reveals, many members of the Tupamaros had no qualms about expressing admiration for both Che Guevara and James Bond, two characters seemingly on different sides of the ideological spectrum.

Unlike other more doctrinaire leftist groups, the Tupamaros' struggle for the betterment of Uruguay did not necessarily require them to reject everything associated with the United States and Europe. Therefore, if supporting neoliberal economic policies benefited the middle class in Uruguay and helped them to win the centrist vote, then the Tupamaros would see no reason to cling to strict Marxist economic models that could, in the estimation of some, harm the country. Proving the complexities of economic policies and ideologies in Uruguay, after the election of Vázquez and the passage of an amendment making water management the responsibility of the state, Uruguayans celebrated leftist victories with an increase in consumption and increased leisure. For example, travel agency manager Juan Ihno Gruber noted that after the election of Vázquez, Uruguayans began to book more vacations. He argued, "Even though people have the same difficulties, just the fact that they have hope makes them consume more."[17] Thus, middle-class consumption in Uruguay did not necessarily decrease because of the election of leftists. Furthermore, while some from the Uruguayan left express concern about their government's policies, evidence indicates that Uruguay's free-market policies during the last eight years have increased the country's economic growth. Under Vázquez's government, Uruguay's agricultural-based economy grew at an average rate of over 7 percent annually from 2004 to 2008.[18] After recovering from the financial crisis in 2010, Uruguay's GDP soared to nearly 9 percent growth. However, the Tupamaros' support of neoliberal policies has led some to assert the familiar criticism that the Tupamaros favor nationalism and their country's interests over an international Marxist movement.[19]

The Tupamaros as Nationalists

Although for some it seemed contradictory, the Tupamaros conceptualized their politics as inspired by international movements as well as their own national history. While the group wanted to create "many Vietnams," they also focused on Uruguay's history and national heroes.[20] Thus, my research indicates that transnational historical actors such as the Tupamaros can also maintain deep nationalist roots. While the MLN-T supported an international socialist movement, they also supported a nationalistic rhetoric and espoused the popular refrain throughout Uruguay of their country's exceptional nature. Thus, the idea that Uruguay contained more "educated" and "civilized" citizens than the rest of Latin America influenced group members to believe that their organization practiced superior warfare techniques, tempered by a higher respect for human life. In turn, many in the US left believed in the overall technical and structural superiority of the Tupamaros when compared with other Latin American guerrilla groups.

Ironically, the revolutionaries that many Tupamaros admired also disdained nationalistic rhetoric as it deviated from the larger struggle of international Marxist transformation. Che Guevara, an inspiration for many in the Tupamaros, seemed to support a different and more traditional Marxist conception of the international nature of revolution. According to Guevara, imperialism was a world system that could be defeated only in a global confrontation.[21] Guevara also hoped for a proletarian internationalism populated by proletarian armies. Guevara's call for an international proletarian army in the countryside deviated from the realities of the often nationalistic, middle-class Tupamaros. Instead, the Tupamaros pointed to their distinctive urban situation and their need to respond most immediately to the increasingly authoritarian Uruguayan state. Thus, while the MLN-T supported internationalism and forged connections with other radicals, the middle-class urban Tupamaros reacted first and foremost to their specific repression within Uruguay.

Urban versus Rural Guerrillas

The Tupamaros implemented urban guerrilla warfare in large part because of their country's unique terrain and demographics. The notion that the MLN-T achieved exemplary success as urban guerrillas earned them admiration from revolutionaries throughout the world. Although the question of what sort of transnational relationship guerrillas in the countryside formed with other radicals has still not been answered, evidence presented in this work indicates personal connections and communication between radicals in urban areas in Uruguay and the US. Bringing together seemingly disparate sources sheds light on the complex web of previously unexplored connections between the US and Uruguay. My research also indicates that Uruguayans did not only communicate with US activists but forged connections with Canadians and others throughout the world.

Although scholars have explored the history of rural guerrillas more extensively than that of their urban counterparts, significant work remains to be done concerning all types of guerrilla movements in Latin America. One unexamined topic even within the study of rural guerrilla movements concerns how militants communicated and established links of solidarity with other revolutionaries. How and to what extent urban and rural guerrillas participated in a transnational discourse remains poorly understood. Only recently have scholars begun to examine the topic.[22] While evidence indicates a relationship between leftists in the US and Uruguay, the nature of the connections between the Latin American left and European activists remain unknown. Even aspects of Cuban influence on the politics and culture of not only US radicals but leftists throughout Latin America proves rich for historical inquiry.[23] More historical research should be done to examine how groups with sometimes dissimilar agendas forged transnational alliances throughout Latin America, Europe, and the US during the Cold War.

Although important works have emerged concerning the experience of female guerrillas, historians still need to explore in more depth the discontent and gendered representation of Latin American militants. My work contributes to the understanding of these critical topics through a discussion of the daily lives of Tupamaras, their representation within US leftist movements, and their place in the Tupamaro hierarchy. Thus, taking into account issues of culture and sexuality offers a more multifaceted understanding of the gendered experiences of female militants in guerrilla movements. Future research about women in guerrilla movements should also consider how issues of culture, representation, and sexuality shaped the experiences of the female militant.

More scholarly work should also be done to explore how issues of race influenced urban and rural guerrilla movements in Latin America.[24] My research indicates that transnational alliances and acts of solidarity occurred between African American activists and the Uruguayan left. By claiming that the black civil rights struggle was "their struggle," many leftist Uruguayans consciously created a hemispheric solidarity with activists in the United States. However, besides Cuba, little is known about the connections between the US civil rights movement and leftists in Latin America. Focusing on the perspective of Latin American historical actors, this manuscript demonstrates that the US civil rights movement had an important impact on the activism and imagination of the Tupamaros as well as the greater Uruguayan left.

IN A 1994 ARTICLE about the state of Latin American history after the end of the Cold War, historian Florencia Mallon lamented, "It is not an easy time for scholars who work on Latin America."[25] According to Mallon, the emergence of governments that supported free markets, the electoral defeat of the Sandinistas in 1990, and disillusionment with the Cuban government as a coveted model of socialism represented just a few of many examples of the unraveling of important and inspirational historical narratives for Latin American historians. While these narratives have come undone in many ways, I contend that rejecting the rigid framework of Cold War politics also offers a whole new way of conceptualizing Latin American history. By using new sources and variant approaches, historians are now able to explore previously marginalized historical actors and events in Latin America during the Cold War. It is my sincere hope that this work contributes to an alternative narrative of US–Latin American relations and that it provides a better understanding of the complexities of revolutionary groups that have been misunderstood or wrongly classified in simplistic Cold War binaries.

The Tupamaros show that Latin American guerrilla groups during the Cold War did more than take sides in a battle between Soviet Union and US ideologies. The MLN-T, refusing to limit themselves to dichotomous categories, created homegrown and unique forms of revolution. They conceptualized changing Uruguayan society on their own terms, without worrying what "-ism" they supported in the process. Despite

Cold War narratives that forced Latin America into impenetrable ideological and political boundaries, my research reveals that the Tupamaros allied with and sometimes expressed admiration for US activists. These connections show the existence of rarely explored, non-paternalistic alliances of solidarity between Latin American and US historical actors. The Uruguayan left and the Tupamaros participated in a transnational network of movements and individuals determined to incite radical change on both the national and international levels. Beyond their willingness to connect with leftists in the US, the Tupamaros have helped to create new definitions of the left in Latin America. These complex and at times contradictory definitions do not replicate conventional Cold War models. Instead, the new left in Uruguay demonstrates not only a willingness to integrate multiple ideologies into their politics, but a rare ability to self-reflect on both their mistakes and successes.

The ability of the Tupamaros to reflect on their flaws comes in part from the years MLN-T members spent in prison, tortured by a government determined to enact its own rigid and radical ideologies. Resolved not to repeat the mistakes of the past, the Tupamaros survived terrible traumas in prison and emerged with a creative political plan. Participating in electoral solutions allowed for the Tupamaros to achieve large-scale political triumph within just a few decades of their release from prison. Thus, Tupamaro victories occurred in large part because of the group's willingness to learn from the rigid ideologies of the Cold War. The Tupamaros now seem to understand that little positive change can be accomplished in a world divided into absolutes. Such ideological flexibility and political adaptability has allowed MLN-T members to occupy government and institutional positions that once supported their repression. Only because of the Tupamaros' ability to integrate various ideologies and tactics in their politics was the group able to transform definitions of revolution, democracy, and the left in Uruguay.

In the preface to his novel *The Devil and Miss Prym*, Brazilian author Paulo Coelho complicates the struggle between polar opposites (in this case "good" and "evil") to show that at times we all must make difficult decisions and perform a balancing act between two seemingly irreconcilable poles. Coelho writes, "When we least expect it, life sets us a challenge to test our courage and willingness to change; at such a moment, there is no point in pretending that nothing has happened or in saying that we are not yet ready. The challenge will not wait."[26] The Tupamaros constantly faced challenges that demanded immediate resolution. Almost daily since the 1960s, they have had to wrestle with the dilemma of how to define themselves as well as find the best mechanisms to create a more equitable Uruguay. The current electoral success of the Tupamaros proves that while revolutions may wax or wane, reflecting on the memory and meaning of the struggle remains an essential part of the left's ever-evolving history. The Tupamaros demonstrate that only through constant reinvention can revolution survive.

Notes

INTRODUCTION

The epigraph is a popular Uruguayan nationalistic expression. Alexandra Barahona de Brito, *Human Rights and Democratization in Latin America*, 18.

1. *Liberation News Service (LNS)*, no. 279 (August 12, 1970), Marshall Bloom papers.

2. Carlos Núñez, "The Tupamaros—Theory and Practice," 16, in *The Tupamaros: Urban Guerrilla Warfare in Uruguay*. New York: Liberated Guardian, 1970. Rpt. *Uruguay: North American Congress on Latin America (NACLA) Archive of Latin Americana* (Wilmington, DE: Scholarly Resources, 1998) (hereafter cited as NACLA), reel 4.

3. For more on the founding of the Tupamaros, see Eleuterio Fernández Huidobro, *Historia de los Tupamaros*.

4. Some important work has been done concerning female guerrillas in other Latin American revolutionary groups. See Karen Kampwirth, *Feminism and the Legacy of Revolution: Nicaragua, El Salvador, Chiapas*; and Kampwirth, *Women and Guerrilla Movements Nicaragua, El Salvador, Chiapas, Cuba*; and Julie Shayne, *The Revolution Question: Feminisms in El Salvador, Chile and Cuba*.

5. See Labrousse, *The Tupamaros*, 145, and Movimiento de Liberación Nacional (MLN-T), "Documentos y antecedentes: Documento No. 5," (December 1970), BNU.

6. For the purposes of this manuscript, I define those on the "left," broadly, as supporting social change in order to create a more egalitarian society. This includes concern for the empowerment of workers and often other historically marginalized social groups as well as a disdain for plutocracy.

7. "Letter to the Editor," *Marcha*, January 7, 1972, 1, BNU.

8. See for example "Angela Davis y la guerrilla urbana en Estados Unidos," *Marcha*, second section, November 20, 1970, 4, BNU; James Petras, "Estado Unidos: El preludio de una lucha politica armada: Especial para *Marcha*," *Marcha*, May 22, 1970, 19–20, BNU.

9. The concrete connections between the Uruguayan left and European activists have yet to be fully explored.

10. For more on the concept of imagined communities, see Benedict Anderson, *Imagined Communities: Reflections on the Origins and Spread of Nationalism*.

11. Anderson, *Imagined Communities*, 6.

12. Anderson, *Imagined Communities*, 7.

13. Anderson, *Imagined Communities*, 134.

14. Anderson, *Imagined Communities*, 25.

15. Edy Kaufman, *Uruguay in Transition*, 46. During this time, the majority of

Uruguayan citizens enjoyed a decent standard of living, health care, and literacy, and for most of the twentieth century a level of democracy unknown throughout the Southern Cone. See Martin Weinstein, *Uruguay: The Politics of Failure*, xiii.

16. I define "radical" movements and people as those that hope for fundamental, abrupt, and drastic changes to current political and societal norms. Uruguayan and US radicals refused to work within their governments' systems and called for alternative solutions, often through the use of violence. See for example "Poder Negro," *Cuadernos de Marcha*, no. 12 (April 1968), CEDINCI.

17. NINOLA, "Untitled," vol. 1, no. 1 (February 1970), 4, Marshall Bloom Papers.

18. See for example CAGLA, "Frente Amplio: Reprinted from *Marcha*," February 12, 1971, trans. Ed Sunshine, Marshall Bloom Papers.

19. Cynthia A. Young, *Soul Power: Culture, Radicalism, and the Making of a US Third World Left*, 9.

20. Young, *Soul Power*, 9. For more on the radicalization of Latin America during the 1960s, see Diana Sorenson, *A Turbulent Decade Remembered*.

21. Young, *Soul Power*, 9.

22. Graciela Taglioretti, *Women and Work in Uruguay*, 14.

23. See Jeffrey Gould, "Solidarity under Siege: The Latin American Left, 1968," 354–55; Jeffrey J. Ryan, "Turning on Their Masters: Unlearning Democracy in Uruguay," 280; and Astrid Arrarás, "Armed Struggle, Political Learning, and Participation in Democracy: The Case of the Tupamaros (Uruguay)," 51.

24. For accounts of Uruguay's exceptional nature, see also S. G. Hanson, *Utopia in Uruguay*; R. H. Fitzgibbon, *Uruguay: Portrait of a Democracy*; Milton Vanger, *The Model Country: José Batlle y Ordóñez of Uruguay 1907–1915*; *Uruguay: the Tupamaros in Uruguay*, 45.

25. Arrarás, "Armed Struggle," 35.

26. R. C. Longworth, "Uruguay Follows Argentina's Path," *Chicago Tribune*, January 26, 1978, 13.

27. See for example *Marcha*, June 11, 1971, 18, BNU; and Comité de Informacion Sobre La Represion en Uruguay, "The Uruguayan University and the Today's Anti-Uruguay," 1974, NACLA, reel 6.

28. For more, see Luis Eduardo Gonzalez, *Political Structures and Democracy in Uruguay*.

29. Vania Markarian, *Left in Transformation*, 10–11.

30. Christine Ehrick, *The Shield of the Weak*, 71.

31. Markarian, *Left in Transformation*, 20–24.

32. M. H. J. Finch, *An Economic History of Uruguay Since 1870*, 227–29.

33. Alain Labrousse, *The Tupamaros: Urban Guerrillas in Uruguay*, 45.

34. Arrarás, "Armed Struggle," 72.

35. Julio Fabregat, *Elecciones Uruguayas*, 13.

36. *Black Panther* 3, no. 5 (July 29, 1972), Marshall Bloom Papers.

37. Arrarás, "Armed Struggle," 50.

38. For more on how fear of the power of organized labor inspired the rise of dictatorships in the Southern Cone, see Paul W. Drake, *Labor Movements and Dictatorships*.

39. *LNS*, no. 295 (November 5, 1970), Marshall Bloom Papers. See also Gonzalo

Aguirre Ramrez, "El Che y los Tupamaros," *El Pais*, December 23, 2008. *historico.elpais.com.uy/08/12/23/predit_389027.asp*.

40. "Falleció esposa de Arbelio Ramírez, asesinado por una bala para el Che," *La Republica* 12, no. 2797 (January 22, 2008), *www.larepublica.com.uy/politica/295033-fallecio-esposa-de-arbelio-ramirez-asesinado-por-una-bala-para-el-che*.

41. Alba Roballo, "El Primer Disparo" in *Sesenta y ocho*. Oscar Maggiolo, ed. (Montevideo: El Popular, 198[?]). See also Eduardo Galeano, *El asesinato de Arbelio Ramírez*. (Montevideo: Comite de Intelectuales y Artistas de Apoyo a Cuba, 1961) and Victor L. Bacchetta, *El asesinato de Areblio Ramírez: la República a la deriva*. (Montevideo: Doble clic Editores, 2010).

42. *Granma*, July 30, 1967, Marshall Bloom Papers.

43. Huidobro, *Historia*, 16–18.

44. Núñez, "The Tupamaros," 19.

45. Arrarás, "Armed Struggle," 63.

46. *Granma*, July 26, 1970, Marshall Bloom Papers.

47. While some work has been done concerning the transnational connections between Cubans and guerrilla groups in South America, the relationship between Cubans and the Tupamaros has not yet been fully explored. See Jean Rodrigues Sales, "O impacto da revolução cubana sobre as organizações comunistas brasileiras (1959–1974)."

48. Arrarás, "Armed Struggle," 215–16.

49. "Create Two, Three Many Vietnams," *Granma*, April 9, 1972, 5, Marshall Bloom Papers.

50. Jorge Castañeda, Utopia Unarmed: The Latin American Left after the Cold War, 79.

51. Richard Gillespie, "A Critique of the Urban Guerrilla: Argentina, Uruguay and Brazil," *Journal of Conflict Studies* 1, no. 2 (1980): 39–53.

52. Daniel Costabilde and Alfredo Errandonea, *Sindicato y sociedad en el Uruguay*, 136.

53. For more on how fear of the power of organized labor inspired the rise of dictatorships in the Southern Cone, see Paul W. Drake, *Labor Movements and Dictatorships*.

54. Núñez, "The Tupamaros," 18.

55. Comité de Información Sobre la Represión en Uruguay, "Uruguay; los rehenes del fascismo," 1974, NACLA, reel 6.

56. Raúl Sendic, "Un Revolver o la Constitucion?" *El Sol*, March 22, 1963.

57. Arrarás, "Armed Struggle," 63.

58. Huidobro, *Historia*, 45.

59. Núñez, "The Tupamaros," 29.

60. Huidobro, *Historia*, 69–71; 75.

61. Prudencio Corres, "Tupamaros: Organization and Solidarity," *Prensa Latina Features*, 1971, Marshall Bloom Papers.

62. *LNS*, no. 202 (October 11, 1969), Marshall Bloom Papers.

63. Núñez, "The Tupamaros," 25.

64. For more on double militancy, see Najma Chowdhury and Barbara J. Nelson, eds. *Women and Politics Worldwide*, 665–67.

65. Ana María Araújo, *Tupamaras: Des femmes de l'Uruguay*, 156.

66. Arturo C. Porzecanski, *Uruguay's Tupamaros: The Urban Guerrillas*, 30–31.
67. Barbara Dane, ed., "Cancion Protesta: Protest Songs of Latin America," New York, 1970, Bobbye Ortiz Papers.
68. Núñez, "The Tupamaros," 23.
69. "Robin Hood," *Marcha*, May 23, 1969, 21, BNU.
70. *Guerrilla*, no. 19 (March 1971), Marshall Bloom Papers.
71. Núñez, "The Tupamaros," 37.
72. Prudencio Corres, "Tupamaros: Organization and Solidarity," *Prensa Latina Features*, 1971, Marshall Bloom Papers.
73. Sonia Pacheco Agraz, "Like a Fish in the Water," *Granma*, June 6, 1971, 11. Marshall Bloom Papers.
74. Núñez, "The Tupamaros," 13–15.
75. The coup took place slowly; in 1972 the government declared a "state of internal war," which temporarily suspended constitutional protections. See American Commission of Human Rights, *Report on the Situation of Human Rights in Uruguay*, 11.
76. Ryan, "Turning on Their Masters," 285.
77. See Markarian, *Left in Transformation*, 5; and Carlos Fortuna, Nelly Niedworok, and Adela Pellegrino, *Uruguay y la emigracion de los 70.*
78. Arrarás, "Armed Struggle," 215–16.
79. Markarian, *Left in Transformation*, 68–69.
80. Markarian, *Left in Transformation*, 103; 112.
81. See Judith Butler, "Imitation and Gender Subordination."
82. Butler, "Imitation and Gender Subordination," 313.
83. María Josefina Saldaña-Portillo, *The Revolutionary Imagination in the Americas and the Age of Development*, 273. See also Ileana Rodríguez, *Women, Guerrillas, and Love: Understanding War in Central America.*
84. See for example Timothy Brown, ed., *When the AK-47s Fall Silent: Revolutionaries, Guerrillas, and the Dangers of Peace*; Laura Enríquez, *Agrarian Reform and Class Consciousness in Nicaragua*; Samuel Farber, *The Origins of the Cuban Revolution Reconsidered*; Michael D. Gambone, *Capturing the Revolution: The United States, Central America and Nicaragua, 1961–1972*; Michael J. Gonzales, *The Mexican Revolution, 1910–1940*; Lynn Horton, *Peasants in Arms: War and Peace in the Mountains of Nicaragua, 1979–1994*; Friedrich Katz, *The Life and Times of Pancho Villa*; Alan Knight, *The Mexican Revolution*; Morris H. Morley, *Washington, Somoza and the Sandinistas: State and Regime in US Policy toward Nicaragua 1969–1981*; Misagh Parsa, *States, Ideologies, and Social Revolutions: A Comparative Analysis of Iran, Nicaragua, and the Philippines*; Thomas C Paterson, *Contesting Castro: The United States and the Triumph of the Cuban Revolution*; Louis Pérez Jr., *Cuba and the United States: Ties of Singular Intimacy*; Marfeli Pérez-Stabli, *The Cuban Revolution: Origins, Course, and Legacy*; Isaac Saney, *Cuba: A Revolution in Motion*; John Womack, *Emiliano Zapata and the Mexican Revolution*; Thomas Wright, *Latin America in the Era of the Cuban Revolution*; Matilde Zimmerman, *Sandinista: Carlos Fonseca and the Nicaraguan Revolution.*

CHAPTER 1

The epigraph is my translation; the original reads: "Patria pa' todos o pa' nadie." Alain Labrousse, "Tupamaros: De la guerrilla al partido de masas," undated pamphlet.

1. My translation; the original reads: "El resultado es que cada Tupamaro capaz de entrar en acción, es un complete "samurai": músculos de acero, mente alerta, reflejos inverosímiles, dominio complete de las armas, resistencia al dolor, etc." Antonio Mercader and Jorge de Vera, *Tupamaros: estrategia y acción*, 104–5.

2. For more on urban guerrilla groups in Latin America, see Julia Sweig, *Inside the Cuban Revolution: Fidel Castro and the Urban Underground*; João Quartim, *Dictatorship and Armed Struggle in Brazil*, trans. by David Fernbach (London: New Left; and Michael Löwy, ed., *Marxism in Latin America from 1909 to the present: An Anthology*.

3. See Anderson, *Imagined Communities*, esp. 15–16; and William French, "Imagining and the Cultural History of Nineteenth-Century Mexico."

4. See for example Eugene Stockwell, "Uruguay: Do We Subsidize Repression?" *Christianity and Crisis*, October 2, 1972, 211, NACLA, reel 6.

5. Taglioretti, *Women and Work*, 18.

6. Marighella's and Guillén's ideas of urban guerrilla warfare were very similar. However, Guillén looked primarily to Uruguay while Marighella focused on Brazil. See Carlos Marighella, *Minimanual of the Urban Guerrilla*.

7. Abraham Guillén, *Philosophy of the Urban Guerrilla*, 8.

8. Abraham Guillén, *Estrategia de la guerrilla urbana: Principios básicos de guerra revolucionaria*.

9. Guillén, *Philosophy of the Urban Guerrilla*, 6.

10. The Fidelistas, inspired by Fidel Castro's strategies in the Cuban Revolution, hoped to incite revolution by using guerrilla warfare tactics in the countryside. They planned to use rural tactics even in Uruguay, which had a primarily urban population.

11. Guillén, *Estrategia de la guerrilla urbana*, 17.

12. Abraham Guillén, "El pueblo en armas: Estrategia revolucionaria" (Montevideo: unpublished m.s., 1972), 35.

13. Abraham Guillén, *Desafío al pentagono*, 149.

14. Guillén, *Estrategia de la guerrilla urbana*, 81–82.

15. See Guillén, *Desafío al pentagono*, esp. chapter 3.

16. Guillén, "El pueblo en armas," 47.

17. Guillén, *Philosophy of the Urban Guerrilla*, 26.

18. "Tiny West German Group Vows to Overthrow State," *New York Times* (*NYT*), June 17, 1970, 7.

19. *L.A. Times*, April 25, 1975, 6.

20. See for example "Honkies Hunt Hunderground," *UPS News Service* 3, no. 7 (March 31, 1972); and "German Guerrillas Strike," *UPS News Service* 2, no. 24 (December 10, 1971), Marshall Bloom Papers.

21. Red Army Faction, "Serve the People," in *The Red Army Faction, A Documentary History: Projectiles for the People*, ed. J. Smith and André Moncourt, 157.

22. "Eight Greeks Are Put on Trial Charged with Being Urban Guerrillas," *NYT*, August 4, 1972, 3.

23. "The Voice of Palestine: Call to Revolution," *L.A. Times*, November 19, 1972, D9.
24. *Uruguay: The Tupamaros in Action*, 52, NACLA, reel 4.
25. Keith Reader, *Régis Debray: A Critical Introduction*, 6.
26. Reader, *Debray*, 8–10.
27. Reader, *Debray*, 15.
28. Quoted in Castañeda, *Utopia Unarmed*, 79.
29. Movimiento de Liberación Nacional (MLN-T), *Los Tupamaros en acción relatos testimoniales de los guerrilleros*; prólogo de Regis Debray, 7.
30. MLN-T, *Los Tupamaros en acción*, 13.
31. MLN-T, *Los Tupamaros en acción*, 19.
32. *LNS*, no. 471 (October 11, 1972), Marshall Bloom Papers.
33. The idea that the Tupamaros employed a nonhierarchal revolutionary model proved patently false. For a fuller discussion, see Chapters 2 and 5.
34. MLN-T, *Los Tupamaros en acción*, 28.
35. MLN-T, *Los Tupamaros en acción*, 30–31. See also Robert J. Alexander, *A History of Organized Labor in Uruguay and Paraguay*.
36. Other practitioners or urban guerrilla warfare such as Marighella agreed with the notion of an alliance with the people. See the chapter "Popular Support" in *Minimanual of the Urban Guerrilla*.
37. Guillén, *Philosophy of the Urban Guerrilla*, 272.
38. MLN-T, *Los Tupamaros en acción*, 17.
39. "Text of the FBI Affidavit Charging Four in University of Wisconsin Bombing," *NYT*, September 3, 1970, 25.
40. "Political Kidnapping Plot Tied to White Panthers," *NYT*, March 17, 1971, 51.
41. Robert Brainard Pearsall, ed., *The Symbionese Liberation Army: Documents and Communications*, 10.
42. Pearsall, *The Symbionese Liberation Army*, 32.
43. Spelling America with a *k* reinforced the Weather Underground's solidarity with people of color, as the *k* represented a critique of America's racist past and present. The *k* indicted American society for the Ku Klux Klan, and also conjured images of the swastika and skinheads. For both the Weather Underground and the Black Panther Party, this *k* disavowed the nation for its current policy as well as its past ills.
44. "A Radical 'Declaration' Warns of an Attack by Weathermen," *NYT*, May 25, 1970, 27
45. "Live Like Them," *New Left Notes*, October 2, 1969, 3, Marshall Bloom Papers.
46. Ellen Hume, "Heavy US Radicals Keep Low Profile," *L.A. Times*, September 24, 1975.
47. For more on the Weather Underground, see Ron Jacobs, *The Way the Wind Blew: A History of the Weather Underground*; and Jeremy Varon, *Bringing the War Home: The Weather Underground, the Red Army Faction and Revolutionary Violence in the Sixties and Seventies*.
48. Robert Cohen, "Tupamaros: A Movement without a Head to Cut Off," *Alternative Features Service*, no. 66 (September 1972): 1, NACLA, reel 4.
49. Cohen, "Tupamaros: A Movement without a Head to Cut Off," 1–2.
50. Uruguay Information Group, *Uruguay News*, no. 1 (April 1, 1979): 19, NACLA, reel 5.
51. See Drew Middleton, "Urban Guerrillas Studied in West," *NYT*, July 30, 1972,

16; Joseph Novitski, "A Strategy of Long, Dangerous Political Warfare," *NYT*, September 12, 1971, E6; Joseph Novitski, "Urban Guerrillas in Uruguay Seem to Have Modified Tactics," *NYT*, July 7, 1971, 6; and "Uruguay Decides to Censor Press," *NYT*, December 7, 1969, 122.

52. Marvine Howe, "South America Drifts Right and the Left Goes Along," *NYT*, February 3, 1974, 177.

53. "Spreading Fad," *L.A. Times*, September 12, 1971, F5.

54. *Chicago Tribune*, September 5, 1972, 20

55. *Chicago Tribune*, May 1, 1972, A3.

56. Claire Sterling, *The Terror Network: The Secret War of International Terrorism*, 18–24.

57. Jon Cleary, *Peter's Pence*, 82.

58. Carlos Wilson, *The Tupamaros: The Unmentionables*, 31. Created in 1961, the Agency for International Development (AID) is a US federal governmental agency that focuses on development and assistance to countries throughout the world. However, critics have charged the organization with helping only to advance military and political allies rather than genuinely attempting to support humanitarian causes. See Ryan, "Turning on their Masters," 282–84.

59. Wilson, *The Tupamaros*, 32.

60. Markarian, *Left in Transformation*, 80.

61. For more on how the US used Latin America as a training ground for later counterinsurgency missions in the Middle East and throughout the world, see Greg Grandin, *Empire's Workshop: Latin America, the United States and the Rise of the New Imperialism*.

62. Wilson, *The Tupamaros*, 9.

63. Labrousse, *The Tupamaros*, 36.

64. The MLN later denounced the "expropriation" of the food. They argued that distributing food for Christmas gave people only "bread for today and hunger for tomorrow." The Tupamaros came to believe that the majority of the population did not benefit from the Christmas Eve action. It was useless to share food with a small number of citizens as expropriations were needed to finance the revolution. Labrousse, *The Tupamaros*, 36

65. "Robin Hood," *Marcha*, May 23, 1969, BNU, 21.

66. *Granma*, April 18, 1971, 11, Marshall Bloom Papers.

67. Servicio Paz y Justicia (SERPAJ), *Uruguay Nunca Más: Human Rights Violations, 1972–1985*, xx.

68. *Granma*, July 19, 1970, 11, Marshall Bloom Papers.

69. "Tupamaros," *UPS News Service* 2, no. 26 (December 24, 1971) Marshall Bloom Papers.

70. *LNS*, no. 266 (June 20, 1970), Marshall Bloom Papers.

71. Ryan, "Turning on Their Masters," 282.

72. A good deal of what we know about Operation Condor comes from the uncovering of the so-called archives of terror in Paraguay in 1992 and 1993. These archives contained thousands of records of kidnapped and disappeared people from many countries in Latin America. For more on the US government's involvement in Southern Cone dictatorships during the 1960s through the 1980s, see J. Patrice McSherry, *Predatory States: Operation Condor and Covert War in Latin America*.

73. Ryan, "Turning on Their Masters," 281–84.
74. *LNS*, no. 266, (June 20, 1970) Marshall Bloom Papers.
75. *Granma*, June 24, 1979, 11, Marshall Bloom Papers.
76. "106 Person Escape," *Chicago Tribune*, September 7, 1971, A7.
77. *LNS*, no. 376 (September 18, 1971), Marshall Bloom Papers.
78. "Free Political Prisoners," *The Red Papers: Women Fight for Liberation*, no. 3 (1970), Bobby Ortiz Papers.
79. "The Tupamaros," *Right On! Revolutionary People's Community Network*, August 1971, Marshall Bloom Papers.
80. *LNS*, no. 370 (August 25, 1971), Marshall Bloom Papers.
81. Labrousse, *The Tupamaros*, 70.
82. "Uruguay Guerrillas Kidnap 3 and Sieze 6 Million in Gems at Bank," *L.A. Times*, November 14, 1970, W5.
83. *LNS*, no. 304 (December 19, 1970), Marshall Bloom Papers.
84. *LNS*, no. 224 (April 1970), Marshall Bloom Papers.
85. *LNS*, no. 233 (February 11, 1970), Marshall Bloom Papers.
86. *LNS*, no. 266 (June 20, 1970), Marshall Bloom Papers.
87. *LNS*, no. 202 (October 11, 1969), Marshall Bloom Papers.
88. "Live Like Them," *New Left Notes*, October 2, 1969, 3, Marshall Bloom Papers.
89. Arrarás, "Armed Struggle," 148; 153–54.
90. *Granma*, October 17, 1971, 6, Marshall Bloom Papers.
91. Labrousse, *The Tupamaros*, 74–76 and *Granma*, January 31, 1971, 8, Marshall Bloom Papers.
92. Chicago Area Group on Latin America (CAGLA), "Tupamaros: From Guerrilla to Mass Based Party" (April/May 1972): 10, NACLA, reel 4.
93. Prudencio Corres, "Tupamaros: Organization and Solidarity" *Prensa Latina Features*, 1971, Marshall Bloom Papers.
94. Cohen, "Tupamaros: A Movement without a Head to Cut Off," 1.
95. Arrarás, "Armed Struggle," 95.
96. Arrarás, "Armed Struggle," 97.
97. In 1968, Guatemalan radicals killed US ambassador John Gordon Mein on the street and later in the year others killed military officials from the US.
98. "Most Foreigners Are Undaunted by Latin Violence," *NYT*, December 2, 1973, 24.
99. "The Tupamaros: 1972 and Beyond," (May/June 1972): 21, NACLA, reel 4.
100. *Prairie Fire* 2, no. 4 (November 17, 1970), Marshall Bloom Papers.
101. "The People's Petition," *Black Panther*, October 23, 1971, Marshall Bloom Papers.
102. *LNS*, no. 279 (August 12, 1970), Marshall Bloom Papers.
103. *LNS*, no. 376 (September 18, 1971), Marshall Bloom Papers.
104. *LNS*, no. 202 (October 11, 1969), Marshall Bloom Papers.
105. *Prairie Fire* 2, no. 4 (November 17, 1970), Marshall Bloom Papers.
106. See Shirley Christian, "Uruguayan Clears Up 'State of Siege' Killing," *NYT*, June 21, 1987, 5.
107. Gene Siskel, "And Look Who Loses," *Chicago Tribune*, May 25, 1973, B1
108. "'Siege' an Angry Muckraker," *NYT*, April 22, 1973, 99.
109. Andrew Sarris, "Films in Focus," *Village Voice*, April 19, 1973, 81.
110. As an agent for the US government agency AID, Mitrione worked in Brazil

before arriving in Uruguay. Ryan, "Turning on Their Masters," 286. For more on the repression in Brazil during the years of the dictatorship, see Martha K. Huggins, "Legacies of Authoritarianism: Brazilian Torturers' and Murderers' Reformulation of Memory," *Latin American Perspectives* 27, no. 2 (March 2000): 57–78; Juan E. Corradi, Patricia Weiss Fagen, and Manuel Antonio Garretón, *Fear at the Edge: State Terror and Resistance in Latin America*; and Paul Drake, *Labor Movements and Dictatorships: The Southern Cone in Comparative Perspective.*

111. "Kennedy Center Drops Disputed Film," *NYT*, March 30, 1973, 33.

112. See for example Richard Glatzer, "'Siege'—Censorship of Art?" *Michigan Daily*, April 19, 1973, 3.

113. Judy Klemesrud, "I'm Not Anti-American," *NYT*, April 22, 1973, 107.

114. Anna Mayo, "The Beekman 538—Or Last Week's Central Event of Our Time," *Village Voice*, April 19, 1973, 81.

115. Andrew Sarris, "Films in Focus," *Village Voice*, April 19, 1973, 82.

116. "McCarthyism from the Left?," *NYT*, May 6, 1973, 155.

117. "State of Siege Speaks a Warning to Us All," *NYT*, June 24, 1973, 117.

118. Sarris, "Films."

119. "Did Sorenson Face Facts?," *NYT*, July 15, 1973, 109

120. Glatzer, "'Siege.'"

121. "Letter to the editor," *NYT*, July 29, 1973, D8.

122. *Guerrilla: The Taking of Patty Hearst*, DVD, directed by Robert Stone (Washington, DC: Public Broadcasting Services, 2004).

123. "Briefs on the Arts," *NYT*, April 19, 1973, 48.

124. OAS, *Report on the Situation*, 60.

125. See Ryan, "Turning on Their Masters," 286.

126. See Manuel Hevia Cosculluela, *Pasaporte 11373: Ocho Anos en la CIA*, 282–87; and A. J. Langguth, *Hidden Terrors: The Truth about US Police Operations in Latin America*, 250–53; 286–87.

127. See Ryan, *Turning on Their Masters*, 282; and Wolfgang Heinz and Hugo Fruhling, *Determinants of Gross Human Rights*, 316–19.

128. Klemesrud, "I'm Not Anti-American."

129. Chicago Area Group on Latin America (CAGLA), "Tupamaros: From Guerrilla to Mass Based Party" (April/May 1972): 1, NACLA, reel 4.

130. Part of this may have derived from the bombardment of anti-Soviet propaganda those in the US constantly viewed growing up during the 1950s. Furthermore, the Soviet Union's invasion of Czechoslovakia also caused many young leftists to see the repressive nature of the Soviet Union and its similarities with the much-maligned US. See Elbaum, *Revolution in the Air*, 48.

131. Elbaum, *Revolution in the Air*, 45.

132. CAGLA, "Tupamaros," 1. While many in the Uruguayan left approved of the Tupamaros' practice of moving toward armed struggle, the PCU rejected most of the strategies of the Tupamaros. See Markarian, *Left in Transformation*, 35.

133. *Prairie Fire 2*, no. 4 (November 17, 1970), Marshall Bloom Papers.

134. Ellen Hume, "Heavy US Radicals Keep Low Profile." *L.A. Times*, September 24, 1975, A1.

135. CAGLA, "Tupamaros," 4.
136. María Esther Gilio, *La Guerrilla Tupamara*, 112–26.
137. Christopher Hewitt, "Terrorism and Public Opinion: A Five Country Comparison," 141.
138. *Granma*, March 9, 1969, 12, Marshall Bloom Papers.
139. Gilio, *La Guerrilla Tupamara*, 117–19; 126.
140. Labrousse, *The Tupamaros*, 113.
141. CAGLA, "Tupamaros," 5.
142. The Montoneros were named after those who fought against the Spanish on horseback. For more, see Paul H. Lewis, *Guerrillas and Generals: The Dirty War in Argentina*.
143. The FSLN was named after Augusto César Sandino, who led the fight against the conservative President Díaz and the intervention of the US during the 1920s and early 1930s, until his death in 1934. The FMLN was named after Farabundo Martí, a important founder of the communist party who led workers and rural peasants in an uprising against the government in 1932. For more, see Cynthia McClintock, *Revolutionary Movements in Latin America: El Salvador's FMLN and Peru's Shining Path*; and Matilde Zimmermann, *Sandinista: Carlos Fonseca and the Nicaraguan Revolution*.
144. Labrousse, *The Tupamaros*, 17.
145. Comité de Informacion Sobre La Represion en Uruguay, "The Uruguayan University and Today's Anti-Uruguay," 1974, NACLA, reel 6.
146. Labrousse, *The Tupamaros*, 149.
147. Labrousse, *The Tupamaros*, 55.
148. Labrousse, *The Tupamaros*, 16.
149. "Preguntas," *Marcha*, February 19, 1971, 10, BNU.
150. Ehrick, *The Shield of the Weak*, 39. For more on the Tupamaros and the influence of anarchist thought concerning sexuality and marriage, see chapter 5.
151. "Preguntas," 10.
152. Labrousse, *The Tupamaros*, 145.
153. MLN-T, *Los Tupamaros en acción*, 24.
154. Markarian, *Left in Transformation*, 35.
155. Guillén, *Philosophy*, 272–76.
156. CAGLA, "The Tupamaros," 5–7.
157. Castañeda, *Utopia Unarmed*, 69.
158. Castañeda, *Utopia Unarmed*, 16.
159. Weinstein, *Uruguay*, 2.
160. Silvia Soler, *La Leyenda de Yessie Macchi*, 81.
161. *Tupamaros*, DVD, directed by Heidi Specogna and Rainer Hoffman (New York: First Run/Icarus Films, 1996).
162. *Prairie Fire*, 2, no. 4 (November 17, 1970), Marshall Bloom Papers.
163. Núñez, "The Tupamaros," 29.
164. MLN-T, "La Carta de los presos y otros documentos" (Montevideo: MLN-T, 1985), BNU.
165. *Tupamaros* DVD, 1996.
166. Socialist International, "Resolution on the International Situation," June 24, 1969, SPA Papers.

167. Socialist International, "Meeting of the Bureau of the Socialist International," December 20, 1969, SPA Papers.
168. Irwin Swall, "Bombings and Terrorism as a Political Tactic," 1971, SPA Papers.
169. Stockwell, "Uruguay," 212.
170. Audre Lorde, *Sister Outsider: Essays and Speeches*, 112.
171. Wilson, *The Tupamaros*, 44.
172. *Guerrilla*, no. 19 (March 1971), Marshall Bloom Papers.
173. OAS, *Report on the Situation*, 60.
174. Wilson, *The Tupamaros*, 55.
175. Labrousse, *The Tupamaros*, 126. See also Stephen Gregory, *Intellectuals and Left Politics in Uruguay, 1958-2006*.
176. CAGLA, "The Tupamaros," 17.
177. Sonia Pacheco Agraz, "Like a Fish in the Water," *Granma*, June 6, 1971, 11, Marshall Bloom Papers.
178. Markarian, *Left in Transformation*, 6.

CHAPTER 2

The epigraph is from Guillén, *Philosophy of the Urban Guerrilla*, vii.
1. Markarian, *Left in Transformation*, 35. For more on the complexities of the Uruguayan left, see Eduardo Rey Tristan, *La Izquierda Revolucionaria Uruguaya: 1955-1973*.
2. Arrarás, "Armed Struggle," 85.
3. For more on the Black Panther Party and Black Power, see Kate Quinn, *The Politics of Black Power in the Anglophone Caribbean*; Paul Alkebulan, *Survival Pending Revolution: The History of the Black Panther Party*; and Curtis Austin, *Up Against the Wall: Violence in the Making and Unmaking of the Black Panther Party*.
4. "Poder Negro," *Cuadernos of Marcha*, no. 12 (April 1968), CEDINCI. In turn, the Uruguayan left knew that US radicals especially looked to the Tupamaros for both revolutionary motivation and in order to mimic their successful tactics. *Marcha* featured quotes from the US left "thanking" the guerrilla fighters of Uruguay. See for example "USA no es excepción," *Marcha*, August 21, 1970, BNU.
5. Labrousse, *The Tupamaros*, 7.
6. See for example "Angela Davis y la guerrilla urbana en Estados Unidos," *Marcha*, second section, November 20, 1970, 4, BNU; James Petras, "Estado Unidos: El preludio de una lucha politica armada: Especial para Marcha," *Marcha*, May 22, 1970, 19, BNU; Stokely Carmichael, "Las falacias el liberalismo," *Marcha*, February 28, 1969, 16, BNU; "La guerra genocida en Vietnam," *Marcha*, January 5, 1973, 23, BNU; and *Marcha*, January 8, 1971, 18, BNU. *Marcha* editor Carlos Quijano admired the Tupamaros but overall did not support their methods, particularly kidnapping. He advocated socialism but called for "the people" to make true changes in society. Quijano did not completely reject violence but argued that every legal possibility should be used before direct violent action occurred. See Markarian, *Left in Transformation*,59.
7. In the 1960s, support from *Marcha* was integral to the founding of the Frente Amplio. Markarian, *Left in Transformation*, 40.
8. Araújo, *Tupamaras*, 211.

9. See for example "Testimonio apasionate," *Marcha*, November 6, 1970, 3, BNU; Eldridge Cleaver, "Una nacion surgia de la brutalidad," *Marcha*, February 9, 1973, 16–17, BNU; George Jackson, "Las cartas de George Jackson," *Marcha*, second section, October 22, 1971, 14–15, BNU; "El asesinato de George Jackson," *Marcha*, September 4, 1971, 24–25, BNU; and "La respuesta de los negros," *Marcha*, January 24, 1969, 24, BNU.

10. Guillén, *Philosophy of the Urban Guerrilla*, vi–viii. See also Eduardo Galeano, *Open Veins of Latin America: Five Centuries of the Pillage of a Continent* (New York: Monthly Review Press, 1973).

11. By the late 1960s, the press and the left in Uruguay had few freedoms. See Gould, "Solidarity under Siege," 354. Despite the government closure of leftist presses in the Uruguay during the late 1960s, *Marcha* continued to critique the repressive Uruguayan state. The government closed down *Marcha* in 1974. Quijano began publishing the newspaper again from exile in Mexico 1977.

12. Markarian, *Left in Transformation*, 57.

13. Sacvan Bercovitch, *The Rites of Assent: Transformations in the Symbolic Construction of America*, 20.

14. "Preguntas," *Marcha*, February 19, 1971, 10, BNU.

15. Uruguay News Group, "Supplement," February 1978, NACLA, reel 5.

16. Noel Ignatin, "Which Side Are You On? US History in Perspective," in *Students for a Democratic Society (SDS) Papers*.

17. Ignatin, "Which Side Are You On?"

18. "Poder Negro," 1–2; and Pat Conaway, "Confessions of a White Revolutionary," *Students for a Democratic Society (SDS) Papers*.

19. Guillén, *Philosophy of the Urban Guerrilla*, vi.

20. In *Open Veins of Latin America*, Uruguayan writer and activist Eduardo Galeano also explores the notion of the "internal" and "external proletariat" in Latin America and the US.

21. Guillén, *Philosophy of the Urban Guerrilla*, 293.

22. Guillén, *Philosophy of the Urban Guerrilla*, vii–viii.

23. James Petras, "Estado Unidos: El preludio de una lucha politica armada: Especial para Marcha," *Marcha*, May 22, 1970, 19, BNU.

24. See for example "Angela Davis y la guerrilla urbana en Estados Unidos," *Marcha*, second section, November 20, 1970, 4, BNU; *Marcha*, June 18, 1971, 19, BNU; and "Estados Unidos: Opinan los jóvenes," *Marcha*, December 24, 1970, 23, BNU.

25. *Marcha*, June 18, 19, 1971, BNU. See also "Estados Unidos" and "Los Yanquis en Camboya," *Marcha*, May 8, 1970, 5, BNU.

26. "Angela Davis y la guerrilla urbana," 4.

27. For their leftist supporters in Uruguay, the fact that six people on the FBI's Most Wanted list came from militant revolutionary groups showed the might and pervasiveness of subversive groups in the US.

28. "Angela Davis y la guerrilla urbana," 4.

29. James Petras, "Estado Unidos: El preludio de una lucha politica armada: Especial para Marcha" *Marcha*, May 22, 1970, 19, BNU.

30. For more on the US involvement in Cambodia, see "Los Yanquis en Camboya" *Marcha*, May 8, 1970, 5, BNU.

31. "Estados Unidos: Opinan los jovenes," *Marcha*, December 24, 1970, 23, BNU.

32. *Marcha*, January 8, 1971, 18, BNU.
33. "La hermana Angela," *Marcha*, June 9, 1972, 21, BNU. In the 1970s, Davis became embroiled in a campaign for prisoners' rights and focused on the defense of Fleeta Drumgo, John Clutchette, and George Jackson, also known as the Soledad Brothers. Upset that his brother was imprisoned, Jonathan Jackson brought guns into a California courtroom and with the help of three prisoners took the district attorney, the judge, and members of the jury hostage. Later some of the hostages died in a shootout with San Quentin guards. Though Davis was not in Northern California during the shooting, the guns used in the crime were registered under her name. See Joy James, ed., *The Angela Y. Davis Reader*. See also "Salvar a Angela Davis," *Marcha*, November 12, 1971, 7, BNU; "El hombre se creía juez," *Marcha*, second section, September 4, 1970, 4–5, BNU; and "Yo vi a Angela Davis en la prison," *Marcha*, second section, November 19, 1971, 19, BNU.
34. "La hermana Angela," *Marcha*, June 9, 1972, 21, BNU.
35. For example, "Salvar a Angela Davis" *Marcha*, November 12, 1971, 7, BNU; "El hombre se creía juez, *Marcha*, second section, September 4, 1970, 4–5, BNU.
36. *Angela Davis Reader*, 11. For more on COINTELPRO, see David Cunningham. "The Patterning of Repression: FBI Counterintelligence and the New Left," *Social Forces* 81 (September 2003): 212.
37. "Yo vi a Angela Davis en la prison," *Marcha*, second section, November 19, 1971, 19, BNU.
38. Todd Gitlin, *The Sixties: Years of Hope, Days of Rage*, 386.
39. Elmer Geronimo Pratt, "The New American Urban Guerrilla," *BLA: Third World Edition* 7, no. 3, 1973, Marshall Bloom Papers.
40. Susan Stern, *With the Weathermen*, 144.
41. Alice Echols, *Daring to Be Bad: Radical Feminism in America, 1967–75*, 132.
42. Echols, *Daring to Be Bad*, 126.
43. "Angela Davis y la guerrilla urbana," 4.
44. *Marcha*, January 22, 1971, BNU.
45. See for example Guillén, *The Philosophy of the Urban Guerrilla*, vi–vii.
46. *Granma*, April 9, 1967, 11, Marshall Bloom Papers.
47. For examples of criticisms of Rockefeller in the Uruguayan press see, "Rockefeller: Responsible del la matanza," *Marcha*, September 29, 1972, BNU; "Los Rockefeller en America Latina," *Marcha*, September 12, 1969, BNU; "Porque y para que la misión Rockefeller," *Marcha*, April 3, 1970, BNU. There was also an entire issue of *Cuadernos de Marcha* devoted to the politician's report, "El Informe Rockefeller," *Cuadernos de Marcha*, no. 33 (January 1970), CEDINCI.
48. For more, see Nelson A. Rockefeller, *The Rockefeller Report on the Americas: The Official Report of a US Presidential Mission for the Western Hemisphere*, New York Times ed. (Chicago: Quadrangle Books, 1969).
49. For more about Rockefeller's involvement in other Latin American countries, see Darlene Rivas, *Missionary Capitalist: Nelson Rockefeller in Venezuela*.
50. "Uruguay Riot Greets Rocky," *Chicago Tribune*, June 22, 1969, 1.
51. *Uruguay: The Tupamaros in Action*, 56.
52. Arrarás, "Armed Struggle," 147.
53. Labrousse, *The Tupamaros*, 147.

54. For example, *Marcha* reviewed a Spanish translation of Eldridge Cleaver's work *Soul on Ice* and deemed it the most ardent and passionate work of 1970 concerning African American activism. See Cristina Peri Rossi, "Testimonio Apasionate," *Marcha*, November 6, 1970, 3, BNU.

55. Eldridge Cleaver, "Una nacion surgia de la brutalidad," *Marcha*, February 9, 1973, 16–17, BNU; George Jackson, "Las cartas de George Jackson," *Marcha*, second section, October 22, 1971, 14–15, BNU; and Rap Brown, "Revienta negro podrido, revienta," second section, *Marcha*, July 3, 1970, 2–4, BNU. Eldridge Cleaver served as minister of information for the BPP and authored the popular work *Soul on Ice*. Rap Brown was chairman of the civil rights organization Student Non-violent Coordinating Committee (SNCC) and served as justice minister of the BPP. George Jackson, a convicted felon, became a communist and member of the BPP while in prison. For more, see Eric Cummins, *The Rise and Fall of California's Radical Prison Movement*.

56. "El asesinato de George Jackson," *Marcha*, September 4, 1971, 24–25 BNU. On August 21, 1971, three days before his trial Jackson was shot by a San Quentin prison guard during an alleged escape attempt. However, some claimed that a weapon was planted in Jackson's cell, while others have argued that there was no weapon at all.

57. "La respuesta de los Negros," *Marcha*, January 24, 1969, 24, BNU.

58. "Primer desertor o ultimo patriota?," *Marcha*, November 5, 1971, 12, BNU.

59. James Westheider, *The Vietnam War*, 175.

60. "Primer desertor," 12.

61. For example, a letter to the editor of *Marcha* linked the recruitment of individuals for the war in Vietnam to issues of racism. See "Reclutamiento de Uruguayos," *Marcha*, November 21, 1969, 3, BNU.

62. Markarian, *Left in Transformation*, 36.

63. Stokely Carmichael, "Las falacias del liberalismo," *Marcha*, February 28, 1969, 16, BNU.

64. Gilio, *La Guerrilla Tupamara*, 112–26.

65. Markarian, *Left in Transformation*, 58.

66. OAS, *Report on the Situation*, 60.

67. "Poder Negro," *Cuadernos de Marcha*, no. 12 (April 1968), CEDINCI.

68. The Black Panthers themselves claimed to derive strength from what they saw as a long history that began in Africa. See Judith Newton, *From Panthers to Promise Keepers: Rethinking the Men's Movement*, 57.

69. "Poder Negro," 20–21.

70. "Poder Negro," 2.

71. "Poder Negro," 17.

72. "Poder Negro," 22.

73. Romero Jorge Rodríguez, "The Afro Populations of America's Southern Cone: Organization, Development, and Culture in Argentina, Bolivia, Paraguay and Uruguay," 323.

74. US Library of Congress, "Education," *countrystudies.us/uruguay/42.htm*. As recently as the early 2000s, according to a study by the Uruguayan Organizacion Mundo Afro (OMA), 89.6 percent of Afro-Uruguayan women worked in the service sector, with half in domestic service. Only one-half of one percent of Afro-Uruguayan women received higher education or worked

in managerial positions. Of the educated, nearly half remained unemployed or occupied jobs for which they were overqualified. See Gabriela Malviasio "Black Women in Uruguay: Ethnic Differences," *Women's Health Journal* (January–March 2004).

75. "Poder Negro," 1.

76. The only recorded attempt of the Afro-Uruguayan population to construct a political party solely on the basis of ethnic interests was the Partido Autóctono Negro (PAN), founded in Montevideo in 1936. PAN attempted to fight labor discrimination against Afro-Uruguayans and promote their electoral participation and representation. However, the group had no electoral success. See Rodríguez, "Afro Populations of America's Southern Cone," 324.

77. Alejandrina da Luz, "Uruguay," 342. See also George Reid Andrews, *Blackness in the White Nation: A History of Afro-Uruguay*.

78. Rodríguez, "Afro Populations of America's Southern Cone," 314–15.

79. One of the most well-known organizations to promote Afro-Uruguayan culture and societal acceptance is Mundo Africa, founded in 1988.

80. "Preguntas," *Marcha*, February 19, 1971, 10, BNU.

81. See Bordaberry letter to Kenneth Golby, February 12, 1975, NACLA, reel 5.

82. See for more on racism in Cuba and Brazil, see Ada Ferrer, *Insurgent Cuba: Race, Nation and Revolution, 1868–1898*; Alejandro de la Fuente, *A Nation for All: Race, Inequality, and Politics in Twentieth Century Cuba;* Edward Telles, *Race in Another America: The Significance of Skin Color in Brazil;* and Charles Hamilton, ed., *Beyond Racism: Race and Inequality in Brazil, South Africa, and the United States.*

83. Rodríguez, "Afro Populations of America's Southern Cone," 325.

84. Elbaum, *Revolution in the Air*, 67. See also Jennifer B. Smith, *An International History of the Black Panther Party.*

85. *Black Panther*, July 4, 1970, Marshall Bloom Papers.

86. *Black Panther*, September 6, 1970, Marshall Bloom Papers.

87. *Right On! Black Community Newsletter*, no. 12, February 15, 1972, Marshall Bloom Papers.

88. *The Black Panther*, June 14, 1969, Marshall Bloom Papers.

89. "Apoyo," *Marcha*, May 9, 1969, 2, BNU.

90. Center for Cuban Studies, "Daniel Viglietti: Canciones para mi America," Bobbye Ortiz Papers.

91. Barbara Dane, ed., "Cancion Protesta: Protest Songs of Latin America," New York, 1970, Bobbye Ortiz Papers.

92. For more on "Duerme Negrito," see Samina Hadi-Tabassum, *Language, Space and Power: A Critical Look at Bilingual Education*, 260–65.

93. "Daniel Viglietti," 6.

94. For more on the AIM, see Paul Chaat Smith and Robert Allen Warrior, *Like a Hurricane: the Indian Movement from Alcatraz to Wounded Knee.*

95. "El Despertar de los Indios," *Marcha*, April 6, 1973, 16–17 BNU.

96. "Entrevista," *Marcha*, June 11, 1971, 25, BNU.

97. See for example Sir Geoffrey Jackson, *Surviving the Long Night: An Autobiographical Account of a Political Kidnapping;* and *Dialogue before Death* (Washington, DC: Squirrel, 1971), NACLA, reel 4.

98. Roger Ebert, "Zabriskie Point," *Chicago Sun Times*, January 1, 1970.

99. *Dialogue before Death*, 15–16. For more on other US films that inspired the gendered worldview of the Tupamaros, see Chapter 5.

100. *Prairie Fire* 2 no. 4, November 17, 1970, Marshall Bloom Papers.

101. Movimiento de Liberación Nacional (MLN-T), "Documentos y antecedentes: Documento No. 5," December 1970, BNU.

102. Jackson, Surviving the Long Night, 125.

103. Elbaum, *Revolution in the Air*, 36. The Tupamaros could have learned about the pro-violence Rap Brown from *Marcha*, which translated and published part of his work about Black Power. See for example Rap Brown, "Revienta negro podrido, revienta," *Marcha*, second section, July 3, 1970, 2–4, BNU.

104. Jackson, *Surviving the Long Night*, 134–35.

105. Jackson, *Surviving the Long Night*, 138–-39.

106. See for example "Estados Unidos en la mira de la locura," *Presencia* 1, no. 3 (April 1981), CEDINCI; "Poder Negro," 22; and "Yo vi a Angela Davis en la prison," *Marcha*, second section, November 19, 1971, 19, BNU.

107. "Estados Unidos en la mira de la locura."

108. "Yo vi a Angela Davis en la prison, 19."

109. My translation, the original reads, "Otros . . . Si nacen Negros y en Estados Unidos . . . son matados como perros." IdeaVlariño, "Agradecimiento," *Marcha*, May 10, 1968, 30, BNU.

110. *LNS*, no. 281, August 19, 1970, Marshall Bloom Papers.

111. Labrousse, *The Tupamaros*, 15.

112. See Joseph, "Close Encounters," 15.

113. Luz, "Uruguay," 342.

114. *Dialogue Before Death*, 17.

115. *Marcha*, June 24, 1971, 23, BNU.

116. In *Colonialism Past and Present: Reading and Writing about Colonial Latin America Today*, Alvaro Félix Bolaños and Gustavo Verdesio argue that Latin Americans of European descent at times identify with an indigenous past for political purposes.

117. For example, in the black power issue of *Cuadernos de Marcha*, the Uruguayan left aligned with the Third World.

118. Center for Cuban Studies, "Daniel Viglietti: Canciones para mi America," Bobbye Ortiz Papers.

119. *Palante* 2, no. 16 (December 11, 1970), Marshall Bloom Papers.

120. "Latin American Vanguard: The Tupamaros," *Palante* 2, no. 2, May 8, 1970, Marshall Bloom Papers.

121. "Vietnam y el conflicto racial," *Marcha*, September 4, 1970, 19, BNU.

122. *Granma*, May 30, 1971, 12, Marshall Bloom Papers.

123. "Create Two, Three Many Vietnams," *Granma*, April 9, 1972, 5, Marshall Bloom Papers.

124. For more on this phenomenon within Europe, see Reinhold Wagnleitner, *Coca-Colonization and the Cold War: The Cultural Mission of the United States in Austria after the Second World War*.

125. *Granma*, March 21, 1971, 10, Marshall Bloom Papers.

126. Núñez, "The Tupamaros," 48.

127. Republica Oriental Del Uruguay: Ministerio Del Interior, *7 meses de lucha*

antisubversiva: Acción del estado frenta a la sedicion desde el 1 de Marzo al 30 de Septiembre de 1972 (Montevideo: 1972), 289.

128. *7 meses de lucha*, 250; 246; 273.
129. Gould, "Solidarity under Siege," 354–57.
130. James Petras, "Los Estados Unidos en 1971: Especial para *Marcha*," *Marcha*, January 21, 1972, 22, BNU.
131. "EE.UU: 16 condenas aun solo Pantera Negra," *Marcha*, December 5, 1969, 2–3, BNU.
132. Ryan, "Turning on Their Masters," 281; and Petras, "Los Estados Unidos en 1971," 22.
133. See OAS, *Report on the Situation*, 60.
134. "Estados Unidos: El preludo de una lucha politica armada."
135. Gould, "Solidarity under Siege," 354–57.

CHAPTER 3

The epigraph is from Grupo de Apoyo a la Resistencia Uruguay (GARU), *Banda Oriental*, no. 4 (January 1975), NACLA, reel 1.

1. Stockwell, "Uruguay," 213.
2. Amnesty International, "Uruguay Campaign," December 1975, NACLA, reel 5.
3. Uruguay News Group, *Uruguay News*, no. 1, April 1, 1977, NACLA, reel 5.
4. Amnesty International, "Uruguay Campaign," November 1975, NACLA, reel 5.
5. Within Latin America, the commission also condemned Argentina, Bolivia, and Paraguay.
6. Labrousse, *The Tupamaros*, 153.
7. Alan Riding, "For Freed Leftists in Uruguay, Hidden Terrors," *NYT*, March 7, 1985.
8. Markarian, *Left in Transformation*, 2.
9. It is important to note that in the 1970s, the idea of "human rights" was still considered a radical idea.
10. See for example GARU, *Banda Oriental*, no. 1 (September 1974), NACLA, reel 1; GARU, *Banda Oriental*, no. 3 (December 1974), NACLA, reel 1; GARU, *Banda Oriental*, no. 4 (January 1975), NACLA, reel 1; GARU, *Banda Oriental*, no. 5 (April 1975), NACLA, reel 1; CLAMOR, *Human Rights in Uruguay*, no. 10 (August 1980), NACLA, reel 6; Uruguay Information Group, *Uruguay News* (August 1979), NACLA, reel 5; CAGLA, "Uruguay: Special Elections Issue," (November 1974), NACLA, reel 3; and Uruguay News Group, *Uruguay News* (January 1978), NACLA, reel 5.
11. For more about the experience of leftist Uruguayan exiles during the dictatorship, see Markarian, *Left in Transformation*, esp. chapter 3.
12. See for example Uruguayan Association against Racism and Apartheid, "The Policy of Co-Operation with the South African Regime in Uruguay," Date Unknown, NACLA, reel 4.
13. Letter to Bobbye Ortiz from Yvelise Macchi, August 30, 1984, Bobbye Ortiz Papers.
14. "Uruguay Informations: Pour l'isolement de la dictadura en uruguayenne," 1977, NACLA, reel 2.

15. See, Committee in Solidarity with the Uruguayan People (CSUP), *Uruguay Newsletter* vol. 2, no. 1 (January 1981), NACLA, reel 6.

16. CSUP, *Uruguay Newsletter*, 1, no. 2 (June 1979), NACLA, reel 6.

17. CSUP, *Uruguay Newsletter* 2. See also the front page of all of issues published by Grupo Uruguayo de Informacion (Uruguay Information Group), "Noticias Del Uruguay News," 1970s–1985, NACLA, reel 5.

18. Committee for the Defense of Human Rights in Uruguay (CDHRU), *Newsletter*, no. 17 (October 1976): 16, NACLA, reel 5.

19. CSUP, Uruguay Newsletter" 1, no. 5 (August 1980): 5, NACLA, reel 6.

20. For more on the CDU, see Edy Kaufman, "The Role of Political Parties in the Redemocratization of Uruguay," in *Repression, Exile and Democracy: Uruguayan Culture*, ed. Louise B. Popkin and Saúl Sosnowski (Durham: Duke University Press, 1993), 37.

21. CDHRU, *Objectives*, no. 17 (October 1976): 17, NACLA, reel 5. The group originated to continue the work started by the Committee for the Defense of Political Prisoners in Uruguay (CDPPU).

22. Letter from Kenneth Golby to Juan María Bordaberry, January 23, 1975, NACLA, reel 5.

23. One method activists used to critique human rights violations in Uruguay was comparing the country's prisons to Nazi concentration camps. An article entitled "Los campos de concentracio de la dictadura Uruguaya" ("The Concentration Camps of the Uruguayan Dictatorship") argues that as a percentage of the population, there were more political prisoners in Uruguay than in Hitler's Germany. Thus, activists grouped the regime with Nazi Germany in order to stress the extreme ways human rights had been violated in the country. See "Los Campos de Concentracio de la Dictadura Uruguaya," *De Frente*, no. 8, Date Unknown, 18–19, NACLA, reel 6.

24. Golby to Bordaberry.

25. Letter from Juan María Bordaberry to Kenneth Golby, February 12, 1975. NACLA, reel 5.

26. Bordaberry to Golby.

27. See Wilson, *The Tupamaros*, 33.

28. Bordaberry to Golby.

29. Rodríguez, "Afro Populations of America's Southern Cone," 325.

30. Markarian, *Left in Transformation*, 78.

31. Letter from Zelmar Michelini to Kenneth Golby, March 24, 1975, NACLA, reel 5.

32. Markarian, *Left in Transformation*, 38.

33. Michelini to Golby.

34. CDHRU, "The Situation," 12–15.

35. Michelini to Golby.

36. Markarian, *Left in Transformation*, 76–81.

37. Louise Popkin established international solidarity with Uruguayan activists after spending a sabbatical year in Buenos Aires. After learning that a friend was jailed because of her ties with the Tupamaros, Popkin wanted to help uncover the brutal mistreatment of Uruguayan political prisoners. Popkin was put in contact with Michelini and tried to arrange his journey to

Washington, DC. She also translated and disseminated Michelini's writings to US organizations concerned with human rights. See Markarian, *Left in Transformation*, 79.

38. Uruguay Information Group, *Uruguay News*, August 1979, 1, NACLA, reel 5.

39. Uruguay Information Group, *Uruguay News*, 5.

40. Uruguay Information Group, *Uruguay News*, 15.

41. CAGLA, "Uruguay: Special Elections Issue," November 1974, 28, NACLA, reel 3.

42. Lucy Komisar, "Junta Leaves a Fiscal Trap in Uruguay," *Chicago Tribune*, September 15, 1983, B1.

43. Uruguay News Group, *Uruguay News*, January 1978, 5, NACLA, reel 5.

44. *Granma*, September 3, 1978, 11, Marshall Bloom Papers.

45. New York Circus, *Uruguay: An Imprisoned Democracy*, no. 3 (197[?]): 13, NACLA, reel 6.

46. Uruguayan Association against Racism and Apartheid (UAARA), "The Policy of Co-Operation with the South African Regime in Uruguay," date unknown, NACLA, reel 4.

47. UAARA, "The Policy," 2–6.

48. UAARA, "The Policy," 12.

49. UAARA, "The Policy," 23. For more on the relationship between Uruguay and South Africa, see Penny Lernoux, "Apartheid Sails West: White Africans in Latin America," *Nation*, September 23, 1978.

50. Letter from Yvelise Macchi to Bobbye Ortiz, August 30, 1984, Bobbye Ortiz Papers.

51. In this instance, I use Nancy Cott's broad and classic definition of feminism, which uses three criteria: a belief in sexual equality, a belief that women's roles are socially constructed, and the support for women as a distinct social grouping. See Nancy Cott, *The Grounding of Modern Feminism*, 4–5.

52. Wire statement, Plenary Session, New York Women's Studies Association, April 27–29, 1984, Bobbye Ortiz Papers.

53. Wire statement.

54. For example: Helen Safa, *Women, Production, and Reproduction in Industrial Capitalism: A Comparison of Brazilian and US Factory Workers* (1979); Lourdes Casal, *Revolution and Conciencia: Women in Cuba* (1980); and Patricia Howell Aguilar and Eugenia Piza, *The Double Workday of Poor Women in Costa Rica* (1982). WIRE also compiled speeches, poetry, and eyewitness testimony such as *Women and War: El Salvador and Nicaraguan Women and the Revolution*.

55. WIRE pamphlet.

56. The problem of articulating "experience" has been debated within the field of Latin American history, particularly in the controversy surrounding Rigoberta Menchú's memoir, *I, Rigoberta Menchú*, which was awarded the Nobel Peace Prize. In these debates, scholars questioned the "truth" of Menchú's recollection of her experiences in Guatemala. For more on the controversy surrounding Menchú, see Arturo Arias, ed., *The Rigoberta Menchú Controversy.* See also Joan Scott, "The Evidence of Experience," *Critical Inquiry* 17, no. 4 (Summer 1991): 773–97; and Chandra Talpade

Mohanty, "Feminist Encounters: Locating the Politics of Experience" in *Destabilizing Theory: Contemporary Feminist Debates*, 74–93.

57. Ideas about "global sisterhood" are explored in Robin Morgan, ed., *Sisterhood Is Global: The International Women's Movement Anthology;* and Angela Rose Miles, *Integrative Feminisms: Building Global Visions 1960s–1990s.*

58. Macchi to Ortiz.

59. NACLA, *Latin America and Empire Report* 5, no. 10 (December 1972): 1.

60. See for example Comité de Información Sobre la Represión en Uruguay, "Uruguay; los rehenes del fascismo," 197[?], NACLA, reel 6.

61. For a fuller discussion about male dominated leadership in the Tupamaros, see Chapter 5.

62. Comité de Información Sobre la Represión en Uruguay, "Uruguay," 15.

63. GARU, *Banda Oriental*, no. 1 (September 1974), NACLA, reel 1. See also the Toronto-based Committee for the Defense of Human Rights in Uruguay (CDHRU), *Objectives*, no. 17 (October 1976), NACLA, reel 5.

64. GARU, *Banda Oriental*, no. 2 (October/November 1974): 14, NACLA, reel 1.

65. GARU, *Banda Oriental*, no. 3 (December 1974): 3–5, NACLA, reel 1.

66. GARU, *Banda Oriental*, 2.

67. GARU, *Banda Oriental*, no. 2 (October/November 1974): 7–8, NACLA, reel 1.

68. CLAMOR, *Human Rights in Uruguay*, no. 10 (August 1980): 8, NACLA, reel 6.

69. *Granma*, September 19, 1976, Marshall Bloom Papers.

70. "The Tragedy of Female Political Prisoners," *Granma*, October 2, 1977, 11, Marshall Bloom Papers.

71. *Granma*, September 26, 1976, 11, Marshall Bloom Papers.

72. *Granma*, December 9, 1973, 12, Marshall Bloom Papers.

73. Macchi to Ortiz.

74. Fabián Werner, "Entrevista a Yessie Macchi: Hacía años que yo no hablaba," *Montevideo Comm*, March 2, 2009, *www.montevideo.com.uy/notnoticias_76979_1.html/.*

75. Macchi to Ortiz.

76. For more, see Michelle Bonner, *Sustaining Human Rights: Women and Argentine Human Rights Organizations* (University Park: Pennsylvania State University Press, 2007).

77. Macchi to Ortiz.

78. Soler, *La Leyenda*, 12.

79. Soler, *La Leyenda*, 69.

80. Most political prisoners had been released in the years leading up to the end of the dictatorship. See Alan Riding, "For Freed Leftists in Uruguay, Hidden Terrors," *NYT*, March 7, 1985.

81. *LNS*, no. 465, September 13, 1972, Marshall Bloom Papers.

82. *La Cacerola* 2, no. 4 (May 1985): 1, CEDINCI.

83. SERPAJ, *Uruguay nunca más*, xx.

84. *La Cacerola* 1, no. 1 (1984): 3, CEDINCI. While the "casserole" represented subversion during the dictatorship, according to GRECMU, Uruguayan society also thought the casserole or domestic work to have a "natural" association with women. GRECMU's members hoped to move beyond confining notions of femininity by redefining the casserole not as a symbol of subordination but as an emblem of liberation.

85. The group's first office opened in Mexico in 1975.
86. La Tribuna/La Cacerola, *Mujer y Coinciencia*, 4.
87. La Tribuna/La Cacerola, *Mujer y Coinciencia*, 16–17.
88. La Tribuna/La Cacerola, *Mujer y Coinciencia*, 43.

CHAPTER 4

The epigraph is my translation. The original reads, "Une femme n'est aussi egale a un homme que lorsqu'elle a un P 45 en main." Araújo, *Tupamaras*, 146. Araújo's edited transcription of interviews is the only source uncovered that features several Tupamaras speaking specifically about feminism and gender issues. While there are obvious weaknesses and limitations to this source, I corroborate much of the information with other sources.

1. Jackson, *Surviving the Long Night*, 28.
2. Ibid., 39.
3. See for example "La Montevideana ante los cambios sociales," *Marcha*, July 10, 1970, BNU. By the 1980s, feminism showed diversity in adherents and ideology and moved away from so-called western feminism. These activists used the terms "Third World feminism" and "black feminism" in order to describe new aspects in feminist thought. Though "Third World feminism" has often been critiqued for its implicit reinforcement of the supposed supremacy of the West, in her book *Loving in the War Years: Lo que nunca pasó por sus labios*, 119–23, feminist Cherríe Moraga defined Third World feminism as a global feminism that understands the racialized and sexualized "simultaneity of oppression." Black feminism and its critique of white, Western feminism also influenced the creation of a Third World feminist movement. See also Chila Bulbeck, *One World Women's Movement*. For more, see Chela Sandoval, *Methodology of the Oppressed*; Chandra Mohanty, *Third World Women and the Politics of Feminism*; Gloria E. Anzaldúa and Cherríe Moraga, eds., *This Bridge Called My Back: Writings by Radical Women of Color*; and Gloria Anzaldúa and Analouise Keating, eds., *This Bridge We Call Home: Radical Visions for Transformation*.
4. "State of Siege," Unidad Latina 3, no. 5, (July 14–30, 1973), Marshall Bloom Papers.
5. *Uruguay: The Tupamaros in Action*, 60.
6. Arturo C. Porzecanski, *Uruguay's Tupamaros: The Urban Guerrilla*, 31.
7. Wilson, *The Tupamaros*, 85.
8. Labrousse, *The Tupamaros*, 43.
9. MLN-T, *Los Tupamaros*, 57.
10. Wilson, *The Tupamaros*, 85.
11. In their critique of feminine drudgery in the home and of mothers, the MLN-T differed from other groups in Latin America, such as the Asociación Madres de Plaza de Mayo (Mothers of the Plaza de Mayo) in Argentina and the Sandinistas in Nicaragua, who invoked women's "natural" instincts as mothers to inspire them to participate in politics. For more on issues of motherhood and activism in Latin America, see Marguerite Guzman Bovard, *Revolutionizing Motherhood: The Mothers of the Plaza de Mayo*; Ulises Gorini, *La rebelión de las madres: Historia de las Madres de Plaza de Mayo* (Buenos Aires: Grupo Editorial Norma, 2006); Marjorie Agosin,

ed., *Surviving beyond Fear: Women, Children and Human Rights in Latin America.*

12. Lorraine Bayard de Volo, *Mothers of Heroes and Martyrs: Gender Identity Politics in Nicaragua, 1979-1999*, 16.

13. Bayard de Volo, *Mothers of Heroes*, 15.

14. Bayard de Volo, *Mothers of Heroes*, 41.

15. Bayard de Volo, *Mothers of Heroes*, 42

16. Guillén, *Philosophy of the Urban Guerrilla*, 71.

17. Wilson, *The Tupamaros*, 86.

18. Margaret Gonzalez-Perez, "Guerrilleras in Latin America: Domestic and International Roles," 318-19. See also Jane S. Jaquette, "Women in Revolutionary Movements in Latin America," 351; and Linda Reif, "Women in Latin American Guerrilla Movements." Considering that in 1966, women made up less than 10 percent of the group, the rhetoric of equality likely encouraged women to join the organization. The considerable change in the number of female combatants also demonstrates willingness on the part of Tupamaro members to recruit women and make their participation a significant part of their movement.

19. "La Montevideana ante los cambios sociales," *Marcha*, July 10, 1970, BNU.

20. Wilson, *The Tupamaros*, 85.

21. Robert E. Biles, "Women and Political Participation in Latin America: Urban Uruguay and Colombia," Working Paper No. 25, Michigan State University, Latin American Studies Association (LASA) Conference, Washington, DC, March 4-6, 1982.

22. See for example Frente Amplio, "Analicemos Juntas Las Medidas de Gobierno Del Frente Amplio para la Mujer y el Niño," 1971, NACLA, reel 4.

23. Araújo, *Tupamaras*, 223-24.

24. See SERPAJ, *Uruguay nunca más*, 327-34.

25. Maxine Molyneux, *Women's Movements in International Perspective* (London: Palgrave Press, 2001), 159.

26. Karen Kampwirth, *Women and Guerrilla Movements: Nicaragua, El Salvador, Chiapas, Cuba*, 14.

27. Kampwirth, *Women and Guerrilla Movements*, 32.

28. Kampwirth, *Women and Guerrilla Movements*, 22.

29. Kampwirth, *Women and Guerrilla Movements*, 43.

30. See SERPAJ, *Uruguay nunca más*, 335.

31. See for example "La Montevideana ante los cambios sociales," *Marcha*, July 10, 1970, BNU.

32. SERPAJ, *Uruguay nunca más*, 106.

33. "Women and Revolution in Latin America," *World University Service*, no. 1 (Summer 1979), Bobbye Ortiz Papers.

34. *Marcha*, April 16, 1971, 5, BNU.

35. "La Montevideana ante los Cambios Sociales," *Marcha*, July 10, 1970, BNU. After his death, the Uruguayan left made Arce into a symbol of the struggle against the ever-worsening dictatorship.

36. The Uruguayan government's perception of the Movimiento Femenino proved to be similar to the Argentine government's notions about the Mothers of the Plaza de Mayo, as both had difficulty determining how to respond to the

protests of female activists. Like the Movimiento Femenino, the Mothers of the Plaza de Mayo were mostly middle-aged housewives who denounced military values of obedience and hierarchy and instead advocated pacifism and cooperation. See Marguerite Guzman Bovard, *Revolutionizing Motherhood*, 1.

37. "La Montevideana ante los Cambios Sociales," 22.
38. "Marcha del la Mujer Uruguaya," *Marcha*, May 25, 1972, 13, BNU.
39. Laura Duhan Kaplan, "Feminism and Peace Theory: Women as Nurturers US Women as Public Citizens," in *In the Interest of Peace*, ed. Kenneth Kunkel and Joseph Klein (Wakefield, NH: Hollowbrook, 1990), 253.
40. "Marcha del la Mujer Uruguaya," 13.
41. "Protesta Femenina," *Marcha*, June 2, 1972, BNU.
42. "Del Comité Femenino Del Frente Izquierda," *Marcha*, January 7, 1972, BNU.
43. "No Entregarnos al Extranjero," *Marcha*, December 19, 1969, BNU.
44. See for example Frente Amplio, "Mujer Uruguaya," 1971, NACLA, reel 4.
45. Frente Amplio, "Analicemos Juntas Las Medidas de Gobierno Del Frente Amplio para la Mujer y el Niño," 1971, NACLA, reel 4.
46. Frente Amplio, "Analicemos Juntas."
47. "Frente Amplio," *Cuadernos de Marcha*, no. 46 (February 1971): 21, CEDINCI.
48. Frente Amplio, "Analicemos Juntas."
49. See Carina Perelli, "Putting Conservatism to Good Use: Women and Unorthodox Politics in Uruguay from Breakdown to Transition," 99.
50. Comisión de Mujeres Uruguayas (CMU), "Mujer y Política," June 1986, CEDINCI.
51. Perelli, "Putting Conservatism to Good Use," 109.
52. Molyneux, *Women's Movements*, 145.
53. Molyneux, *Women's Movements*, 151.
54. Karen Offen, *European Feminisms, 1700–1950: A Political History*, 21–22. See also María Luisa Femenías and Amy A. Oliver, eds., *Feminist Philosophy in Latin America and Spain*; and Jane Jaquette, ed., *Feminist Agendas and Democracy in Latin America*.
55. Perelli, "Putting Conservatism to Good Use," 99.
56. The Uruguayan government imprisoned Viglietti in 1972, but released the singer a few months later, in part because of an international campaign to free him. Viglietti had many well-known supporters, including Jean Paul Sartre, who signed petitions for his freedom. Center for Cuban Studies, "Daniel Viglietti: Canciones para mi America," Bobbye Ortiz Papers.
57. Araújo, *Tupamaras*, 149
58. Center for Cuban Studies, "Daniel Viglietti."
59. See Jackson, *Surviving the Long Night*.
60. See for example Jackson, *Surviving the Long Night, part 4: Mind, Men and Women*.
61. See for example Araújo, Tupamaras.
62. Jackson, *Surviving the Long Night*, 159–67.
63. Jackson, *Surviving the Long Night*, 76–77.
64. Jackson, *Surviving the Long Night*, 136.
65. Jackson, *Surviving the Long Night*, 141.
66. Jackson, *Surviving the Long Night*, 141.
67. Jackson, *Surviving the Long Night*, 77–78.

68. Sonia Pacheco Agraz, "Like a Fish in the Water," *Granma*, June 6, 1971, 11, Marshall Bloom Papers.

69. Araújo, *Tupamaras*, 125.

70. Comite de Informacion Sobre La Represion en Uruguay, "The Uruguayan University and Today's Anti-Uruguay," 1974, NACLA, reel 6.

71. Araújo, *Tupamaras*, 137.

72. Araújo, *Tupamaras*, 146; 245.

73. Rodríguez, *Women, Guerrillas and Love*, 50.

74. Arrarás, "Armed Struggle," 92.

75. MLN-T, *Los Tupamaros*, 58–59.

76. Nita Samuniski, e-mail message to the author, April 20, 2009.

77. Araújo, *Tupamaras*, 162–63; 223; 200.

78. Labrousse, *The Tupamaros*, 43.

79. In actuality, women's organizing has produced many unique permutations in Latin America. For more on Latin American feminism(s), see Karen Kampwirth and Victoria Gonzalez, eds., *Radical Women in Latin America: Left and Right*; Marysa Navarro-Aranguren et al., "Feminisms in Latin America: From Bogota to San Bernadino,"; Sonia Alvarez et al., "Encountering Latin American and Caribbean Feminisms"; June Nash and Helen Safa, *Women and Change in Latin America*; Lorraine Bayard de Volo, *Mothers of Heroes and Martyrs: Gender Identity Politics in Nicaragua 1979–1990*; Karen Kampwirth, *Feminism and the Legacy of Revolution: Nicaragua, El Salvador, Chiapas*; Maxine Molyneux, *Women's Movements in International Perspective*; Julie D. Shayne, *Feminisms in El Salvador, Chile and Cuba*.

80. Araújo, *Tupamaras*, 197; 169.

81. Echols, *Daring to Be Bad*, 120.

82. See for example "La Montevideana ante los cambios sociales," *Marcha*, July 10, 1970. BNU.

83. Araújo, *Tupamaras*, 177.

84. Araújo, *Tupamaras*, 216. The phenomenon of romanticizing the blonde revolutionary also occurred in Brazil after the release of the film Bonnie and Clyde. In 1968, in Brazil there emerged a plethora of sexualized images of militant women, particularly after a bank robbery that was linked to Carlos Marighella and a blonde woman named Silvia. See Langland, "Birth Control Pills and Molotov Cocktails." See also Hilary Neroni, *The Violent Woman: Femininity, Violence and Narrative in Contemporary American Cinema*.

85. Araújo, *Tupamaras*, 216. For more on cultural influences of the US on Latin America during the Cold War, see Jean Franco, *The Decline and Fall of the Lettered City: Latin America in the Cold War* (Cambridge, MA: Harvard University Press, 2002).

86. *Dialogue Before Death*, 9.

87. Araújo, *Tupamaras*, 217. For more on James Bond as a cultural and philosophical influence, see James B. South and Jacob M. Held, eds., *James Bond and Philosophy*.

88. "La Montevideana ante los cambios sociales," *Marcha*, July 10, 1970, BNU.

89. For more on Alba Roballo, see Guillermo Chifflet, *Alba Roballo: Pregon por el tiempo Nuevo* (Montevideo: Ediciones TAE, 1992).

90. See also "La Montevideana ante los cambios sociales," 11.
91. See Elmer Geronimo Pratt, "The New American Urban Guerrilla." BLA: *Third World Edition* 7, no. 3 (1973), Marshall Bloom Papers. Though the description is somewhat positive, in this aforementioned article, Pratt refers to militant women as "Amazons."
92. Gilda Zwerman, "Participation in Underground Organizations: Conservative and Feminist Images of Women Associated with Armed, Clandestine Organizations in the United States," 136–37.
93. Zwerman, "Participation," 137.
94. Araújo, *Tupamaras*, 217.
95. Saldaña-Portillo, *The Revolutionary Imagination*, 78.
96. The Weather Underground, "Honky Tonk Women," 383–84.
97. See Jane Macafee and Myrna Wood, "Bread and Roses," 417.
98. "Jóvenes: entre la violencia y la sociedad ideal," *Marcha*, June 13, 1969, 12, BNU. See also Araújo, *Tupamaras*, 224.
99. Che also advocated for asceticism for revolutionaries. Ilena Rodríguez argues that Che's guerrilla subject used, "the terminology of protestant personal repression." See Ileana Rodríguez, *Women, Guerrillas, and Love*, 44.
100. Jackson, *Surviving the Long Night*, 169.
101. Ehrick, *Shield of the Weak*, 40. For more on sexual mores within the left during Southern Cone dictatorships, see Langland, "Birth Control Pills and Molotov Cocktails," 308–49.
102. "Jóvenes, 12."
103. Araújo, *Tupamaras*, 224; 192.
104. Versions of the Trotsky-oriented PST existed in other countries such as Argentina, Peru, Colombia, Mexico, and the United States. For more, see Jorge Alonso, *La tendencia al enmascaramiento de los movimientos politicos: El caso del Partido Socialista de los Trabajadores.*
105. Partido Socialista de los Trabajadores (PST), *Mujeres en Movimiento*, June 1983, CEDINCI.
106. PST, *Mujeres en Movimiento*, 1.
107. PST, *Mujeres en Movimiento*, 40.
108. PST, *Mujeres en Movimiento*, 41. For more on issues of forced sterilization in Latin America, see Nancy Leys Stepan, *The Hour of Eugenics: Race, Gender and Nation in Latin America*, 102–34.
109. *La Cacerola* 2, no. 5 (October 1985): 1–2, CEDINCI.
110. *La Cacerola*, 3.
111. SERPAJ, *Uruguay nunca más*, 12.
112. Alan Riding, "For Freed Leftists in Uruguay, Hidden Terrors," *NYT*, March 7, 1985.
113. SERPAJ, *Uruguay nunca más*, 12.
114. Araújo, *Tupamaras*, 233.
115. SERPAJ, *Uruguay nunca más*, 99.
116. OAS, *Report on the Situation*, 38.
117. SERPAJ, *Uruguay nunca más*, 16; 101.
118. See Araújo, *Tupamaras*, 164.
119. Araújo, *Tupamaras*, 163; 200.

120. Ximena Bunster-Burotto, "Surviving beyond Fear: Women and Torture in Latin America," in *Women and Change in Latin America*, ed. June Nash and Helen Safa (South Hadley, MA: Bergin and Garvey, 1986), 276.

121. In her work *Myths of Modernity: Peonage and Patriarchy in Nicaragua*, Elizabeth Dore argues that patriarchy and not merely capitalism provided the organizing principle for Nicaragua's economic system during the late nineteenth and early twentieth centuries. For more on how issues of patriarchy influence politics and the economy and vice versa, see also Patty Kelly, *Lydia Open Door: Inside Mexico's Most Modern Brothel*.

122. Bunster-Burotto, "Surviving beyond Fear," 276.

123. "Mujeres Uruguayas Víctimas Del Fascismo," Bobbye Ortiz Papers.

124. "Mujeres Uruguayas."

125. *Granma*, November 21, 1976, 11, Marshall Bloom Papers.

126. Bunster-Burotto, "Surviving beyond Fear," 283. For a literary account of torture in Uruguay based on factual research, see Carlos Moreno, *El infierno*.

127. Araújo, *Tupamaras*, 125.

128. Arrarás, "Political Participation," 103–4; 168.

129. *Granma*, January 24, 1971, Marshall Bloom Papers.

130. Araújo, *Tupamaras*, 180.

131. "Free Political Prisoners," *The Red Papers: Women Fight for Liberation*, no. 3, 1970, Bobbye Ortiz Papers.

132. Araújo, *Tupamaras*, 146–47.

133. MLN-T, *Tres Evasiones de Tupamaros: Operaciones Estrella Abuso Gallo* (Santiago: Prensa Latinoamericana, 1973), 36.

134. SERPAJ, *Uruguay nunca más*, 121.

135. My translation; the original reads, "El homosexualismo crea a diario problemas de todo tipos." "Cárceles: Más allá de los muros," *Marcha*, July 2, 1971, 11, BNU. For more about same sexual desire in prison in Latin America, see Chris Girman, *Mucho Macho: Seduction, Desire and the Homoerotic Lives of Latin Men*; Pablo Piccato, "'Such a Strong Need': Sexuality and Violence in Belem Prison,"; Carlos Aguirre, *The Criminals of Lima and their Worlds: The Prison Experience, 1850–1935*; and Jacobo Schifter, *Macho Love: Sex behind Bars in Central America*.

136. "Cárceles: Más allá de los muros," *Marcha*, July 2, 1971, 11, BNU.

137. "Prision y fueros," *Marcha*, January 12, 1973, 11, BNU.

138. SERPAJ, *Uruguay nunca más*, 106; 150; 159.

139. Jean Franco, "Gender, Death and Resistance: Facing the Ethical Vacuum," 109. Both male and female Jewish prisoners also received particular humiliation and ire from guards, who repeated anti-Semitic statements to those prisoners. See SERPAJ, *Uruguay nunca más*, 101.

140. Franco, "Gender, Death and Resistance," 108–9.

141. Araújo, *Tupamaras*, 224.

142. CSUP, "Uruguay Newsletter," vol. 1, no. 2 (October 1979), NACLA, reel 6.

143. Ettore Pierri and Luciana Possamay, eds., *Hablan los otros* (Montevideo: Proyección, 1987), 24. For another look at issues of homosexual repression in Uruguay and the rest of the Southern Cone, see Carlos Basilio Muñoz, *Uruguay homosexual: Culturas, minorías y discriminación desde una*

sociología de la homosexualidad; and James Green, *Beyond Carnival: Male Homosexuality in 20th Century Brazil.*

144. Pierri and Possamay, *Hablan los otros,* 23–24.

145. Pierri and Possamay, *Hablan los otros,* 16.

146. Pierri and Possamay, *Hablan los otros,* 20–21.

147. Pierri and Possamay, *Hablan los otros,* 61.

148. See for example Margaret Randall, *Our Voices, Our Lives: Stories of Women from Central America and the Caribbean.* As a US feminist and expatriate living in Latin America between 1960 and 1984, Margaret Randall moved from romantic representations of the Nicaraguan and Cuban revolutions to a critique of the sexism and homophobia within socialism. Nevertheless, she argued that the idea of equality in socialist movements enabled and inadvertently supported a space for the subversion of traditional ideologies concerning gender and sexual identity.

CONCLUSION

The epigraph is from Carlos Núñez, "The Tupamaros," 29.

1. Similar to Vania Markarian on the Uruguayan left, Astrid Arrarás has posited that another reason the MLN-T eventually accepted democratic ideas and institutions was the transnational connections its members forged while in exile. While in exile, Tupamaros had access to new ideas, media, and interactions with nonviolent leftist groups. These transnational connections and exchanges helped many in the Tupamaros reevaluate their beliefs about the political expediency of violence. Furthermore, the Tupamaros embraced democracy also because it offered a better alternative to the previous repressive dictatorship. Thus, Arrarás also suggests that the trauma Tupamaro members experienced under the dictatorship and their large rates of incarceration challenged group members to rethink previous ideologies and tactics. See Arrarás, "Armed Struggle," 23–24.

2. At the end of the dictatorships during the 1980s and 1990s, guerrilla groups throughout the Southern Cone turned to electoral politics, though with less success than the Tupamaros. In Brazil, members of the Ação de Libertacio Nacional joined other leftist political organizations; the former Argentine Montoneros became the "Peronismo Revolucionario" within the Peronist movement; previous members of the Movimiento de Izquierda Revolucionario (MIR) in Chile joined a "refurbished" section of the Socialist party. See Charles Gillespie, *Negotiating Democracy: Politicians and General in Uruguay,* 232.

3. Larry Luxner, "Uruguay Is the Latest South American Country to Veer Left," *Uruguayan-American Chamber of Commerce in the USA,* December 2004, *www.uruguaychamber.com/press_15.php/.*

4. Jorge Castañeda, "Latin America's Left Turn," *Foreign Affairs,* May/June 2006, *www.foreignaffairs.com/articles/61702/jorge-g-castaneda/latin-americas-left-turn/.*

5. Andres Stapff, "Former Guerrilla Leader Elected President in Uruguay," *USA Today,* November 29, 2009, *www.usatoday.com/news/world/2009-11-29-uruguay-elects-new-president_N.htm/.*

6. Ernesto "Che" Guevara, *Guerrilla Warfare,* 213.

7. Labrousse, *The Tupamaros*, 145.
8. Labrousse, *The Tupamaros*, 20.
9. Ehrick, *Shield of the Weak*, 6.
10. Francisco Panizza, "Late Institutionalization and Early Modernisation: The Emergence of Uruguay's Liberal Democratic Political Order," *Journal of Latin American Studies* 29 (October 1997): 667–91. See also Fernando López-Alves, *Between the Economy and the Polity in the River Plate: Uruguay 1811–1890;* Fernando López-Alves and David Rock, "State Building and Political Systems in Nineteenth Century Argentina and Uruguay," 177–202.
11. Arrarás, "Armed Struggle," 23–24.
12. Richard Gillespie, "The Urban Guerrilla in Latin America," in *Terrorism, Ideology and Revolution*, ed. Noel O' Sullivan (Sussex: Harvester Press, 1986), 38.
13. *The Tupamaros: Urban Guerrilla Warfare in Uruguay* (New York: Liberation Guardian, 1970), 29. NACLA, reel 4.
14. "Uruguay Approves Gay Civil Unions," *BBC News*, December 19, 2007, *news. bbc.co.uk/2/hi/americas/7151669.stm*
15. "Former guerilla fighter Mujica wins Uruguay's presidential election," *Telegraph*, November 30, 2009, *www.telegraph.co.uk/news/worldnews/ southamerica/uruguay/6687767/Former-guerrilla-fighter-Mujica-wins-Uruguays-presidential-election.html/.*
16. "The Tupamaro Guerrilla," *Liberation News Service*, no. 384 (October 20, 1971): 11, NACLA, reel 4.
17. Luxner, "Uruguay Is the Latest South American Country to Veer Left."
18. Kevin Gray, "Ex-guerrilla Fighter Mujica to Rule Uruguay," *Reuters*, November 30, 2009, *www.reuters.com/article/idUSN3042521220091130/.*
19. See for example Michael Fox, "Uruguay's Frente Amplio: From Revolution to Dilution," *Upside Down World*, June 26, 2007, *upsidedownworld.org/main/ uruguay-archives-48/788-uruguays-frente-amplio-from-revolution-to-dilution/.*
20. Núñez, "The Tupamaros," 32.
21. Guevara, *Guerrilla Warfare*, 209. In contrast, in his *Minimanual of the Urban Guerrilla*, Carlos Marighella focuses specifically on urban guerrilla warfare and the liberation of Brazil.
22. See for example Jerry Davila, "A Brazilian Exiled in Angola: Maria do Carmo Brito, 1976–77," (Paper presented at the annual meeting of the American Historical Association, San Diego, California, January 9, 2010).
23. Some scholars have already initiated the important research. See for example Jean Rodrigues Sales, "O impacto da revolução cubana sobre as organizações comunistas brasileiras (1959–1974)."
24. See Greg Grandin's *Empire's Workshop: Latin America, the United States and the Rise of the New Imperialism;* and Grandin, *The Last Colonial Massacre: Latin America in the Cold War* for works that include race in the examination of the Latin American left and the Cold War.
25. Florencia E. Mallon, "The Promise and Dilemma of Subaltern Studies: Perspectives from Latin American History."
26. Paulo Coelho, *The Devil and Miss Prym*, 9.

References

ARCHIVAL SOURCES

Biblioteca Nacional, Montevideo, Uruguay (BNU)

Bobbye Ortiz Papers, Sallie Bingham Center for Women's History and Culture in the David M. Rubenstein Rare Book and Manuscript Library, Duke University, Durham, North Carolina (Bobbye Ortiz Papers)

Centro de Documentación e Investigación de la Cultura de Izquierdas, Buenos Aires, Argentina (CEDINCI)

Marshall Bloom Alternative Press Collection, 1967–2002, Archives and Special Collections, Amherst College Library, Amherst, Massachusetts (Marshall Bloom Papers)

Socialist Party of America Papers, Chicago and New York, Rare Book, Manuscript and Special Collections Library, Duke University, Durham, North Carolina (SPA Papers)

Uruguay Papers, North American Congress on Latin America, Archive of Latin Americana (NACLA)

PRINTED SOURCES

Acosta-Belén, Edna, and Christine E. Bose. "US Latina and Latin American Feminisms: Hemispheric Encounters." *Signs: A Journal of Women in Culture and Society* 25, no. 4 (2000): 1113–19.

Aguirre, Carlos. *The Criminals of Lima and their Worlds: The Prison Experience, 1850–1935*. Durham: Duke University Press, 2005.

Agosín, Marjorie, ed. *Surviving beyond Fear: Women, Children and Human Rights in Latin America*. Fredonia, NY: White Pine, 1993.

Alexander, Robert J. *A History of Organized Labor in Uruguay and Paraguay*. Westport, CT: Praeger, 2005.

Alkebulan, Paul. *Survival Pending Revolution: The History of the Black Panther Party*. Tuscaloosa: University of Alabama Press, 2007.

Alonso, Jorge. *La tendencia al en mascaramiento de los movimientos políticos: El caso del Partido Socialista de los Trabajadores*. Mexico City: Centro de Investigaciones y Estudios Superiores en Antropología Social, 1985.

Alvarez, Sonia, et al. "Encountering Latin American and Caribbean Feminisms." *Signs: A Journal of Women in Culture and Society* 28, no. 2 (2003): 538–79.

———. "Translating the Global." *Meridians: Feminism, Race, Transnationalism* 1, no. 1 (Middletown, CT: Wesleyan University Press, 2000): 29–67.

American Commission of Human Rights. *Report on the Situation of Human Rights in Uruguay*. Organization of American States: Washington, DC, 1978.

Anderson, Benedict. *Imagined Communities: Reflections on the Origins and Spread of Nationalism*. New York: Verso, 1983.

Andrews, George Reid. *Blackness in the White Nation: A History of Afro-Uruguay*. Chapel Hill: University of North Carolina Press, 2010.

Anzaldúa, Gloria, and Analouise Keating, eds. *This Bridge We Call Home: Radical Visions for Transformation*. New York: Routledge, 2002.

Anzaldúa, Gloria, and Cherríe Moraga, eds. *This Bridge Called My Back: Writings by Radical Women of Color*. New York: Kitchen Table, Women of Color Press, 1983.

Araújo, Ana María. *Tupamaras: Des femmes de l'Uruguay*. Paris: Des Femmes, 1980.

Arenas, Reinaldo. *Before Night Falls: A Memoir*. New York: Penguin, 2000.

Arias, Arturo, ed. *The Rigoberta Menchú Controversy*. Minneapolis: University of Minnesota Press, 2001.

Arrarás, Astrid. "Armed Struggle, Political Learning, and Participation in Democracy: The Case of the Tupamaros in Uruguay." PhD diss., Princeton University, 1998.

Austin, Curtis. *Up against the Wall: Violence in the Making and Unmaking of the Black Panther Party*. Fayetteville: University of Arkansas Press, 2006.

Bacchetta, Victor. *El asesinato de Areblio Ramírez: La República a la deriva*. Montevideo: Doble clic Editores, 2010.

Barahona de Brito, Alexandra. *Human Rights and Democratization in Latin America: Uruguay and Chile*. Oxford: Oxford University Press, 1997.

Bayard de Volo, Lorraine. *Mothers of Heroes and Martyrs: Gender Identity Politics in Nicaragua 1979—1990*. Baltimore: Johns Hopkins University Press, 2001.

Bolaños, Alvaro Félix, and Gustavo Verdesio. *Colonialism Past and Present: Reading and Writing about Colonial Latin America Today*. New York: State University of New York Press, 2001.

Bonner, Michelle. *Sustaining Human Rights: Women and Argentine Human Rights Organizations*. University Park: Pennsylvania State University Press, 2007.

Bovard, Marguerite Guzman. *Revolutionizing Motherhood: The Mothers of the Plaza de Mayo*. Wilmington, DE: Scholarly Resources, 1994.

Bejel, Emilio. *Gay Cuban Nation*. Chicago: University of Chicago Press, 2001.

Bercovitch, Sacvan. *The Rites of Assent: Transformations in the Symbolic Construction of America*. New York: Routledge, 1993.

Berger, Henry, ed. *A William Appleman Williams Reader: Selections from his Major Historical Writings*. Chicago: I. R. Dee, 1992.

Biles, Robert E. "Women and Political Participation in Latin America: Urban Uruguay and Colombia." Working Paper No. 25, Michigan State University, Latin American Studies Association (LASA) Conference, Washington, DC, March 4–6, 1982.

Brown, Timothy, ed. *When the AK-47s Fall Silent: Revolutionaries, Guerrillas, and the Dangers of Peace*. Stanford, CA: Hoover Institution Press, 2000.

Bulbeck, Chila. *One World Women's Movement*. London: Pluto, 1988.

Bunster-Burotto, Ximena. "Surviving beyond Fear: Women and Torture in Latin America." In *Women and Change in Latin America*, edited by June Nash and Helen Safa, 297–325. South Hadley, MA: Bergin and Garvey, 1986.

Butler, Judith. *Gender Trouble: Feminism and the Subversion of Identity*. New York: Routledge, 1990.

———. "Imitation and Gender Subordination." In *The Lesbian and Gay Studies*

Reader, edited by Henry Abelove, Michele Aina Barale, and David M. Halperin. New York: Routlege, 1993.

———. "Performative Acts and Gender Constitution: An Essay in Phenomenology and Feminist Theory." In *Performing Feminisms: Feminist Critical Theory and Theatre*, edited by Sue-Ellen Case, 270–82. Baltimore: Johns Hopkins University Press, 1990.

Castañeda, Jorge. *Utopia Unarmed: The Latin American Left after the Cold War.* New York: Alfred A. Knopf, 1993.

Caulfield, Sueann. "The History of Gender in the Historiography of Latin America." *Hispanic American Historical Review* 81, no. 3–4 (August–November 2001): 449–90.

Chowdhury, Najma, and Barbara J. Nelson, eds. *Women and Politics Worldwide.* New Haven: Yale University Press, 1994.

Chifflet, Guillermo. *Alba Roballo: Pregon por el tiempo nuevo.* Montevideo: Ediciones TAE, 1992.

Cleary, Jon. *Peter's Pence.* New York: William Morrow, 1974.

Coelho, Paulo. *The Devil and Miss Prym.* Translated by Amanda Hopkinson and Nick Caistor. London: Harper Collins, 2000.

Conseulluela, Manuel Hevia. *Pasaporte 11373: Ocho años en la CIA.* Havana: Editoral de las Ciencias Sociales, 1978.

Corradi, Juan, Patricia Weiss Fagen, and Manuel Antonio Garretón, eds. *Fear at the Edge: State Terror and Resistance in Latin America.* Berkeley: University of California Press, 1992.

Costabilde, Daniel, and Alfredo Errandonea. *Sindicato y sociedad en el Uruguay.* Montevideo: Biblioteca de Cultura Universitaria, 1969.

Cott, Nancy. *The Grounding of Modern Feminism.* New Haven, CT: Yale University Press, 1987.

Cummins, Eric. *The Rise and Fall of California's Radical Prison Movement.* Stanford, CA: Stanford University Press, 1994.

D' Emilio, John. "Capitalism and Gay Identity." In *Powers of Desire: The Politics of Sexuality*, edited by Ann Snitow, Christine Stansell, Sharon Thompson, 100–113. New York: Monthly Review Press, 1983.

Dore, Elizabeth. *Myths of Modernity: Peonage and Patriarchy in Nicaragua.* Durham: Duke University Press, 2006.

Drake, Paul. *Labor Movements and Dictatorships: The Southern Cone in Comparative Perspective.* Baltimore: Johns Hopkins University Press, 1996.

Echols, Alice. *Daring to Be Bad: Radical Feminism in America, 1967–1975.* Minneapolis: University of Minnesota Press, 1989.

Ehrick, Christine. *The Shield of the Weak: Feminism and the State in Uruguay, 1903–1933.* Albuquerque: University of New Mexico Press, 2005.

Elbaum, Max. *Revolution in the Air: Sixties Radicals Turn to Lenin, Mao and Che.* New York: Verso, 2002.

Endy, Christopher. *Cold War Holidays: American Tourism in France.* Chapel Hill: University of North Carolina Press, 2004.

Enríquez, Laura. *Agrarian Reform and Class Consciousness in Nicaragua.* Gainesville: University of Florida Press, 1997.

Evans, Sara. *Personal Politics: The Roots of Women's Liberation in the Civil Rights Movement and the New Left.* New York: Knopf, 1979.

Fabregat, Julio. *Elecciones Uruguayas.* Vol. 4. Montevideo: Cámara de Senadores del Uruguay, 1964.

Farber, Samuel. *The Origins of the Cuban Revolution Reconsidered.* Chapel Hill: University of North Carolina Press, 2006.

Femenías, María Luisa, and Amy Oliver, eds. *Feminist Philosophy in Latin America and Spain.* Amsterdam: Rodopi, 2007.

Ferrer, Ada. *Insurgent Cuba: Race, Nation, and Revolution, 1868–1898.* Chapel Hill: University of North Carolina Press, 1999.

Finch, M. H. J. *An Economic History of Uruguay since 1870.* New York: St. Martin's, 1981.

Fitzgibbon, R. H. *Uruguay: Portrait of a Democracy.* New Brunswick, NJ: Rutgers University Press, 1954.

Fortuna, Carlos, Nelly Niedworok, and Adela Pellegrino. *Uruguay y la emigracion de los 70.* Montevideo: CIEU/EBO, 1988.

Franco, Jean. *The Decline and Fall of the Lettered City: Latin America in the Cold War.* Cambridge, MA: Harvard University Press, 2002.

———. "Gender, Death and Resistance: Facing the Ethical Vacuum." In *Fear at the Edge: State Terror and Resistance in Latin America*, edited by Juan Corradi, Patricia Weiss Fagen, Manuel Antonio Garretón, 104–20. Berkeley: University of California Press, 1992.

French, William. "Imagining and the Cultural History of Nineteenth-Century Mexico." *Hispanic American Historical Review* 79, no. 2 (May 1999): 249–67.

Fruhling, Hugo and Wolfgang Heinz. *Determinants of Gross Human Rights: Violations by State and State-Sponsored Actors in Brazil, Uruguay, Chile, and Argentina, 1960–1990.* International Studies in Human Rights, 59. Cambridge, MA: M. Nijhoff, 1999.

Fuente, Alejandro de la. *A Nation for All: Race, Inequality, and Politics in Twentieth Century Cuba.* Chapel Hill: University of North Carolina Press, 2001.

Gaddis, John Lewis. *The Cold War: A New History.* New York: Penguin, 2005.

———. *The United States and the Origins of the Cold War, 1941–1947.* New York: Columbia University Press, 1972.

———. *We Now Know: Rethinking Cold War History.* New York: Oxford University Press, 1997.

Gambone, Michael. *Capturing the Revolution: The United States, Central America and Nicaragua, 1961–1972.* Westport, CT: Praeger, 2001.

Galeano, Eduardo. *El asesinato de Arbelio Ramírez.* Montevideo: Comite de Intelectuales y Artistas de Apoyo a Cuba, 1961.

———. *Open Veins of Latin America: Five Centuries of the Pillage of a Continent.* New York: Monthly Review Press, 1973.

Gerstle, Gary. *American Crucible: Race and Nation in the 20th Century.* Princeton: Princeton University Press, 2001.

Gilio, María Esther. *La guerrilla Tupamara.* Havana: Casa de las Americas, 1970.

Gillespie, Charles. *Negotiating Democracy: Politicians and Generals in Uruguay.* New York: Cambridge University Press, 1991.

Gilligan, Carol. *In a Different Voice: Psychological Theory and Women's Development.* Cambridge, MA: Harvard University Press, 1982.

Girman, Chris. *Mucho Macho: Seduction, Desire and the Homoerotic Lives of Latin Men.* New York: Harrington Park, 2004.

Gitlin, Todd. *The Sixties: Years of Hope, Days of Rage.* Toronto: Bantam, 1987.

Gobat, Michel. *Confronting the American Dream: Nicaragua under US Imperial Rule.* Durham: Duke University Press, 2005.

Gonzales, Michael. *The Mexican Revolution, 1910–1940.* Albuquerque: University of New Mexico Press, 2002.

Gonzalez, Luis Eduardo. *Political Structures and Democracy in Uruguay.* Notre Dame: University of Notre Dame Press, 1991.

Gonzalez, Victoria, and Karen Kampwirth, eds. *Radical Women in Latin America: Left and Right.* University Park: Pennsylvania State University, 2001.

Gonzalez-Perez, Margaret. "Guerrilleras in Latin America: Domestic and International Roles." *Journal of Peace Research* 43, no. 3 (May 2006): 318–19.

Gorini, Ulises. *La rebelión de las madres: Historia de las madres de Plaza de Mayo.* Buenos Aires: Grupo Editorial Norma, 2006.

Gosse, Van. *Where the Boys Are: Cuba, Cold War America and the Making of a New Left.* London: Verso, 1993.

Gott, Richard. *Guerrilla Movements in Latin America.* New York: Seagull Books, 2008.

Gould, Jeffrey. "Solidarity under Siege: The Latin American Left, 1968." *American Historical Review* 114, no. 2 (April 2009): 354–55.

Grandin, Greg. *Empire's Workshop: Latin America, the United States and the Rise of the New Imperialism.* New York: Metropolitan, 2006.

———. *The Last Colonial Massacre: Latin America in the Cold War.* Chicago: University of Chicago Press, 2004.

Green, James. *Beyond Carnival: Male Homosexuality in 20th Century Brazil.* Chicago: University of Chicago Press, 1999.

Gregory, Stephen. *Intellectuals and Left Politics in Uruguay, 1958–2006.* England: Sussex, 2009.

Guevara, Ernesto "Che." *Guerrilla Warfare.* Lincoln: University of Nebraska Press, 1985.

Guillén, Abraham. *Desafío al pentagono.* Montevideo: Editorial Andes, 1969.

———. *Estrategia de la guerrilla urbana: Principios básicos de guerra revolucionaria.* Montevideo: Ediciones Liberacion, 1969.

———. *Philosophy of the Urban Guerrilla.* Translated by Donald C. Hodges. New York: William Morrow, 1973.

Guy, Donna, Mrinalini Sinha, and Angela Woollacott, eds. *Feminisms and Internationalism.* Maiden, MA: Wiley Blackwell, 1999.

Hamilton, Charles, ed. *Beyond Racism: Race and Inequality in Brazil, and the United States.* Boulder, CO: Lynne Rienner, 2001.

Hanson, S. G. *Utopia in Uruguay.* New York: Oxford University Press, 1938.

Hewitt, Christopher. "Terrorism and Public Opinion: A Five Country Comparison." In *Terrorism: The Third or New Left Wave,* edited by David C. Rapoport. New York: Routlege, 2006.

Hobson, Emily. "Imagining Alliance: Queer Anti-imperialism and Race in California, 1966–1990." PhD diss., University of Southern California, 2009.

Horton, Lynn. *Peasants in Arms: War and Peace in the Mountains of Nicaragua, 1979–1994.* Athens: Ohio University Center for International Studies, 1998.

Huggins, Martha. "Legacies of Authoritarianism: Brazilian Torturers' and

Murderers' Reformulation of Memory." *Latin American Perspectives* 27, no. 2 (March 2000): 57–78.

Huidobro, Eleuterio Fernández. *Historia de los tupamaros.* 3 vols. Montevideo: TAE, 1986–87.

Jacobs, Ron. *The Way the Wind Blew: A History of the Weather Underground.* New York: Verso, 1997.

Jackson, Geoffrey. *Surviving the Long Night: An Autobiographical Account of a Political Kidnapping.* New York: Vanguard, 1973.

James, Joy, ed. *The Angela Y. Davis Reader.* Malden, MA: Blackwell, 1998.

Jaquette, Jane, ed. *Feminist Agendas and Democracy in Latin America.* Durham: Duke University Press, 2009.

———. "Women in Revolutionary Movements in Latin America." *Journal of Marriage and the Family* 35 (1973): 344–54.

Jenness, Linda, ed. *Feminism and Socialism.* New York: Pathfinder, 1972.

Johns, Andrew. *Vietnam's Second Front: Domestic Politics, the Republican Party, and the War.* Lexington: University Press of Kentucky, 2010.

Johns, Andrew, and Kathryn C. Statler, eds. *The Eisenhower Administration, the Third World, and the Globalization of the Cold War.* Lanham, MD: Rowman and Littlefield, 2006.

Jones, Charles, ed. *The Black Panther Party (Reconsidered).* Baltimore: Black Classic Press, 1998.

Joseph, Gilbert, Catherine C. LeGrand, and Ricardo D. Salvatore, eds. *Close Encounters of Empire: Writing the Cultural History of US-Latin American Relations.* Durham: Duke University Press, 1998.

Kampwirth, Karen. *Feminism and the Legacy of Revolution: Nicaragua, El Salvador, Chiapas.* Athens: Ohio University Press, 2004.

———. *Women and Guerrilla Movements: Nicaragua, El Salvador, Chiapas, Cuba.* University Park: Pennsylvania State University Press, 2002.

Kaplan, Laura Duhan. "Feminism and Peace Theory: Women as Nurturers US Women as Public Citizens." In *In the Interest of Peace,* edited by Kenneth Kunkel and Joseph Klein. Wakefield, NH: Hollowbrook, 1990.

Katz, Friedrich. *The Life and Times of Pancho Villa.* Stanford: Stanford University Press, 1998.

Kaufman, Edy. *Uruguay in Transition: From Civilian to Military Rule.* New Brunswick, NJ: Transaction, 1979.

Kelly, Patty. *Lydia's Open Door: Inside Mexico's Most Modern Brothel.* Berkeley: University of California Press, 2008.

Knight, Alan. *The Mexican Revolution.* 2 vols. Lincoln: University of Nebraska Press, 1990.

Labrousse, Alain. *The Tupamaros: Urban Guerrillas in Uruguay.* London: Penguin, 1970.

LaFeber, Walter. *America, Russia, and the Cold War, 1945–1992.* New York: McGraw-Hill, 1993.

Langguth, A. J. *Hidden Terrors: The Truth about US Police Operations in Latin America.* New York: Pantheon, 1978.

Langland, Victoria. "Birth Control Pills and Molotov Cocktails: Reading Sex and Revolution in 1968 Brazil." In *In from the Cold: Latin America's New Encounter with the Cold War*, edited by Gilbert Joseph and Daniela Spenser, 308–49. Durham: Duke University Press, 2008.

Lavrin, Asunción. *Women, Feminism, and Social Change in Argentina, Chile, and Uruguay, 1890–1940*. Lincoln: University of Nebraska Press, 1995.

Lewis, Paul. *Guerrillas and Generals: The Dirty War in Argentina*. Westport, CT: Praeger, 2002.

López-Alves, Fernando. *Between the Economy and the Polity in the River Plate: Uruguay 1811–1890*. London: University of London Institute of Latin American Studies.

López-Alves, Fernando, and David Rock. "State Building and Political Systems in Nineteenth Century Argentina and Uruguay." *Past and Present* 167 (2000): 177–202.

Lorde, Audre. *Sister Outsider: Essays and Speeches*. New York: Crossing, 1984.

Löwy, Michael, ed. *Marxism in Latin America from 1909 to the Present: An Anthology*. Translated by Michael Pearlman. Atlantic Highlands, NJ: Humanities Press, 1992.

Lumsden, Ian. *Machos, Maricones and Gays: Cuba and Homosexuality*. Philadelphia: Temple University Press, 1996.

Luz, Alejandrina da. "Uruguay." In *No Longer Invisible: Afro-Latin Americans Today*, edited by Minority Rights Group, 332–44. London: Minority Rights Publications, 1995.

Macafee, Jane, and Myrna Wood. "Bread and Roses." In *Voices from Women's Liberation*, edited by Leslie B. Tanner. New York: Signet Press, 1971.

Mallon, Florencia. "The Promise and Dilemma of Subaltern Studies: Perspectives from Latin American History." *American Historical Review* 99, no. 5 (December 1994): 1491–515.

Marighella, Carlos. *Minimanual of the Urban Guerrilla*. Translated by Robert Moss. London: International Institute for Strategic Studies, 1971.

Markarian, Vania. *Left in Transformation: Uruguayan Exiles and the Latin American Human Rights Networks, 1967–1984*. New York: Routledge, 2005.

Martin, Gus. *Understanding Terrorism: Challenges, Perspectives and Issues*. Thousand Oaks, CA: Sage, 2006.

McClintock, Cynthia. *Revolutionary Movements in Latin America: El Salvador's FMLN and Peru's Shining Path*. Washington, DC: United States Institute of Peace Press, 1998.

McMahon, Robert. *The Cold War: A Very Short Introduction*. New York: Oxford University Press, 2003.

———. *The Cold War on the Periphery: The United States, India, and Pakistan*. New York: Columbia University Press, 1994.

———. *The Limits of Empire: The United States and Southeast Asia since World War II*. New York: Columbia University Press, 1999.

McPherson, Alan. *Yankee No! Anti-Americanism in US-Latin American Relations*. Cambridge, MA: Harvard University Press, 2003.

McSherry, Patrice. *Predatory States: Operation Condor and Covert War in Latin America*. Lanham, MD: Rowman and Littlefield, 2005.

Menchú, Rigoberta. *I, Rigoberta Menchú: An Indian Woman in Guatemala*. Translated by Ann Wright. London: Verso, 1984.

Mercader, Antonio, and Jorge de Vera. *Tupamaros: Estrategia y acción*. Montevideo: Editorial Alfa, 1969.

Miles, Angela Rose. *Integrative Feminisms: Building Global Visions 1960s–1990s*. New York: Routledge, 1996.

Mohanty, Chandra. *Third World Women and the Politics of Feminism*. Indianapolis: Indiana University Press, 1992.

Mohanty, Chandra Talpade. "Feminist Encounters: Locating the Politics of Experience." In *Destabilizing Theory: Contemporary Feminist Debates*, edited by Michele Barrett and Anne Phillips, 74–93. London: Polity, 1992.

Molyneux, Maxine. *Women's Movements in International Perspective*. London: Palgrave, 2001.

Morley, Morris H. *Washington, Somoza and the Sandinistas: State and Regime in US Policy toward Nicaragua 1969–1981*. Cambridge: Cambridge University Press, 2002.

Movimiento de Liberación Nacional (MLN-T). Documentos y antecedentes: Documento No. 5. Montevideo: MLN-T, 1970.

———. *Los Tupamaros en acción relatos testimoniales de los guerrilleros;* prólogo de Regis Debray. Santiago: Ediciones Prensa Latinoamericana, 1972.

———. *Tres Evasiones de Tupamaros: Operaciones estrella abuso gallo*. Santiago: Prensa Latinoamericana, 1973.

———. *La Carta de los presos y otros documentos*. Montevideo: MLN-T, 1985.

Muñoz, Carlos Basilio. *Uruguay homosexual: Culturas, minorías y discriminación desde una sociología de la homosexualidad*. Montevideo: Ediciones Trilce, 1996.

Mohanty, Chandra. *Third World Women and the Politics of Feminism*. Indianapolis: Indiana University Press, 1992.

Moore, Carlos. *Castro, the Blacks and Africa*. Los Angeles: UCLA Center for Afro-American Studies, 1988.

Moraga, Cherríe. *Loving in the War Years: Lo que nunca pasó por sus labios*. Cambridge: South End, 1983.

Moreno, Carlos Martínez. *El infierno*. London: Reader's International, 1981.

Morgan, Robin. *Sisterhood Is Global: The International Women's Movement Anthology*. New York: Feminist, 1996.

Navarro-Aranguren, Marysa, et al. "Feminisms in Latin America: From Bogota to San Bernadino." *Signs: Journal of Women in Culture and Society* 17, no. 2 (1992): 393–434.

Neroni, Hilary. *The Violent Woman: Femininity, Violence and Narrative in Contemporary American Cinema*. Albany: State University of New York Press, 2005.

Newton, Judith. *From Panthers to Promise Keepers: Rethinking the Men's Movement*. Lanham, MD: Rowman and Littlefield, 2005.

Núñez, Carlos. "The Tupamaros—Theory and Practice." In *The Tupamaros: Urban Guerrilla Warfare in Uruguay*. New York: Liberated Guardian, 1970. Rpt. *Uruguay: North American Congress on Latin America (NACLA) Archive of Latin Americana* (Wilmington, DE: Scholarly Resources, 1998).

Offen, Karen. *European Feminisms, 1700–1950: A Political History*. Stanford, CA: Stanford University Press, 2000.

Padula, Alfred, and Lois Smith. *Sex and Revolution: Women in Socialist Cuba*. Oxford: Oxford University Press, 1996.

Panizza, Francisco. "Late Institutionalization and Early Modernisation: The Emergence of Uruguay's Liberal Democratic Political Order." *Journal of Latin American Studies* 29 (1997): 667–91.

Parker, Jason. *Brother's Keeper: The United States, Race, and Empire in the British Caribbean, 1937—1962*. Oxford: Oxford University Press, 2008.

Parsa, Misagh. *States, Ideologies, and Social Revolutions: A Comparative Analysis of Iran, Nicaragua, and the Philippines*. Cambridge: Cambridge University Press, 2000.

Paterson, Thomas. *Contesting Castro: The United States and the Triumph of the Cuban Revolution*. Oxford: Oxford University Press, 1995.

Pearsall, Robert Brainard, ed. *The Symbionese Liberation Army: Documents and Communications*. Amsterdam: Rodopin, 1974.

Perelli, Carina. "Putting Conservatism to Good Use: Women and Unorthodox Politics in Uruguay from Breakdown to Transition." In *The Women's Movement in Latin America: Feminism and the Transition to Democracy*, edited by Jane Jaquette, 95–113. Boston: Unwin Hyman, 1989.

Pérez, Louis, Jr. *Cuba and the United States: Ties of Singular Intimacy*. Athens: University of Georgia Press, 2003.

Pérez-Stabli, Marfeli. *The Cuban Revolution: Origins, Course, and Legacy*. Oxford: Oxford University Press, 1998.

Piccato, Pablo. "'Such a Strong Need': Sexuality and Violence in Belem Prison." In *Gender, Sexuality, and Power in Latin America since Independence*, edited by Katherine Bliss and William French, 87–108. Lanham, MD: Rowman and Littlefield, 2007.

Pierri, Ettore, and Luciana Possamay, eds. *Hablan los otros*. Montevideo: Proyección, 1987.

Porzencanski, Arturo. *Uruguay's Tupamaros: The Urban Guerrillas*. New York: Praeger, 1973

Quartim, João. *Dictatorship and Armed Struggle in Brazil*. Translated by David Fernbach. London: New Left, 1971.

Quinn, Kate. *The Politics of Black Power in the Anglophone Caribbean*. Gainesville: University Press Florida, forthcoming.

Radu, Michael, ed. *Violence and the Latin American Revolutionaries*. New Brunswick, NJ: Foreign Policy Research Institute, 1988.

Randall, Margaret. *Our Voices, Our Lives: Stories of Women from Central America and the Caribbean*. Monroe, ME: Common Courage, 1995.

Rapoport, David, ed. *Terrorism: The Third or New Left Wave*. New York: Routledge, 2006.

Reader, Keith. *Régis Debray: A Critical Introduction*. London: Pluto, 1995.

Red Army Faction. "Serve the People." In *The Red Army Faction, A Documentary History: Projectiles for the People*, edited by J. Smith and André Moncourt. Montreal: Kersplebedeb and PM Press, 2009.

Reif, Linda. "Women in Latin American Guerrilla Movements." *Comparative Politics* 18, no. 2 (January 1986): 147–69.

Republica Oriental Del Uruguay: Ministerio Del Interior, *7 meses de lucha antisubversiva: Acción del estado frenta a la sedicion desde el 1 de Marzo al 30 de Septiembre de 1972*. Montevideo: 1972.

Rivas, Darlene. *Missionary Capitalist: Nelson Rockefeller in Venezuela*. Chapel Hill: University of North Carolina Press, 2002.

Roballo, Alba. "El Primer Disparo." In *Sesenta y ocho*, edited by Oscar Maggiolo. Montevideo: El Popular, 198[?]).

Rockefeller, Nelson. *The Rockefeller Report on the Americas: The Official Report of a US Presidential Mission for the Western Hemisphere*, New York Times ed. Chicago: Quadrangle, 1969.

Rodríguez, Ileana. *Women, Guerrillas, and Love: Understanding War in Central America*. Minneapolis: University of Minnesota Press, 1996.

Rodríguez, Romero Jorge. "The Afro Populations of America's Southern Cone: Organization, Development, and Culture in Argentina, Bolivia, Paraguay and Uruguay." In *African Roots/American Cultures: Africa in the Creation of the Americas*, edited by Sheila S. Walker, 314–31. Lanham, MD: Rowman and Littlefield, 2001.

Rosenthal, Anton. "Streetcar Workers and the Transformation of Montevideo: The General Strike of May 1911." *Americas* 51, no. 4 (1995): 471–94.

Ruddick, Sara. *Maternal Thinking: Towards a Politics of Peace*. Boston: Beacon, 1989.

Ryan, Jeffrey. "Turning on Their Masters: Unlearning Democracy in Uruguay." In *When States Kill: Latin America, the United States and Technologies of Terror*, edited by Cecilia Menjívar and Nestor Rodríguez, 278–303. Austin: University of Texas Press, 2005.

Saldaña-Portillo, María Josephina. *The Revolutionary Imagination in the Americas and the Age of Development*. Durham: Duke University Press, 2003.

Sales, Jean Rodrigues. "O impacto da revolução cubana sobre as organizações comunistas brasileiras (1959–1974)." PhD diss., Universidade Estadual de Campinas (UNICAMP), 2005.

Sandoval, Chela. *Methodology of the Oppressed*. Minneapolis: University of Minnesota Press, 2000.

Saney, Isaac. *Cuba: A Revolution in Motion*. New York: Palgrave, 2004.

Sargent, Lydia, ed. *The Unhappy Marriage of Marxism and Feminism: A Debate on Class and Patriarchy*. London: Pluto, 1986.

Sawyer, Mark. *Racial Politics in Post-revolutionary Cuba*. Cambridge, MA: Cambridge University Press, 2006.

Scheina, Robert. *Latin America's Wars*. Vol. 2, *The Age of the Professional Soldier*. Washington DC: Brassey's, 2003.

Schifter, Jacobo. *Macho Love: Sex behind Bars in Central America*. Binghamton, NY: Haworth, 1999.

Schrecker, Ellen. *Cold War Triumphalism: The Misuse of History after the Fall of Communism*. New York: New Press, 2004.

Scott, Joan. "The Evidence of Experience." *Critical Inquiry* 17, no. 4 (Summer 1991): 773–97.

———. "Gender: A Useful Category of Historical Analysis." *American Historical Review* 91, no. 5 (1986): 1053–75.

Servicio Paz y Justicia (SERPAJ). *Uruguay nunca más: Human Rights Violations, 1972–1985*. Philadelphia: Temple University Press, 1992.

Shayne, Julie. *The Revolution Question: Feminisms in El Salvador, Chile and Cuba*. New Brunswick, NJ: Rutgers University Press, 2004.

Smith, Jennifer. *An International History of the Black Panther Party*. New York: Garland, 1999.

Smith, Paul Chaat, and Robert Allen Warrior. *Like a Hurricane: The Indian Movement from Alcatraz to Wounded Knee*. New York: W. W. Norton, 1996.

Soler, Silvia. *La Leyenda de Yessie Macchi*. Montevideo: Editorial Fin de Siglo, 2001.

Sorenson, Diana. *A Turbulent Decade Remembered: Scenes from the Latin American Sixties*. Stanford, CA: Stanford University Press, 2007.

Sosnowski, Saul, and Louise Popkin, eds. *Repression, Exile, and Democracy: Uruguayan Culture*. Durham: Duke University Press, 1992.

South, James, and Jacob M. Held, eds. *James Bond and Philosophy*. Chicago: Open Court, 2006.

Stepan, Nancy Leys. *The Hour of Eugenics: Race, Gender and Nation in Latin America*. Ithaca, NY: Cornell University Press, 1991.

Sterling, Claire. *The Terror Network: The Secret War of International Terrorism*. New York: Reader's Digest Press, 1981.

Stern, Susan. *With the Weathermen*. New York: Doubleday, 1975.

Students for a Democratic Society (SDS) Papers. Glen Rock, NJ: Microfilming Corporation of America, 1977.

Sweig, Julia. *Inside the Cuban Revolution: Fidel Castro and the Urban Underground*. Cambridge, MA: Harvard University Press, 2002.

Taglioretti, Graciela. *Women and Work in Uruguay*. Paris: United Nations Educational, Scientific and Cultural Organization, 1983.

Telles, Edward. *Race in Another America: The Significance of Skin Color in Brazil*. Princeton: Princeton University Press, 2004.

Thevein, Rose. "'Boundaries of Law and Disorder': The Grand Design of Eldridge Cleaver and the Overseas Revolution in Cuba." In *Diasporic Africa: A Reader*, edited by Michael A. Gomez, 219–50. New York: New York University Press, 2006.

Tristan, Eduardo Rey. *La Izquierda Revolucionaria Uruguaya: 1955–1973*. Seville: University of Seville, 2005.

Trouillot, Michel-Rolph. *Silencing the Past: Power and the Production of History*. Boston: Beacon, 1995.

Uruguay: The Tupamaros in Uruguay. N.p.: Meridian Liberation, 1970.

Wagnleitner, Reinhold. *Coca-Colonization and the Cold War: The Cultural Mission of the United States in Austria after the Second World War*. Chapel Hill: University of North Carolina Press, 1994.

The Weather Underground. "Honky Tonk Women." In *Takin' It to the Streets*, edited by Alexander Bloom and Wini Breines. New York: Oxford University Press, 1995.

Weinstein, Martin. *Uruguay: Democracy at the Crossroads*. Boulder, CO: Westview, 1988.

———. *Uruguay: The Politics of Failure*. Westport, CT: Greenwood, 1975.

Wells, Tom. *The War within: America's Battle over Vietnam*. Berkeley: University of California Press, 1994.

Westheider, James. *The Vietnam War*. Westport, CT: Greenwood, 2007.

Williams, William Appleman. *The Tragedy of American Diplomacy*. New York: Dell, 1972.

Wilson, Carlos. *The Tupamaros: The Unmentionables*. Boston: Branden, 1974.

Womack, John. *Emiliano Zapata and the Mexican Revolution*. New York: Vintage, 1970.

Wright, Thomas. *Latin America in the Era of the Cuban Revolution*. London: Praeger, 2001.

Vanger, Milton. *The Model Country: José Batlle y Ordóñez of Uruguay 1907–1915*. Hanover, NH: University Press of New England, 1980.

Varon, Jeremy. *Bringing the War Home: The Weather Underground, the Red Army Faction and Revolutionary Violence in the Sixties and Seventies*. Berkeley: University of California Press, 2004.

Young, Allen, ed. *Gays under the Cuban Revolution*. San Francisco: Grey Fox, 1981.

Young, Cynthia. *Soul Power: Culture, Radicalism, and the Making of a US Third World Left*. Durham: Duke University Press, 2006.

Zimmermann, Matilde. *Sandinista: Carlos Fonseca and the Nicaraguan Revolution*. Durham: Duke University Press, 2000.

Zwerman, Gilda. "Participation in Underground Organizations: Conservative and Feminist Images of Women Associated with Armed, Clandestine Organizations in the United States." In *International Social Movement Research*. Vol. 4. Edited by Donatella Della Porta. London,: JAI, 1997.

Index